DEADLY FORCE
ENCOUNTERS

This book is dedicated to all the men and women in law enforcement. Every day you put your lives on the line to serve and protect.

DEADLY FORCE
ENCOUNTERS

What Cops
Need to Know
to Mentally
and Physically
Prepare for
and Survive
a Gunfight

Dr. Alexis Artwohl
Loren W. Christensen

PALADIN PRESS • BOULDER, COLORADO

*Deadly Force Encounters: What Cops Need to Know to Mentally and
Physically Prepare for and Survive a Gunfight*
by Dr. Alexis Artwohl and Loren W. Christensen

Copyright © 1997 by Dr. Alexis Artwohl and Loren W. Christensen
ISBN 0-87364-935-4
Printed in the United States of America

Published by Paladin Press, a division of
Paladin Enterprises, Inc.
Gunbarrel Tech Center
7077 Winchester Circle
Boulder, Colorado 80301 USA
+1.303.443.7250

Direct inquiries and/or orders to the above address.

PALADIN, PALADIN PRESS, and the "horse head" design
are trademarks belonging to Paladin Enterprises and
registered in United States Patent and Trademark Office.

Visit our Web site at www.paladin-press.com

Table
of
Contents

Introduction   1

Part One

Chapter 1: The Survival Triangle   13
Chapter 2: Are We Fueling The Fire Here?   21
Chapter 3: Sudden Violence   25
Chapter 4: Those Who Can't Shoot   29
Chapter 5: Fear   33
Chapter 6: The Four Rs Of Deadly Force Training   69

Part Two

Chapter 7: Beyond The Headlines   79
Chapter 8: Psychological Injuries   177

Part Three

Chapter 9: When The Shooting Is Over   191
Chapter 10: Traumatic Incident Debriefings   201
Chapter 11: Psychologically Surviving the Aftermath
      of a Traumatic Event   213
Chapter 12: Family And Trauma   229

Chapter 13: Investigating Officer-Involved Shootings   245
Conclusion: Components of a Police Trauma
    Survival Program   253
References And Suggested Reading   261

Acknowledgments

First and foremost, I want to thank all the law enforcement personnel and their family members who have allowed me to serve them as a police psychologist and law enforcement trainer. It has been an inspiration and a privilege to learn about your unique world and to make a contribution to it.

A special thanks to all the officers and family members who contributed their stories to this books.

I want to thank Sergeant Lonn Sweeney of the Portland Police Bureau. He is a man of courage and compassion who has gone beyond the call of duty to serve his community and help fellow officers. I appreciate his valuable insights into the minds and hearts of street cops.

I appreciate the mentoring I have received from police psychologists Dr. Jim Shaw and Dr. Roger Solomon, and I thank them for their support over the years.

I want to thank my husband, Captain Dave Butzer of the Portland Police Bureau. In his usual cheerful manner, he put up with my having little time to spare for him during the year it took to write this book. As he has risen through the ranks, he has maintained his integrity and stood firm in his dedication to taking care of his troops and treating them with fairness and compassion.

I want to thank my co-author, Officer Loren Christensen of

the Portland Police Bureau for taking the chance to work jointly with me on this project. His wealth of experience as an editor and published author made the task less painful. He has been a pleasure to work with.

Alexis Artwohl, Ph.D.

It is only because of the understanding and support of my family and friends that I am able to write a single word. Thank you for your patience during those times I was completely preoccupied with this book.

This project would not have been possible without my co-author, Alexis Artwohl. Her knowledge of the subject is as boundless as her affection for the officers she serves.

Many thanks to my friend Dave Butzer for giving up so many weekends so his wife, Alexis, and I could work on this project. Now you two can get back to your white-water rafting.

Loren W. Christensen

Introduction

I stepped on an aorta my third night out of the police academy. I didn't know what it was, but an ambulance driver said it was the man's aorta, the man lying in an ever-widening pool of blood 15 feet away at the entrance of the hallway. The aorta, if that's what the spongy piece of meat really was, had been blasted out of his chest by a 12-gauge shotgun. The television was shrieking at full volume, and the man's wife, the boy's grandmother, and four toddlers were screaming and wailing at the top of their lungs as other officers wrestled the 16-year-old stepson into handcuffs. It was while I gagged and scraped the sticky thing off my heel with my other shoe that I asked myself if I was sure that this is what I wanted to do for a living.

Two nights later my coach and I knocked on an apartment door to investigate the sounds of a heated argument called in by neighbors. Although the door opened only a few inches, the man was so large we couldn't have seen in even if it had been wide open. He assured us everything was OK, but then gave a quick look behind him. When my coach asked if we could talk to his wife, he looked startled and began shutting the door. I just stood dumb and useless in my freshly ironed rookie uniform, but my coach jammed his foot in the door and shoved the man aside, giving us our first view inside.

There was an easy chair in the far corner of the room with a woman slumped in it. Her arms flopped about in her lap, her eyes

1

bulged dangerously from her ashen face, and a kitchen knife protruded obscenely from the hollow of her throat.

The big man jumped us as we moved through the door and the fight was on. We thrashed about on the living room floor, crashed into a bedroom, rolled over and off the bed, and fought wildly in a cramped place between the bed and the wall. Then, although we hadn't gained control of him, the big man gave up.

An hour later he was behind bars. Three hours later his wife was released from the hospital emergency room with a small, circular bandage on her neck where the razor-sharp knife had entered cleanly, missing everything vital. An hour after that she bailed her husband out and angrily told a jailer that she was going to sue us for false arrest.

That was my fifth day on the job, and I asked myself again if this is what I wanted to do with my life.

THE JOB

Most police officers get into law enforcement because they want to help people. Of course there are other attractions, such as the excitement of the chase, arresting suspects, the variety of work, being where the action is, doing something positive for the community, working in a perceived glamorous profession, getting attention from friends and the community, getting good medical and hospital plans, and job security. While these are all part of the consideration, most officers are initially attracted to police work because they see it as a place where they can do something positive for others.

Let's take a brief look at an average police career—yours.

Myriad emotions go through your head the first time you put on that stiff, scratchy police uniform and stand before your bedroom mirror. It feels good. Scary, but good. You look good, too, as powerful as Superman in his blue tights and red cape. You also feel like a walking neon sign, all lit up brightly, spelling out: "The Answer Man." But you don't even know the questions.

The first few days of processing into your agency are a

mad, mind-boggling swirl of filling out forms, gathering equipment, meeting new faces, and learning new names, ranks, serial numbers, terms, expressions, procedures, rules, rules, and more rules. The academy begins and suddenly you are immersed in an odd academic world of laws, rules, procedures, psychology, self-defense, driving and shooting skills, CPR, ethnic, racial, sexual, and religious diversity training, and a whole lot of how this and that will be done.

So intense are the many weeks of training that the real world, referred to in police vernacular as "the street," becomes remote, an abstract reality that gets buried under heavy law books, an infinite number of rules and procedures, and paper targets you shoot at 5, 10, 15, and 25 yards.

The instructors talk about shooting people, but they don't *really* talk about it. No one tells you what it's like to thrust a gun at a human being, feel the steel explode in your hand, and watch the human crumple to the floor. No one tells you what it's like to see him writhe and scream and bleed and die. No one tells you what it's like to know that *you* caused that.

Then you graduate and the real world of police work hits you like a freight train. While you got used to wearing your uniform in the confines of the academy, now you have to get used to how it feels wearing it in the street. While you may be a little more equipped to answer the questions now, you realize quickly that what you learned in the academy is no more than a drop of water in the ocean.

Your training coach is your umbilical cord, your lifeline. Technically he is your partner, but not really. He is someone you have to prove yourself to, someone you learn from and emulate. He is always watching you, evaluating you, and making you feel self-conscious. He is the parent and you are the child; you want to show the parent that you can handle things and that you know what you are doing. Your mind is busy with laws and procedures and doing everything right. The thought of having to shoot someone is abstract and sits quietly in a corner of your mind.

You quickly discover that there are people on the street

who like you, even love you, but there are many others who don't. Some hate you and some are indifferent. You are uncomfortable and suspicious around those who love you because you are not sure why they do, if indeed they really do. You are leery of those who hate you, but at least there is comfort in knowing where they stand. The indifferent ones are just there. You figure they are probably people who have money and feel they are superior to you, or criminal types who have been through the liberal justice system dozens of times and are no longer intimidated. On the other hand, maybe they are just so law abiding that the thought of having anything to do with the police is far removed from their thoughts.

How long you spend with a training coach depends on your agency's policy, but when you finally go out on your own, usually after three months to a year, there is still much smoothing out to do and many new things to learn.

After about two years, you feel comfortable with your daily work routine and confident you can handle most situations without having to call a supervisor for advice. At three or four years, it wouldn't be uncommon for you to exhibit an extreme attitude of confidence, maybe even a little cockiness. This is generally a result of feeling comfortable with the police task and a little heady from the power you have come to enjoy. You easily complete each task given, you are arresting street criminals, and you feel you are doing good things for good citizens. You are doing what you said you wanted to do when you applied for police work: you are helping people.

You may or may not have drawn your weapon by now. If you have, it was probably to stop a suspect from fleeing, from retrieving his own weapon, or from hurting you or someone else. But that burning, decisive thought that you were going to squeeze the trigger and blow the life out of a human being was not part of the action. It remains only an abstract thought.

At five years, you will either be completely absorbed in the job or feeling pangs of disillusionment with police work and the justice system. Between 5 and 20 years you might seek a promotion, take a lateral transfer into a specialty field, or decide to ride out your career in a patrol car. At 20 years and beyond, your thoughts, positively or negatively, are on your impending retirement. Between 25 and 30 years you will sign your retirement papers and be off on another journey.

GOOD GUYS AND BAD GUYS

Early in your career, it becomes clear in your mind that there are good guys and bad guys. While different police agencies use different terms—suspect, perp (for perpetrator), crook, and a variety of more colorful terms—you can walk into any police agency and say "bad guy" and everyone will know whom you are talking about. While it may not always be immediately apparent who is who in a situation, facts quickly designate the roles.

In your mind, bad guys break the law. They steal, intimidate, rape, assault, and kill. Sometimes it can be a little fuzzy whether the victim is totally good, but there is never any doubt in your mind that *you* are a good guy and it's your job to go out and catch the bad guys.

Oversimplistic? Perhaps. But if you are like most officers, you will come to think this way because it's the world in which you work. Then when you have to kill someone, no matter how justified, the division between good and bad often becomes confused.

IT'S A NEW ERA

Times change, and so does the nature of police work. Many officers who retired 25 years ago said they had never drawn their service weapon in the line of duty. Today, in active patrol districts in mid-sized cities and larger, officers pull their weapons once or twice a month, sometimes once or twice a week. Street gangs, the proliferation of drugs, and social conditions in general are placing officers in greater peril than any time in recent history. Guns are everywhere, and "shots heard in the area" calls are routine in some neighborhoods. Police officers are on the front line of a war that goes undeclared because of politics and political correctness.

Since there is a greater possibility today that you will have to fire your weapon in self-defense or to defend someone else, you need to ask yourself if you are ready. Are you prepared mentally, physically, and spiritually to do it? Are you prepared for the aftermath?

• • • • •

Deadly Force Encounters was written for officers who have used deadly force and for officers who may some day have to; for police administrators, chaplains and mental health professionals who need to know about the effects of trauma on officers; and for citizens interested in the issue of deadly force and what happens to officers who are forced to use it.

Deadly Force Encounters was not written to titillate, to entertain, or to satisfy readers seeking vicarious thrills. There are plenty of places where the sensationalists can feed and satiate their hunger, such as the weekly made-for-TV-dramas, the cinema, and computer games. These sources offer plenty of bloody fantasies where one can see cops exchange hundreds of shots with snarling bad guys, then go right on with their lives in the next scene as if shooting people is as common as buffing their shoes for duty.

Whereas real law enforcement officers have always cringed at the absurdity of these programs, the public all too often accepts this nonsense as reality. This creates misconceptions about what happens to officers after they have been forced to take the life of another human being. This book will be a real eye-opener to people not involved in law enforcement as to the mental and physical anguish officers often suffer and the struggle they must go through to recover from what is often the most profound experience of their lives.

Many police officers have misconceptions about using deadly force since they too have been fed the same media fantasy as everyone else. Even those officers who have given the possibility serious thought and have come to terms with the issue, the notion of shooting someone may remain an abstract one, something that will never happen to them. This book will help prepare them for the reality of a deadly force encounter and provide them with an opportunity to listen to the experiences of those who have already been there.

Deadly Force Encounters is not a book on tactics. Our intention is to increase your awareness of general issues that are relevant to deadly force encounters and give you suggestions on how you can begin educating and preparing yourself to survive a shooting and the aftermath. For both the uninitiated officer and the officer who has used deadly force, the book is packed with practical techniques, exercises, suggestions, and examples.

The book is divided into three sections. The first one examines the many faces of fear and ways to deal with it, diminish it, and even accept it as an ally. We take a brief look at violence and how some officers get hooked on its addictive nature. Are there other things you can do to prepare for a deadly force encounter besides going to the shooting range? Yes, and we give you physical and mental techniques that will increase the chance of your success and help reduce post-traumatic psychological injuries.

The second section of the book reveals personal stories of officers who have had to kill in the line of duty. You will find their tales engrossing, deeply moving, and sometimes shocking. If you are not in law enforcement or a combat arms branch of the military, you will come to know a phenomena called post-traumatic stress disorder, something television and movies rarely show. If you are an uninitiated officer, you will learn from these officers' experiences how to better prepare for your own. And if you are an officer who has used deadly force, and perhaps have not come to terms with it, you will see yourself in many of their stories and realize you are not alone and you are not crazy. What did they do to help themselves recover? You will learn that here.

While these stories are horrific, the officers have taken the right steps to recover from there incidents in a positive way. We believe that police officers get enough bad publicity, and we didn't want to add to it by telling stories of officers who were unable to recover from their shooting experience. Therefore, our purpose here is to give police officers a positive message of hope and healing along with practical information to help them survive their years in a job that is full of negativity. We praise the officers who tell their stories in this book because they have survived their shootings and they took the right steps to recover from their traumatic experience, or they are still seeking help. There are lots of books and movies that paint a bad picture of police officers. This is not one of them.

The last third of the book is devoted to the aftermath, especially the healing process. You will learn how to take care of yourself and your family, using the help and support of other officers, family, friends, and mental health professionals. If you are an investigator assigned to a police-involved shooting, you will learn some valuable tips to help you understand the officers' reactions and how you can best get the information you need. Family members also have a vote in this book. Their stories are lessons on the impact of police work on families and what they have done to stay intact.

At the back of the book, we have included a "References and Suggested Readings" section. This can be used to locate the original references we used and to give you additional resources to continue your education in this area.

A WORD ON STYLE

Whereas we recognize there are all types of law enforcement officers, we have used the generic term cop and police officer, with no slight meant to sheriffs, deputies, corrections officers, federal agents, security officers, and the wide variety of ranks that protect and serve in various capacities.

Whereas we support and applaud the growing number of women entering police work, we have used *he* for ease of writing and reading and hope no one is offended. We would support and applaud the English language developing a gender neutral term to replace he and she.

Much of the material in this book comes from the voices of the officers and their families. Know that while the anecdotes and all the other war stories are true, we have either omitted or changed the names of each contributor to protect their anonymity and their agencies. Occasionally, minor details of the stories have been changed.

Who Loves The Warrior?

Who loves the warrior?
Not those he has fought for,
For those he has fought for have seen
The stains of battle on his garment.
They draw back when they learn of the deed
He has done to keep them safe.
It is better for them to keep a distance from the warrior
So the stain will not spoil the perception of their dignity.
Yet the warrior continues to give his all.
He must fight the battles to keep those souls he loves
Free from harm and free from the stain of evil,
For he is a warrior,
The only shield between good and evil.
It is only the warrior who loves the warrior.

Sergeant Lonn Sweeney
Portland Police Bureau
Portland, Oregon

Part One

The Number One Rule of Police Work:
Go home alive at the end of your shift.

The Survival Triangle

1

THE SURVIVAL TRIANGLE

Ask any police officer what the first rule of police work is and you will hear, "Go home alive at the end of your shift."

Police officers are justifiably concerned about survival, and when it's discussed, the conversation is usually about physical techniques. But officers also need to consider the legal and psychological aspects. Let's call all three of these the "survival triangle":

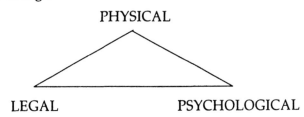

PHYSICAL

LEGAL   PSYCHOLOGICAL

PHYSICAL SURVIVAL

As a profession, police officers have become much better at physical survival over the past 25 years. The infamous Newhall incident of April 5, 1970, was a wake-up call to the law enforcement community. On that dark day, four California Highway Patrol officers were murdered in less than five minutes by two heavily armed suspects. A detailed description of this event is provided by Massad Ayoob in his book *The Ayoob Files: The Book.*

The Newhall incident occurred at a time when law enforcement officers were being slain at the rate of about 35-38 per 100,000 employed officers per year. (The average rate for all occupations is only about five per 100,000). This high rate of death among officers represented the dangers of being murdered in the line of duty and the need for improved officer safety strategies. Law enforcement has reduced the death rate from line-of-duty deaths by homicide to about 10-12 per 100,000 officers. Body armor and better officer-survival skills are primarily responsible for this reduced death rate. (For a detailed statistical analysis of deadly force encounters, see Geller and Scott's book, *Deadly Force: What We Know.*)

Body Armor

In the mid 1970s, my agency acquired a prototype vest. I was curious about it and volunteered to be the guinea pig who would try it out. It was hot and bulky but I decided to stick with it, at least for a while. Four days after I began wearing it, I answered an incomplete "man with a gun" call.

I parked my patrol car near the area and got out. A moment later, I felt something like a giant fist slam into my chest. It knocked me out, and the next thing I remembered was waking up in a gutter, looking up at the sky. I was in a daze and felt like I was in the Twilight Zone. Sights and sounds were distorted and I was in a state of confusion. Someone told me I had been shot and I was transported to a hospital, where I spent the next five days recovering from my injuries.

I found out that the "man with a gun" had been a sniper with a rifle looking for a cop to kill. He was in the second story of a neighborhood house waiting for the first uniform, who was me. He took careful aim from 200 yards away and shot me in the chest without warning. Had I not been wearing that hot, bulky, prototype vest, the bullet would have shattered my heart. As it was, it left a huge bruise and some minor internal injuries that I fully recovered from. I never went back out on the street after that without body armor.

Officer Survival Skills

Improved training in officer-survival skills has saved countless lives. Law enforcement trainers will often tell their students, "When all hell breaks loose, you will do what you have trained to do. You have to learn to trust your training."

Truer words were never spoken. Under the high-arousal states dictated by the natural fear response, you will usually give little or no conscious thought to your actions. Your body has been programmed by Mother Nature to go into autopilot mode, and you respond automatically based on all your training and past experiences. All the officers we spoke with who have been in deadly force encounters said the same thing: "After my incident, I took my training, practice, and preparation a lot more seriously."

One officer who has survived three shootings put it this way: "I told myself, and I tell all the officers I train, to never forget the LANFWM principle: Life Ain't No Fucking Western Movie. You have to train and practice during your whole career because you never know when a real bad guy will try to take your life away from you. There won't be any riding off into the sunset with dramatic music if you get killed. Just a dead cop and a lot of grieving people."

There is nothing mysterious about training to survive a deadly force encounter. It takes knowledge, commitment, and lots of practice.

LEGAL SURVIVAL

Some officers still naively assume that their community and their agency will always be grateful to them for putting their life on the line. They assume that this gratitude will mean that they will automatically be treated fairly so all they need to do is let events unfold and trust in their agency and the community to take care of them. They believe that since they acted according to the laws of their community and the policies and procedures of their agency, they are safe from condemnation and punishment for using deadly force. Sometimes this is true. But since this is not guaranteed, all officers need to educate themselves about the legal risks of their profession.

What are some legal risks? You could be disciplined by your agency, anything from a written reprimand to being fired. You could be indicted on criminal charges in your local jurisdiction. Even if your actions are approved of by your agency and your local government, you could still face federal civil rights violation charges, both criminal and civil. And you could still be sued in civil court even if you have been cleared on all the preceding charges.

Good Job—You're Fired

Five years ago I was forced to shoot an ex-convict who was waving a gun around, under the influence of drugs, and refusing all of my efforts and other officers' efforts to get him under control. I was sure that one of us was going to die, and I didn't want it to be me.

After the shooting I had to go before a grand jury and explain why I was forced to use deadly force. Although I took it seriously, I wasn't too worried. This was standard operating procedure, and it was so obvious to me that I was justified that it never occurred to me there could be any problems with their judgment of me.

Apparently I didn't explain it to their satisfaction because although they cleared me of any criminal charges, they sent a letter to my chief criticizing my tactics. He fired me. I was stunned. That started a nightmare that is still hard for me to believe. I knew I had done nothing wrong so I sued to get my job back. After an elaborate investigation with mountains of evidence, the arbitrator ruled that the shooting was justified and my agency was forced to reinstate me. However, this took almost three years by the time the lawyers got through with all their legal wrangling. I had to find temporary employment, and had it not been for the generosity of friends, peers, and relatives, my family and I would have lost our house.

We will never fully recover financially, and I don't know yet if we will ever fully recover emotionally. I still feel guilty about how much my wife, kids, and other relatives suffered during this ordeal. Police work will never be the same for me. It's still a job I believe in, but much of the joy ended for me, probably forever.

Here are a few things you can do to protect yourself legally.

*   Don't assume that someone else will do it for you.
*   Start educating yourself *right now* as to your legal rights and responsibilities during and after a deadly force encounter. Read your general orders and local laws. Look for training seminars on the topic of shootings and their legal implications. Will Aitchison, a labor attorney in Portland, Oregon, who represents multiple police unions, has written a book entitled, *The Rights of Law Enforcement Officers* (Third Edition). Although not specific to deadly force encounters, some of the material is relevant to this situation. (See our References and Suggested Reading section in the back of this book.)
*   Find out what the shooting review procedures in your community are and how they work.
*   Talk to other officers who have already been there to find out what worked and what didn't.
*   Understand the sensory and cognitive distortions that are a normal part of traumatic events.
*   Remember that no one will be as concerned about your welfare as you.
*   Don't underestimate the emotional stress that can be caused by legal and civil proceedings. Many officers and family members have found these events to be harder to cope with than the shooting itself. The plaintiff's attorney will usually do his best to paint you as a vicious, incompetent coward no matter how justified and even heroic your actions may have been. These are times for officers and their families to seek out the support of peers, friends, family and, if needed, counseling.

• Assemble a list of attorneys in your area who represent police officers. Keep it in a file just in case.

PSYCHOLOGICAL SURVIVAL

Deadly force encounters can leave scars that can last for years, sometimes destroying careers, even lives. Of course, not all officers involved in shootings are permanently traumatized, and many recover and return to the street. But far too many don't. Many suffer, and so do their families and friends. Some leave law enforcement through resignation or early retirement, while others grit their teeth and hang on by their fingernails, no longer enjoying the work they used to love.

Leaving law enforcement after a deadly force encounter should not automatically be viewed as negative. There are many people in a variety of professions who, for many reasons, become disenchanted with their professions and decide to switch careers. Police officers are no exception. After going through a deadly force encounter and its aftermath, an officer may say to himself, "Once was enough. There aren't enough positives in this job for me to put myself and my family through this again." These officers should be admired for having enough sense to do what is right for them.

In this book you will hear the stories of officers and family members who have done well after shootings, and some who have not. Their stories contain lessons and inspiration for all of us.

PREPARATION

Once you survive a shooting physically, you must fight for your legal and psychological survival. Fortunately, there are many things you can do to help make sure you come out a winner, and this book will give you information to start preparing *now*.

Is the issue of post-traumatic stress blown out of proportion? Some think so.

As a veteran detective chased a holdup man on foot across a six-lane freeway, the suspect pulled a gun from his waistband, turned, and fired. The detective crouched behind the traffic median and fired back, killing the suspect instantly. Several years later, he was asked by an officer if he had ever experienced nightmares about the incident or in any other way been traumatized.

"Hell no," the detective answered, incredulous that the question had even been asked "In fact, I'm looking forward to doing it again."

• • • • •

"Sometimes I think all this hype about post trauma can be dangerous. I think it puts thoughts in officers' minds that they are supposed to feel upset after they shoot someone. I know a lot of officers who have killed and they aren't haunted by it."

• • • • •

An officer who survives a shooting situation should feel great joy. He should not feel sad, or depressed, or in some way horribly traumatized. Hey, he won! He should feel great.

• • • • •

I think some of this so-called post trauma is taught. They tell you in the academy that if you get in a shooting, you are going to be all screwed up from it. You are going to suffer all kinds of problems, like headaches, impotence, and your marriage will go down the tubes. It's all bullshit.

Are We Fueling the Fire Here?

2

There are many officers, supervisors, and leaders who still think as the officers above do, though this thinking is antiquated and out of step with *progressive police agencies* across the country. They think post trauma is b.s. and that officers should feel good about surviving a deadly encounter and just get back to work. But is there any validity to this thinking? Is it possible that if we make too much of the aftermath that we will actually set officers up for post-traumatic stress?

The answer is a resounding NO. As usual, extreme views on both sides of the issue distort the truth. Police officers, like combat soldiers, natural disaster survivors, and others subjected to a wide variety of traumas are susceptible to the psychological injury currently known as PTSD. PTSD among police officers is well documented in professional, psychological literature and we both have seen much of it in our careers.

No officer has ever developed PTSD from the joy of winning a deadly force encounter and sending an evil bad guy to hell. They rightly do experience that joy from time to time, but that is not what traumatizes them. People who believe that officers should not feel trauma after a shooting live in a fantasy world where every officer-involved shooting is like a 1950s western, where the hero shoots the villain and then rides triumphantly and happily into a Technicolor sunset, with the undying gratitude of an adoring town. He never has to worry about the post-shooting investigations, grand juries, lawsuits, upset family members, hostile media, and uncaring command staff, or about becoming a political sacrifice. The hero apparently never has any religious concerns or fears of death, and never has to worry about anything going wrong with disastrous results.

If you are still living in this fantasy world, we hope the stories of *real* officers in this book will jolt you back into reality.

Many people who look at PTSD with disdain inhabit the fantasy world of macho denial where they can pretend that PTSD has never existed, as if it's a brand new idea. Unfortunately, all too many people, even some mental health professionals, want to pretend that people are not supposed to be bothered by ugly and gruesome events. There is a long history of survivors of war, concentration camps, horrible crimes, severe child abuse, and other traumas being ignored and told, "It's in the past, just get over it." Sometimes they are even rejected and ostracized by those who have not experienced anything like it, perhaps as a way of not having to face the horror through the pain and stories of the survivors.

Well, that is not reality. The officers who have suffered after putting their lives on the line deserve better than being told to just shut up and get over it. They need us to listen to them and provide help so they really can get over it. They need the same compassion and the same level of sophisticated intervention and treatment as an officer who has been physically wounded in the line of duty.

Whenever Dr. Artwohl trains officers on surviving a deadly force encounter and its aftermath, veteran officers frequently come up to her afterwards to talk privately about a shooting they were in and to thank her for bringing the topic out in the open. Some are still bothered by these long-ago events, and this is the first time they could talk to someone. Many of them tried to talk about it afterward but were hushed by the denial and ignorance of others and the macho myth of the indestructible cop.

The law enforcement community has nothing to gain by presenting police officers as *Robocops*, efficient killing machines with perfect judgment and no feelings. This extreme view will only lead to false expectations of total perfection that will result in harsh condemnation of any officer who shows feelings or makes the smallest mistake. Most tragically, it will prevent officers and their family members from getting the proper debriefing and treatment that can prevent PTSD after shootings. Police officers and their families are human beings trying to cope with a difficult and demanding profession, and everyone, including cops, needs to understand that.

NOT ALL WILL HAVE PROBLEMS

Officer Collins had been an infantry captain in Vietnam. While on a mission, his squad came under intense fire and within minutes all his men were dead. While still under heavy incoming fire, Collins used his men's bodies like sandbags to build a bunker where he could take cover and continue to return fire. For this he won the U.S. Army's Distinguished Service Cross.

After leaving the service, he became a deputy sheriff. Six months later he came face-to-face with an armed man in a popular restaurant and was forced to shoot the man to death.

Ten years after he had left the horror of Vietnam and five years after the restaurant shooting, Collins had not suffered any psychological trauma and would occasionally discuss the incidents matter-of-factly. He even turned down a writer's request to tell his Vietnam story because, as he put it, "It was no big deal. Other guys had it worse."

The other extreme view is that every officer who gets involved in a shooting will suffer emotional problems. Sometimes this goes even further and says that any officer who fails to have problems is in denial. This is not true. Traumatic events do not traumatize everyone. Although we have seen plenty of officers seriously traumatized from deadly force encounters and other gruesome events, we have also seen plenty of officers who bounce back quickly and have no lasting problems.

The only responsible and truthful statement about shootings and PTSD is that shootings are traumatic events, and *some* officers who get involved in them are at risk for developing PTSD. The best way to deal with this truth is to educate officers and their families about this possibility. Additionally, officers and their families need to be offered debriefings and, if necessary, treatment to help ensure that they will recover from any psychological injury they might sustain.

As for those with contentions that cops are *brainwashed* into believing they should be upset by shootings, don't be fooled by talk about wimpy, weak-minded cops who appear to be from a different planet. The cops we are familiar with are intelligent, skeptical, tough-minded individuals with finely tuned "b.s. detectors" who are innately suspicious of shrinks and other experts. They would never believe in something like PTSD just because a *shrink* told them they should be experiencing it.

Anyone who has given classes to police officers, as both authors have, can tell you that they can be the toughest audience in the world if what you are selling doesn't make sense to them based on their own experience. And if they are not buying it, they are not the least bit shy to tell you that they think you're full of it!

Police officers who have been traumatized, or who have seen someone close to them traumatized, believe in PTSD. Among officers who have not had the experience, there are always a few who don't believe it will happen. That is just human nature. However, by educating all police officers about its possibility, they will have the basic information needed to recognize the problem.

Sudden Violence

3

"My butt hurts," is a typical comment heard by civilians after spending a l-o-n-g, quiet shift with an officer in a police car. A quiet shift can be a monotonous stretch of driving down empty city streets and cruising sleeping neighborhoods. Not a peep comes from the radio, not one car runs a red light, not one home gets burglarized, and every criminal obeys every law. Many ride-a-longs have gone home convinced that police work is painfully boring and a terrible waste of gas.

Sometimes it is. Police work defines an expression popular during the Vietnam War: "War is long stretches of boredom punctuated by moments of sheer terror." Police work can be the same. An entire week can go by without getting a single dangerous call. A month will pass and all you get are a few cold burglaries and a shoplifter. Hard-working officers say they don't depend on radio calls for activity because they can keep busy finding things to do. Nonetheless there are times when even the most industrious officer can't even find a traffic violator.

But veteran officers know this can all change around the next corner, at the next car stop, or at the next seemingly innocuous radio call.

NEIGHBORS

It had been a long, hot summer day and our quiet shift was final-ly ending. My partner and I were hot and bored with the job and bored with eight hours of small talk. Just as we were starting to head in, the sweet voice of the dispatcher asked us to stop by an address and talk to a woman upset about a stray dog in her garden. My part-ner looked at me sleepily and yawned, "We can handle this."

When we rounded the corner onto the street where the lady lived, we expected to see an old woman shooing a stray mutt out of her yard with a broom. Instead, we saw an angry crowd of about 40 peo-ple fighting in the street, on the sidewalks, and in the yards. They were armed with rakes, shovels, boards, and who knows what else. My partner shook his head to clear the fuzzies out of his brain, and I pushed myself up out of my lazy slouch.

Those people who weren't fighting rushed toward our car and beat on the hood demanding that we arrest this person and that per-son. More people arrived in cars, leaped out and joined the fray. Those who had run up to us began to fight, and my partner and I were getting jostled all about as we tried to separate them. A man near me swung a 2x4 board at another man, but it struck me in my upper right arm. Reflexively, I punched the guy in the chops with my left, which turned both sides of the mob against us.

Arriving police cars burped their sirens to clear a path through the ever-growing mob. I yelled to my partner and other officers to grab the agitators and put them in the police cars. If we could get them out of the area, maybe the mini-riot would fizzle.

When we got a half dozen people in our bac seats, we roared off to a parking lot a few blocks away. Once we got the big mouths sep-arated and calmed, we learned that the whole thing had been about the dog. It started with the woman kicking the dog because he had been whizzing on her roses, which led to a heated argument with the dog's owner. They each called their friends, relatives, and neighbor-hood supporters, and all gathered to brawl with each other, then us. Four arrests and three injuries over a dog who just wanted to pee.

It certainly took the doldrums out of a hot, boring day.

The uncertainty of what lies around the next corner causes a variety of emotions among police officers. Some look at it with enthusiastic excitement, and others view it with dreaded anxiety. Both views cause internal knotting that can cause negative physical and psychological effects. It's not uncommon for police officers, especially those in poor physical condition, to suffer everything from strained muscles to heart attacks when suddenly thrust from a quiet moment into an explosive one. Later we will discuss the importance of physical conditioning as one of the best defenses against sudden physical and psychological stress.

ADDICTED TO THE RUSH

As odd as it may seem to the reader who lives a peaceful, sedentary existence, the heart-thumping, eye-watering, sweat-producing, hyperventilating rush of sudden violence can be an addictive drug to some people. Many returning Vietnam veterans found that the relative quiet of stateside duty was just too sedate. They had become addicted to the adrenaline rush of war, an addiction so powerful and hungry that many of them risked their lives for second, third, fourth, and fifth tours. It's irrelevant whether these men and women had this addiction before they were exposed to Vietnam. They had become hooked on adrenaline and they needed to feed its hungry appetite.

There are many police officers who are action junkies and need to get their regular fix. As with the Vietnam soldiers, they may have been thrill seekers before or it was unleashed from within them. In either case, they now actively seek it around every corner, and when their shift ends and they didn't get it, they feel disappointed, ripped off. When they do get the experience, they accept it with open arms because it's what they need.

New officers in particular are generally action junkies because police work is still new to them, an amusement park of thrills and spills. They look at their watches with dread as the time inches toward their shift's end and hope for "the big one," a major incident so they can stay out on the street, regardless that their family is waiting at home. For some officers, it very quickly becomes an addiction.

But sudden violence doesn't just offer thrills. It can also bring tragedy. The unknown, which is just around that next corner, may change the officer's life forever. It may even end it.

Probably Nothing

The police call came out as a suspicious person in a mobile home in a quiet mobile home park. The area was so peaceful and open that it couldn't possibly be a burglar, and the officers probably figured it had to be someone with a valid reason to be there. It was a fairly routine call, but risky enough that the partners needed to be alert.

But as they approached the door of the trailer, a man quickly stepped out with a semiauto pistol and shot them both dead.

Just Routine

It was a routine traffic stop like a thousand others I've done, but as I walked up to the car, the driver came out with a shotgun, the barrel pointed into the air. I drew my Glock and yelled at him to drop it, but he gave me a funny look and started to bring it down toward me. I fired my gun six times and he fell to the pavement, dead.

It's not uncommon for an adrenaline hungry officer to find himself being mentally pulled in opposite directions after experiencing a traumatizing event, particularly where he has had to use deadly force. He still needs the adrenaline rush from whatever may be around the next corner, but now he is frightened, even terrified of it. His need pulls him toward the unknown, but his fear holds him back. This can be an excruciating and debilitating torment.

Those Who Can't Shoot

4

From time to time a police applicant, or a sworn officer who has managed to slip through a police agency's screening system, decides that he cannot and will not kill a human being. Whether the decision is based on religious or deeply held moral reasons or an abhorrence to taking another's life, the person decides he will not use deadly force in a police situation, no matter what the circumstances.

THE POLICE APPLICANT INTERVIEW

Some police agencies conduct an oral board as part of the screening process of police applicants. Generally, a board poses questions and hypothetical scenarios designed to reveal an applicant's ability to think and make sound decisions. Some questions reveal an applicant's ethics, and some are designed to show how thoughts are formulated, regardless of whether the answer is right or wrong. For example, here is a question asked by one police agency:

You are walking along a 15-foot-high cyclone fence and you see a man on the other side kicking a prone, uniformed police officer. The officer is helpless as the man repeatedly kicks him in the head and body. You cannot climb over the fence and you cannot go around it. What are you going to do?

The preferred answer is something like this: Since you know that kicks to the head can be fatal, you would order the assailant to stop immediately. If he continued, you would draw your service weapon and warn him to stop or you will shoot. If he continues, you would shoot him.

TWO OUT OF TEN APPLICANTS WOULDN'T SHOOT

One large agency found that, in an unscientific observation, approximately two out of ten applicants would not shoot the assailant. Some said they would call in a police dog, while others would call for a helicopter. One even said he would dig under the fence to reach the officer. To force these applicants to make a decision whether or not to use deadly force, the panelists added obstacles, such as, there was no dog available, the helicopter was being repaired, and the fence was over concrete. Some applicants reluctantly said they would fire a warning shot, a few said they would shoot to wound, and a small number shrugged and said they didn't know what they would do. Only one or two said they would shoot to kill. The panelists were instructed to write "No Shoot" at the top of an applicant's sheet who would not shoot in the scenario, the equivalent of writing "Fail."

If an applicant reasons that he would wait for a helicopter or take the time to dig a hole instead of defending the immediate threat to another's life, that person has no business in police work. It's a poor argument that the applicant has no knowledge of law and police procedure. The question is designed to test common sense, and common sense should dictate that if an assailant will not stop his deadly action when ordered to, then force should be used to stop him. If the officer cannot reach the assailant to apply hands-on force, then a long range method is necessary—the gun.

THOSE ALREADY HIRED

Some training coaches ask their new trainees if they feel

they are mentally prepared to shoot someone. What coaches want to hear is an immediate *yes* or a *yes* with an explanation, such as "I don't want to, but if I'm in a situation where I have to defend myself or another, I will shoot." Sometimes a coach will find himself with a trainee who has somehow slipped through the screening process and answers *no* with or without an explanation. When this happens, it's not uncommon for a coach to make a U turn and take the trainee back to the precinct and refuse to work with him.

An officer who is uncertain whether he can shoot some-one, or an officer who for religious or moral reasons knows he will not shoot a human being, should not be in a police car and, for that matter, should not be in police work. Such an offi-cer is detrimental to other officers and to the public he is sworn to protect. They all depend on him to do the right thing when the situation calls for it. If that means taking another person's life, they need to know he will do it, and without hes-itation. An unwillingness or the inability to shoot is in no way a bad reflection on him as a person, but it does mean he needs to find another line of work.

Police work is a complex and many-faceted job. Whereas there are many opportunities to help people and make the community a better place, there are also situations where offi-cers' lives are placed at risk. Though it's hard to imagine, there are some people interested in police work who have not con-sidered the risk element. While some of these people are quite intelligent and well-meaning in their goals, their life experi-ences have not introduced them to the violent side of life.

Nice Guys Don't Even Finish

One recruit, a young man who had followed a scholarly pur-suit his entire life and had graduated from an Ivy League univer-sity, was unable to finish his probationary period. He had never been exposed to life's harsher side until he joined a police depart-ment and came face-to-face with it his first week. He demonstrat-ed several times—once nearly getting his coach hurt—that he could not function in "hot" situations. He was given much coun-

*seling and several chances to prove himself, but still he was unable
to do the job.*

*"It is beyond my comprehension that there are people out there
who don't even know me but would still hurt me," he was quoted
as saying, proving his lack of understanding of the harsh reality of
the street.*

He agreed to resign and is now successful in another field.

With the ever-increasing dangers on the street, every person considering a career in law enforcement, every rookie just beginning to experience the reality of police work, and every veteran officer who has discovered that his outlook on life and on the job has changed as the years have passed needs to search his soul to decide whether they can kill another human being. If the applicant answers no, he should not go into a police career. If the recruit discovers this about himself, he needs to talk to someone who can guide him in his next step, whether it be the agency chaplain, a department counselor, a supervisor. If the recruit is unable to change his belief after talking with one or all these people, then he should be discharged before more time and money is invested in someone who could get himself or another hurt or killed. The veteran officer, who for whatever reason realizes he can no longer use deadly force, needs to make this known. He should get counseling and not be allowed to work in a position that will expose him to a deadly force situation.

What is of concern to everyone, however, is when the applicant, recruit, or veteran doesn't express his feelings or lies about them. The result can be tragic.

Fear

5

Fear. Some call it weakness. Some call it cowardice. Others see it as the bogeyman that will destroy them. There is even a good book about fear in law enforcement work with the unfortunate title of *Fear: It Kills*. But fear is actually a gift from Mother Nature, a gift that will keep you alive. Like your gun, it's a powerful survival tool, but only if you understand it and know how to use it.

Fear is an *automatic* physical reaction to a *perceived threat* that will result in predictable *physical, emotional, perceptual, and cognitive* changes because of high physical arousal states. It's important that you understand these automatic reactions, not only for your physical survival, but for your legal and psychological survival as well.

AUTONOMIC NERVOUS SYSTEM

The physical changes that bring on the fear response are controlled by a part of your nervous system called the autonomic nervous system (ANS). The ANS controls the readiness of your body for action, a condition called your arousal state. Your ANS is composed of two parts: the parasympathetic, which controls low arousal states, and the sympathetic, which controls high arousal states.

If you are not perceiving a major threat, your body will be in a state of low arousal and your parasympathetic will be in charge. You are relaxed and your body performs normal housekeeping functions, such as digesting food and maintaining your blood pressure, heart rate, and other bodily functions within normal levels.

But when you perceive a threat, the sympathetic part of your ANS will kick in and your body will start to experience a high arousal state. The greater the perceived danger, the higher your arousal. Sometimes this state is called *excitement* and may be experienced as pleasurable, such as the thrill people get when skydiving and bungee jumping. Many police officers experience the danger and unpredictable nature of police work as an excitement that is enjoyable most of the time.

When I was in boot camp in the army, we had a night training course where we had to crawl out of a ditch and across a stretch of open ground while three .50-caliber machine guns laid a lane of fire about 30 inches off the ground. Well, I ended up between two lanes so that I was crawling safely where there were no bullets going over my head.

This wasn't getting it. Although they had told us that a trainee in the last group had panicked and was killed when he stood up, I wanted to feel the rush of having red tracer rounds scream over my body. So when the drill sergeant wasn't looking, I crawled sideways until I was directly under a stream of bullets, then I crawled toward the .50-caliber. It was scary, really scary with those rounds passing just inches over head. But it was a rush, too. I loved it. It made me feel alive being that close to death.

But once this high arousal state reaches a certain level, it may start to take on negative overtones, a point where we may begin to label it as fear. Fear can gradually build in intensity as a dangerous situation unfolds, or it may explode inside of you with ferocious intensity when you are presented with a sudden and unpredictable threat. It all depends on the situation.

FIGHT, FLIGHT, FREEZE

Fear is not some weird neurosis to be eliminated. It's Mother Nature's way of telling you that your life is in immediate danger and that you better do something to save it. To help you do that, profound chemical changes occur in your body that give you an extra survival edge. These natural changes compel you to instinctively, and without hesitation, do one of three things to save your life: fight, flight, or freeze.

Fight

If you are fighting for your life, Mother Nature usually does not expect you to fight by the rules. She has programmed you to annihilate the threat any way you can. When faced with a life-threatening event, many people find a strength and ferocity they never knew they had. Even small, timid animals can be provoked into all-out attacks when they find themselves cornered.

Flight

This is another survival option that Mother Nature has programmed into all of us. Maybe you can remember a time when you were a kid walking in the dark by yourself. You heard a noise, the hair on the back of our neck stood up, and you were overcome by an overwhelming urge to run away as fast as you could. You took off, crashing through bushes, heedless of scratches and bruises, never stopping until you arrived home panting and shaken. Flight is a major survival option for many prey animals, which is why so many are programmed for speed and flight at the first sign of danger.

Freeze

What if you can't escape by flight and the adversary is too big to defeat in a fight? That is why Mother Nature gave you that third survival option: freeze and play dead. If you go hiking in grizzly country, the rangers say that if a grizzly charges you, fighting is not a good option, nor is flight, since they can run much faster than you. They tell you to freeze and play dead. Hopefully, the bear will get bored and go look for livelier prey.

Based on these powerful instinctive urges to fight like a demon, run like hell, or freeze in place, police officers have a difficult task. You are asked to deliberately go out and look for dangerous situations where your life or someone else's may be threatened. Then when you are faced with a deadly threat, you are prohibited from opting for any of these three options.

You can fight, but not like a demon, unless your opponent is fighting like a demon as well. While you can use force, even deadly force, you can use only enough to stop the threat. This is not an easy task when someone has just tried to kill you and you think that this might be the end. Add to this the difficult task of making a threat assessment during the often confusing conditions that occur in a deadly force encounter.

Flight (tactical retreats and taking cover are not considered a flight response) is not an option for police officers. You are not paid to avoid a dangerous situation but to stay and deal with it. If a gunman invades a building and starts shooting people, the civilian occupants have the luxury of running away; the role of the police is to run to it.

Freezing is rarely a good survival option for a police officer. Many officers and soldiers who have never been under fire harbor one secret hope: I hope I don't freeze when the shit hits the fan.

One day I was parked on a side street writing a report. Halfway into it, dispatch gave the neighboring car a call in my beat since I hadn't cleared my call yet. "See the bartender at Keg 'n More Tavern. Report of a very large, unwanted drunk male assaulting patrons and tearing up the place."

I reached for the mike to tell them I'd take it since I'd just finished my report and I was only four blocks away from the tavern. Then something happened that's never happened before or since: my hand froze when I touched the mike. I literally could not pick it up.

At this point in my career I'd been to hundreds of bar fights, but this time I had a weird, powerful feeling that I was going to get hurt, and hurt badly. I just couldn't get past the thought that the guy was going to attack me and beat me, and I would be hurt and embarrassed in front of my buddies.

I'm six feet two and weigh a hard 220. I've pumped iron since I was a teenager and I'm a self-defense and firearms instructor for the sheriff's office. I'm always first on the scene and I love a good fight. But this time I just froze. My heart was racing as if I'd run a mile and my eyes were watering like crazy. I just sat there, unable to move; it was like I was completely enveloped in pure, raw fear. Dispatch got another car to cover and I prayed they wouldn't drive down the street I was parked on and see me. What would I say, sitting there dumbly and sweating like a fool? I sat for about ten minutes until the feeling passed. I listened as the cars announced their arrival at the tavern, then a few minutes later when they said they had the guy in custody and were going to jail.

That was ten years ago, and this is the first time I've ever mentioned it.

What happened to this officer could happen to anyone. Cops are human beings, and no matter how hard we try, none of us can be perfect every second of our lives. However, officers rarely take flight, rarely freeze, and rarely fight out of control during a deadly force encounter because they continually train to confront problems. They are successful because they are trained to use to their advantage the natural physical, emotional, perceptual, and cognitive changes that occur during the fear response. They use fear not just to survive, but to respond in the specific behavior of a highly skilled law enforcement professional.

If you experience a disturbing incident like the one described here, don't let it eat away at you. Find a mental health professional who has special training and experience in working with police officers. Many of them have the skills and techniques that will help you understand and deal with what happened. This can lead to improved performance.

UNDER THE INFLUENCE

When fear explodes inside of you, your sympathetic nervous system instantly dumps a variety of natural drugs and hormones into your body to cause the high arousal state known as fear. You are literally under the influence of these natural chemicals, so your body operates differently, just as it would under the influence of a chemical you deliberately ingested. Besides such obvious emotional symptoms as anger and fear, this high arousal state causes other changes that can be put into three categories: physical, sensory/perceptual, and cognitive/behavioral.

Physical Changes from Fear
Here are some physical changes you might experience because of a high arousal state.

- Pounding heart
- Muscle tension
- Trembling
- Rapid, shallow breathing
- Dizziness
- Nausea
- Gut-wrenching knot
- Sweating
- Dry mouth
- Goose bumps
- Tingling sensation in limbs and/or face
- Insensitive to pain
- Jumpy, easily startled
- Urge to urinate
- Urge to defecate

These physical changes are designed to galvanize you into action and give you the extra edge to fight as hard and run as fast as you can. You will feel so wound up that you may be trembling and jumpy. These are not signs of cowardice but the inevitable physical reaction to the chemicals that have caused your high arousal state. A pounding heart, rapid breathing, and muscle tension are reactions designed to help you fight and run better. Other changes, such as dry mouth and an urge to urinate and defecate, are side effects of the powerful chemicals surging through your body.

Mother Nature also makes you less sensitive or even totally insensitive to pain during high arousal. The literature on combat is full of stories of soldiers who were seriously injured during firefights but continued to fight, often unaware of the severity or even existence of their wounds until the battle was over. Similarly, it's common for officers to receive cuts, scrapes, and bruises during a fight and be unaware of their injuries until later, when they are no longer aroused.

Perceptual Changes from Fear

The natural drugs that cause the high arousal state also cause your senses to operate differently, sometimes altering your perceptions during a traumatic event. Here are some examples.

• Tunnel Vision: Tunnel vision is a result of the loss of your peripheral vision. Your field of vision may narrow to mere inches and you may lose your depth perception and your ability to see what is behind the threat.

I was entering a house with several other officers. As I was approaching a room, a man suddenly entered from the opposite side of the room and started cranking off rounds in our direction. As I ducked to the side, my gun appeared in my hand and I fired at him until he went down. With my gun at the ready, I moved over to the body, but another officer came up and led me outside as others continued to clear the house and secure the scene of the shooting.

Before I left the location, I went back inside to review the scene. In the room near the body was a Christmas tree all lit up. I was stunned to see it, then I realized that from the moment I became aware we were taking fire I had seen nothing of my surroundings other than the sus-

pect. It's like I was seeing him at the end of a tunnel and everything else in my field of vision was gone. There was nothing there, just grayness.

- Heightened Visual Clarity: While experiencing tunnel vision, you may have a clear picture of details you ordinarily might not notice or remember. You may see a muzzle flash as if in stop action, or even see a bullet in the air. You may have a vivid image of the gun, or even a ring on the suspect's hand, yet not remember his face.

I focused on the weapon pointed at my face from twelve feet away and I could see the bullets in the cylinder of the revolver. I saw the suspect's forearm muscles and tendons tense as he squeezed the gun. I looked down the barrel and knew I was going to get shot somewhere between my nose and neck, probably my teeth. I fired one shot and it struck the suspect.
I couldn't believe I got off a shot before he did.

- Hearing distortions: The most common hearing distortion is diminished sound, which can range from total loss to sounds seemingly muffled and distant. This often happens with gunfire. You may not hear the shots at all, or they may sound like a distant, muffled popping sound. Your ears may not ring afterwards like they usually do when you hear nearby gunfire. This is one of the reasons why officers usually don't know how many shots have been fired. You may not hear people shouting at you, the sound of sirens, and other loud sounds at the scene. Sometimes sounds may seem louder than normal. Sometime you may even experience both types of sound distortion during the same event.

The whole thing began to take on this unreality when I heard the gunshot. My partner and I had chased a bank robber into an empty lot overgrown with trees and bushes. Stan ran toward a long hedge as I ran alongside it in the other direction to cut off the suspect when he got flushed out. When I rounded the corner, I heard the shot.

It wasn't a loud bang, like at the range. It was just a little pop. In fact, I remember thinking as I pushed through the limbs of a huge tree that it couldn't be a shot, it had to be something else. Then I came face to face with the suspect. He had been pushing through the tree branches too, coming toward me, his pistol pointed right at my face. We both froze.

Although we couldn't have stood there for more than a second, I remember the moment very clearly. We were about five or six feet apart and his face looked as surprised as mine probably did. I remember he had a tie-dyed T-shirt on and he was big and bushy-haired. Then we backed away from each other and the branches fell back and blocked my view.

Seeing the guy's gun and not seeing Stan suddenly put an odd twist on everything. There was this sudden feeling that a real shooting was going down, even though I wasn't sure about the pop I'd heard, and I didn't know Stan had been shot. There was a scenario feel to everything; it was like acting.

When I backed out of the tree limbs, it seemed as if I were watching another person. I decided to drop behind a parked car, then I saw myself do it. I crawled to the front of it just as I had seen actors do in the movies. I saw myself stand up behind its hood. I saw the suspect about 30 yards away. He was turning, raising his gun, pointing it at me.

I raised mine. I remember having the thought, "This is wrong. I'm going to get into trouble." There was this feeling I was being watched by an audience. I fired at him.

My shot wasn't very loud either.

• • • • •

"My partner and I were pursuing a stolen vehicle. The suspect was driving very erratically and stopped only when the vehicle spun out of control and crashed into a ditch. My partner had grabbed the shotgun and I had my semiauto drawn as we cautiously approached. When a bullet exploded out one of the windows, I opened fire.

I faintly heard one round go off, then nothing. I could feel the recoil of my own gun, so I knew I was firing, but I didn't hear the shotgun and I was afraid my partner had been shot. When it was all over, it turns out I had fired nine rounds, and my partner, who was five feet away, had fired four shotgun rounds. The suspect also got off two more rounds before we killed him. Neither of us was injured.

I had no idea how many rounds any of us had fired until I was told later. To this day, I still have no memory of hearing any gunfire except that first round."

• Time Distortion: It's common for officers to experience the phenomenon of *slow motion time* during a traumatic event. An event that takes milliseconds may seem like minutes as everyone and everything appears to move in slow motion. Conversely, time may seem to speed up and things happen so fast you can barely perceive them. As with hearing distortions, you can experience both types of time distortion during the same event.

• Dissociation: During high threat situations you may experience a strange sense of detachment, as if the event is a dream, or as if you were looking at yourself from outside your body. You may go from that *oh shit* moment with an intense awareness of fear to feeling almost nothing as you focus only on staying alive. Afterward, when you snap back to reality, it may seem as if the event took place in the Twilight Zone. Even hours later you may have difficulty accepting that it happened, as if some part of you is still in denial that it could really happen to you.

• Temporary Paralysis: You may find yourself momentarily freezing as your body is desperately trying to catch up to the sudden awareness that your life is in danger and that you had better do something right now.

Cognitive/Behavioral Changes
During the high arousal state, the chemical changes in your brain cause you to think and act differently than under normal circumstances.

- Automatic Behavior: Most participants in a traumatic event give little or no thought to their behavior; they just instinctively do what their experience has programmed them to do. This is why officers are told, "You will do what you train to do, so trust your training."

As soon as I saw the suspect's gun, I found myself behind cover returning fire. I don't remember actually moving to the cover position or drawing my gun. It just happened like I had rehearsed in my mind and during training. The whole event happened way too suddenly and quickly for me to even begin to think about what I was doing. I had new respect for training and mental rehearsal after that. It's really true; you'll only do what you have trained to do because there's no time to think up anything else.

- Memory Gaps: It's normal when you are involved in a deadly force encounter to not remember parts of what happened and parts of what you did. Memories of high-threat situations are often like a series of snapshots, some vivid, some blurry, some even missing.

I was in a high-speed pursuit with a bunch of other officers, chasing a known felon with a long history of violent behavior. When he started firing a gun at us out the window, I had the disturbing thought that I may not live through this. In spite of the fear, my training kicked in and I performed well, and we killed the suspect before he killed us.

When I finally got home, my wife made a comment about listening to the pursuit over the phone. I had no idea what she was talking about. It turns out that during the pursuit, I had called her on the cellular phone in my patrol car to tell her I loved her in case I didn't make it. My wife said she told me to hang up and concentrate on my driving.

I had no memory at all of making that call.

- Intrusive Thoughts: Sometimes you will have intrusive

thoughts that may not be immediately relevant to the current tactical situation. You might think of your family, some future event, or a previous event that reminds you of the present one.

I remember thinking, "I don't know this guy. Why is he doing this to me?" I thought that if my family could see this, they would be very upset and frightened. ·

• • • • •

I had a fleeting thought as I pulled the trigger that I would get into trouble with my department. The shooting happened in a park on a holiday and there were hundreds of people present. I had a sense that I was on a stage.

• Memory Distortions: You may think you saw, heard, or experienced something during the event, but later you find out it happened very differently or never really happened at all.

A suspect with a gun got the drop on my partner and was getting ready to shoot him. As I shot the suspect, I could see blood spurting out of my partner as the suspect shot him. After the suspect had been neutralized, I ran over to help my partner, praying that he would survive his gunshot wound. As it turns out, he had also shot the suspect but the suspect had never got off a round. My partner was not only fine but a little annoyed by my overly zealous concern for his welfare.

• • • • •

A heavily armed gunman had invaded an office building and we had him contained in an office with glass walls. Now and then he would crank off a round or two, and I kept expecting to see bullets come through the glass wall in our direction. Well, sure enough, I saw the glass shatter when rounds came flying our way. But when I peeked out from behind my cover, I was shocked to see that the glass was still intact.

In my mind, I can still see it breaking.

• • • • •

A suspect pointed a gun at me and I could feel a bullet hitting my body. Fortunately, I already had my gun out and I returned fire. I injured the suspect and he threw down his gun and gave up. After I cuffed him, I stepped back to check my own wounds. There were none.

The suspect never got a round off.

Cognitive changes that are a result of high arousal states have been outlined in an article written by Dr. Seymour Epstein in the *American Psychologist*, August 1994. Dr. Epstein points out that there are two kinds of thinking: experiential (high arousal) and rational (low arousal).

Rational thinking is the kind you *choose* to do when you are not under an immediate threat and are in a low arousal state. Under this condition, you have the luxury of taking your time to think things through. Rational thinking is conscious, deliberate, reflective, unhurried, and is not action oriented. It allows you to think before you act as you consciously examine all the facts and evidence to reach a logical conclusion based on careful analysis. Your thinking patterns follow a step-by step deductive reasoning process that you can easily explain to others. Think of it as *Star Trek's* Mr. Spock method of thinking.

Experiential thinking is the kind of thinking that will automatically kick in whenever you perceive a threat and your body is flooded with natural drugs that induce the high arousal state. Under threat conditions, experiential thinking will dominate and reduce or even eliminate your ability to think in a rational, creative, and reflective manner. It's effortless, automatic, lightning quick, action-oriented, and much more efficient (but not necessarily more accurate) than rational thinking. It's experienced as much more compelling than rational thinking, which is why we tell people who are angry not to make hasty decisions "Wait until you have calmed down," we tell them, "You'll see things differently," or, "Count to ten before you say or do anything."

Experiential thinking is also what you do when you follow your gut instinct. There is nothing mystical about gut instincts, sixth sense, or intuition. Our brain is an incredible computer constantly analyzing subtle bits of information to reach conclusions, information that may not be obvious to our conscious awareness. You know your conclusion is right, but you can't explain exactly how you know that (of course, your conclusion could also be wrong).

Experiential thinking does not follow a step-by-step process to reach a conclusion but reaches it quickly without your knowing how it got there. You must rely on this type of thinking when you don't have enough time or information to reach a carefully reasoned, logical conclusion. Street officers have to rely heavily on their experiential thinking to keep themselves and others safe because they can't be guaranteed the luxury of time and irrefutable evidence to slowly reason their way through all situations.

Deadly force encounters often happen suddenly and unexpectedly and involve irrational and dangerous suspects. Since there is not enough time for rational thinking, you can't count to ten and wait until you and the suspect have calmed down. Instead, you will shift to experiential thinking based on gut instincts, training, and automatic responses to keep you alive.

Dr. Epstein summarizes the two different types of thinking in the following chart.

EXPERIENTIAL	RATIONAL
1. Based on overall impression	1. Based on thoughtful analysis
2. More compelling, driven by emotion	2. Less compelling, driven by intellect
3. Behavior determined by "vibes" from past events (including training)	3. Behavior determined by conscious analysis of current facts
4. Reality is concrete, based on senses and perceptions	4. Reality is abstract, based on words and symbols
5. Rapid, efficient information processing	5. Slow, less efficient information processing
6. Oriented toward immediate action	6. Oriented toward delayed action and reflection
7. Change based on repetitive or intense experience (including training) and slower to change	7. Change based on speed of thought and is quick to change
8. Based on generalizations and stereotypes	8. Is more analytical and specific
9. Less integrated: more memory gaps and more scattered	9. More integrated: Fewer memory gaps and more coherent
10. More subconscious: we are "Seized by our emotions"	10. More conscious: we feel in control of our emotions and thoughts
11. Self-validating: "Experiencing is believing"	11. Not self-validating: requires justification via logic and evidence.

Dr. Epstein points out that when thinking experientially, you will respond to what you are perceiving at the moment. Your response will be mostly automatic and strongly based on your past training, experiences, and beliefs. It would be rare for you to think creatively under stress and devise all new responses. That is why it's essential that your training *programs you to win.*

Understanding the cognitive, perceptual, and behavioral changes brought on by the biochemical changes from a high arousal state is not only important for your physical survival but for your legal and psychological survival as well. After the shooting is over, your performance will be reviewed and second guessed by everyone: you, your peers, the media, the courts, your agency, and the community. While you were forced to respond to a sudden, deadly threat based on experiential thinking, your performance will be judged based on rational thinking criteria. Things can look differently in hindsight, especially when hours are spent analyzing the situation from a place of safety and comfort.

It's important that everyone who chooses to judge an officer's performance in a high-threat situation such as a shooting understand these differences. If they don't, they may harshly judge the officer for not making rational decisions, though the situation was a high-threat one that called for an immediate response.

For instance, it's common for an officer to be criticized for shooting a suspect threatening, crouching, and reaching as if for a gun. If the officer waits to see the gun come out of a jacket, he may be making a fatal error. If the officer shoots, based on his past experience that the suspect's behavior is indicative of someone reaching for a concealed weapon, but it turns out the suspect was not armed, the officer may be criticized for overreacting.

In a nonthreatening situation, the officer would have the luxury of wondering if the suspect was reaching for a gun or just had a sudden urge to pull out a pack of gum. He would have the luxury of taking the time to actually see the gun so he could make a logical decision based on careful analysis of the facts. But in a high-threat situation, that kind of delay could get the officer killed. "It is better to be judged by twelve than carried by six," goes the law enforcement axiom.

Although many street officers may not have read Dr. Epstein's article, those who have faced a deadly threat know the difference between the two types of thinking. All of us who judge their performance should understand it too.

As part of our research for this book, we asked officers who had been involved in deadly force encounters to fill out a survey to find out what percentage of them had experienced some perceptual and cognitive distortions mentioned above.

Seventy-two officers volunteered to fill out the survey with the following results.

PERCEPTUAL DISTORTION SURVEY

Number of officers responding to survey: 72

Percentage Who Answered in the Affirmative—Distortion

88 DIMINISHED SOUND: You did not hear some sounds at all, or the sounds had an unusual distant, muffled quality. (This applies to sounds you ordinarily would hear, such as gunfire, shouting, nearby sirens, etc.)

82 TUNNEL VISION: Your vision became intensely focused on the perceived threat and you lost your peripheral vision.

78 AUTOMATIC PILOT: You responded automatically to the perceived threat, giving little or no conscious thought to your actions.

65 HEIGHTENED VISUAL CLARITY: You could see some details or actions with unusually vivid clarity and detail.

63 SLOW MOTION TIME: Events seemed to be taking place in slow motion and seemed to take longer to happen than they really did.

61 MEMORY LOSS FOR PARTS OF THE EVENT: After the event you came to realize that there were parts of it that you could not remember.

60 MEMORY LOSS FOR SOME OF YOUR ACTIONS: After the event you came to realize that you could not remember some of your own actions.

50 DISSOCIATION: There were moments when you had a strange sense of detachment, as if the event were a dream, or like you were looking at yourself from the outside.

36 INTRUSIVE DISTRACTING THOUGHTS: You had some thoughts not directly relevant to the immediate tactical situation, such as thinking about loved ones, future plans, etc.

19 MEMORY DISTORTION: You saw, heard, or experienced something during the event that you later found out had not happened.

17 INTENSIFIED SOUNDS: Some sounds seemed much louder than normal.

17 FAST MOTION TIME: Events seemed to be happening much faster than normal.

11 TEMPORARY PARALYSIS: There was a brief time when you felt paralyzed.

HARNESSING THE POWER OF FEAR

What can you do to harness the awesome power of these changes Mother Nature has given you?

You can learn to survive a stressful situation by *inoculating* yourself against it. Just as you receive vaccinations to inoculate yourself against getting a disease, you can inoculate yourself against being overwhelmed by a stressful situation through a process called Stress Inoculation Training (SIT). SIT is a concept developed by psychologist Donald Meichenbaum, Ph.D, which is based on research on the psychology of how people learn. Using well-known principles, SIT outlines methods of teaching people the cognitive, behavioral, and emotional skills they need to cope effectively with a predicted stressor, in this case a deadly force encounter. You can use SIT to prepare yourself for any kind of stressor.

SIT consists of three phases:

* Conceptualization of the stressor
* Skills acquisition and rehearsal
* Application and follow-through

PHASE ONE: CONCEPTUALIZATION OF THE STRESSOR

During this phase you should try to do three things:

* Anticipate the stressor

- Understand the problems it will present to you
- Assess your current skill level

You need to have a clear idea of what you are up against, both externally and internally, so that you can formulate your survival plan based on real threats. This phase can include the following:

- Understand and accept the effects of fear: Rather than thinking of fear as a negative, think of it as a warning device that keeps you alert and prepares you to survive. Fear is a positive and powerful source of energy and strength, as opposed to panic, which is poorly managed fear.

Once you understand all the physical, cognitive, perceptual, and emotional changes caused by the biochemistry of the high-arousal state, you will not fear them, be confused by them, or be distracted by them. To help control your arousal level, learn the controlled breathing techniques and physical relaxation methods described in this section to help keep your arousal level down and your energy focused.

I've been involved in three shootings. Before the first two, I had no training in what to expect. I performed well, but felt shocked, disoriented, confused, and at times out of control by all the weird stuff that I experienced during and after the shooting. I didn't know what to think, and that made it harder to cope during and after the event.

After the second shooting, I sought counseling and learned about all that weird stuff I'd been experiencing. The doctor also taught me the principles of Stress Inoculation Training and I started using it to prepare myself for the future.

Then when I got into another situation, that training made all the difference in the world. This time I knew what to expect and I was even able to control and compensate somewhat for the tunnel vision, sound distortions, and other strange things my mind and emotions were going through. I also bounced back a lot quicker because I knew I wasn't crazy and I knew what to do to take care of myself.

- Anticipate being in a deadly force encounter: It's imperative that you anticipate the possibility of getting into a
deadly force encounter. To orient yourself toward this reality, read accounts of and review audio and videotapes of
real incidents, discuss shootings with officers who have
been there, and seek out high-quality training that will
help you prepare.

Because of the nature of violence, many police officers are
shocked and surprised when it's directed at them, even when
there is high anticipation for it. When a man bursts from a
closet, screaming and slashing at you with a kitchen knife, it's
going to set into motion a startle reflex, even though you were
guardedly searching the house looking for a burglar. You may
work in a virtual war zone of gang violence, shootings, store
robberies, street muggings, and so on, but violence is still not
a constant condition, a minute-by-minute norm. It's sporadic.
When a life-threatening act happens to you, when a gun is
suddenly pulled from a waistband and thrust in your direction, it's not the norm; it's the exception. And as such, it comes
as a surprise.

Logic dictates, however, that the intensity of the surprise is
related to how much you anticipate it happening. How well
you respond is dependent upon your preparation in the areas
discussed here and on your total acceptance that you may
have to shoot another human being.

*Dispatch said the guy was screaming his head off, brandishing a
pistol, and running up and down the fifth floor of the Holiday Inn.
He was described as shirtless, shoeless, and mentally ill.*

*We did a floor-by-floor search and found only the guy's shirt and
shoes. By the time we worked our way down to the lobby, the counter
people were in a panic. The guy had just run out into the parking lot,
where the whipping rain and wind had reduced visibility to about 30
feet. We stepped cautiously out into the downpour and scanned the
jammed parking lot.*

Two more officers joined us and we began making a plan, but we were interrupted by a shout. "Hey! You want me?" The shirtless man was standing behind the hood of a car about 20 feet away, his hands out of sight. "Here I am. Come on."

The four of us spread out and took cover behind cars and pointed our weapons at him. I centered my sights on his heart. He shouted something I couldn't hear over the rain, then a moment later slowly moved away from the car, both hands in his pockets. "Come and get me so I can shoot you," he screamed. "Come on, are you afraid?" He leaned forward as if to draw a weapon out of his pocket. "Come on, I'm ready. Let's do it."

I slowly squeezed the trigger on my revolver to the first click. Seconds passed but the man didn't move. Rain streamed down his face and over his bare chest. He looked at the guns pointed at him and laughed maniacally. "Come on," he threatened.

I was mentally, physically, and spiritually ready to shoot the guy. I just knew he was going to pull his gun because I could see it in his eyes. And there was no way I was going to wait for him to fire. I would dump him the instant it cleared his pocket.

Then he screamed and jerked both hands out of his pockets. My adrenaline fired through my arm to my trigger finger. But something made me hesitate.

His right hand held a book of matches, his left was empty. He raised them into a crucifix pose, looked up into the rain and laughed uproariously.

He was taken into custody without incident

· · · · ·

Officer Doyle was annoyed at having to sit through a two-hour in-service class on how to mentally prepare to survive a deadly force encounter. Although the class was high quality, he thought it was stupid to be talking about an event that was very unlikely to happen to the average officer. He even told the instructor that the class was a big waste of time.

A month later he was involved in a shooting.

· Be honest with yourself about your skill level: A deadly

force encounter is a complex event requiring the converging of many different skills to perform successfully. You may be able to b.s. your way through many events in life, but a deadly force encounter isn't one of them.

If you currently lack confidence in your skills, do something about it *before* you need it. Be glad that you are aware of your limitations and use that awareness to study, learn, and improve.

PHASE TWO: SKILLS ACQUISITION AND REHEARSAL

During this phase you will use all the information you gained above to formulate your training plan to get the skills you will need to survive a deadly force encounter.

- Learn the technical skills needed to perform.
- Learn the psychological skills needed to perform.
- Training should be done systematically, building one acquired skill onto another in a gradual, systematic manner that encourages a sense of confidence and mastery.
- Training should follow the general principles outlined in Chapter 6 ("The 4 Rs of Deadly Force Training").

Consider the following areas of training and rehearsal.

- Physical fitness: A strong, healthy body generally means a strong, healthy outlook. Without argument, good health and fitness go a long way toward helping you survive a shooting and the emotional and physical stress that may follow. No, you don't have to look like Arnold Schwarzennegger, but when you are healthy and in good shape, you have more strength and energy reserves to help you through the long ordeal.

It's beyond the scope of this book to provide you with an exercise program. There are lots of them out there to choose from—aerobics, stretching, yoga, weight training, swimming, and a variety of sports—and all are of value to police officers when they are practiced regularly together with a healthy diet. Choose one or two and practice them systematically at least twice a week for a minimum of 30 minutes at a time. Ideally, you should choose one that strengthens your muscles and one that works your cardiovascular system. Toned muscles provide you with endurance and physical strength, while a strong cardiovascular system helps to keep your heart strong, your cholesterol count under control, and your body weight where it should be. Both types of exercise are stress eaters.

Considering the police life-style: the terrible hours, the frequently missed meals, the court time. Is it idealistic to suggest that you get involved in a good exercise program, eat correctly, and get sufficient sleep? No, it isn't. In fact, it's all the more reason to do these things. It's not always going to be easy, but it can be done with planning and effort.

• Tactic skills training: People are much more likely to feel high levels of fear or even panic when they are unprepared to deal with a threat. The actual threat is not nearly as important as the level of preparation. The more prepared you are, the more in control you feel, and the less fear you will experience. It's important that deadly force training be as realistic as possible and that it programs you to win.

It's vital that you maintain proficiency in all areas of your job. Strive to keep current on new and innovative techniques for conducting car stops, building searches, defensive tactics, suspect approaches, dealing with the mentally ill, prisoner transport, shooting techniques, and all other high-risk police duties. Volunteer to take every training opportunity that comes along. If your agency refuses a request that you know is beneficial, be willing to pay for it out of your own pocket.

Try to become an instructor in as many areas of police work as your agency allows. Most instructors would agree that there is no better way to learn a skill than to teach it. Students' questions will keep you on your toes so that you need to know every minute detail of the subject.

As a defensive tactics instructor, I've taught the straight baton for years. Then my agency went to the side-handle baton, which I've always hated. But as an instructor I had to teach it and, to my surprise, I got good with it. I didn't want to be good with it because that would be the same as admitting that I liked it. But after teaching the thing for years, answering hundreds of questions about it, and designing a variety of drills, I got pretty darn good with it.
But I still don't like it.

We live in the information age now, and even if you work for a small agency in an isolated place, there is still material available to increase your knowledge of the job.

- There are dozens of books and videotapes on police tactics that can be found listed in police catalogues, police union newspapers, and on the shelves of police supply stores. There is lots of information just floating around in cyberspace waiting for you to connect with it. You can use it to talk with officers in other parts of the country and even other parts of the world. Here are three excellent web sites where you can gather more information about policing and related subjects than you might ever have time to use.

- **The Police Officer's Internet Directory** (Http://www.officer.com) contains links to hundreds of other sites, which link to more sites, and so on.
- **LWC Books** (Http://www.aracnet.com/~lwc123/) is Loren Christensen's web site, which offers exciting literature on law enforcement, martial arts, and personal safety. LWC Books also offers links to other sites.
- **The Paladin Press Web Site** (Http://www.paladin-press.com) is an on-line catalog offering hundreds of action books and videos. Paladin Press is a leading pub-

lisher of police science books and videos. Their web site also offers links to related sites.

If you want to search the Internet even further, simply go to Http://www.search-it.com. This site offers a number of search engines where you can simply type in keywords that will unveil loads of information on law enforcement. Here are some good keywords:

> police—cops—jails—law enforcement
> sheriffs—prisons—police departments
> police agencies—police shootings—glock
> firearms—cop links—police training
> public safety—police statistics

- If you can't get your agency to subscribe to the many police magazines, newsletters, bulletins, and intelligence reports, cough up the money yourself.

- Read the newspapers and news magazines to see what crime trends are happening in your area and around the country.

- Contact other law enforcement agencies to see what they teach about car stops, barricaded suspects, and knife defense. Many will gladly send you a notebook or FAX you their literature and teaching outlines.

- If you are a training officer, bombard your boss with memos and purchase requests for new training material and classes. If you are a street officer, bombard your training unit with memos and purchase requests. If you are told there isn't a budget for these things, or you get turned down for another reason, examine ways to get what you want. Are other officers willing to pool their money? Are you willing to spend yours? Can you get a tax write-off if you do?

If the training is worth it, do whatever you have to do to get it.

- Your state of mind: It's important to educate yourself about the psychological aftermath of traumatic events on you and your family. If your agency does not require or provide you with psychological debriefing, be sure that you and your family find it on your own.

Since there is life outside police work (that will come as a surprise to some officers), know that outside stress can influence your job performance. Whether it's a fight with a spouse, money problems, or having to live with a teenager, all can effect how you relate to your partner or how you do in a shooting.

Since problems at home are inevitable, it's important to learn how to deal with them.

- Legal survival: Educate yourself about your legal rights and responsibilities before you get into a deadly force encounter.

- Mental survival: You must decide right now that no matter what, you will win a deadly force encounter. Your most critical survival weapon is not hanging on your gun belt; it's between your ears. A determined and winning attitude will keep you alive and you need to cultivate that determination now—and keep it forever.

- Mental imagery: Besides maintaining a winning mental attitude, you can also use your mind to rehearse any number of dangerous scenarios. Let's take a look at mental rehearsal—commonly called mental imagery—and see how it is made even more effective when combined with deep relaxation exercises. Then we will look at how you practice mental imagery in the privacy of your own home and even in your patrol car.

Much has been written on mental imagery in recent years as more people discover its importance for improving physical skill. Many Olympic athletes include mental imagery in their training and devote a significant portion of their time to visualizing gymnastic routines, high dives, downhill ski runs, or whatever their sport may be. They know from experience that it's an effective, easy-to-do supplement to their physical training that often makes the difference between winning and losing.

Studies have been conducted using basketball players, dart players, and other people who engage in sports that require precision skill. The studies broke the participants into three groups: those who physically practiced every day, those who didn't practice at all, and those who only visualized daily practice sessions. After several weeks the groups were tested, with always the same results. As you might expect, the groups that didn't train didn't improve. The groups that only mentally rehearsed their skills improved nearly as much as the ones that physically practiced.

Karate champion and actor Chuck Norris used mental imagery during his competitive years. He says that when he knew he had to fight a particular competitor for the first time, he would watch the man fight his earlier matches to see how he moved and responded. Norris would then find a quiet place where he could conjure mental imagery of his pending fight. He would see the man's roundhouse kick, then see himself block or evade it and counter with a clean, point-winning technique. He would create several mental scenarios and on each exchange see himself score with the winning point.

When Norris actually climbed into the ring, he had a distinct advantage. He had "experience" fighting the man, though the man didn't have experience fighting Norris. Norris' attacks and counterattacks flowed just as he had visualized them, and he made every winning point that he had seen in practice. Norris used mental imagery for all of his competitive years and retired as Middleweight Champion of the World. Then he started visualizing that he would be an actor . . .

Some bodybuilders can "pump," their muscles with blood by visualizing themselves doing an exercise, such as barbell curls. By creating a clear mental image of the repetitions, they can engorge their muscles as if they had physically curled a barbell for three sets of ten repetitions. And think about this for a moment: some bodybuilders claim they developed their chiseled abdominal muscles simply by visualizing sit-up exercises!

Mental imagery practice requires that you form a clear mental picture of the activity. If you are creating a scenario where you walk into a convenience store and interrupt a robbery in progress, you need to fill the entire picture. There is the candy display case to the left, the milk cooler next to that, the cash register along the front wall, magazine displays to its right and left, and a cigarette display case above it. You can smell the wieners in the rotisserie and hear the music. This complete mental image is important to create a situation as close to reality as possible. If you make it vivid enough in your mind, you may even experience a sense of nervousness and an accelerated heart rate.

The "action" should take the same amount of time in your mind as it would in reality. Let's say you visualize yourself walking up behind a man at the counter of a convenience store. He turns toward you, pulls a gun from his waistband, and raises it toward your face. You respond by quick-drawing your weapon, side-stepping, and firing into his chest. In reality this would take about five seconds, which is exactly how long it should take in your mind. If you begin your mental scenario as you pull up to the curb, add five seconds as you see yourself walking into the store.

Since your scene doesn't take much time, you can benefit from high-repetition practice and visualize it dozens of times in a five minute period.

Relaxation Exercises

Whereas you can practice mental imagery anywhere, your mind is more receptive to mental imagery when you are in a quiet place and completely relaxed, such as in your easy chair at home. For some people, the best time is when they first awaken and are completely relaxed. People who practice at other times of the day find that they need to first do a relaxation exercise to prepare themselves for mental imagery.

There are a variety of relaxation exercises taught in yoga, martial arts, and mediation classes. How-to literature can also be found in the self-help section of your local bookstore, particularly in books that discuss stress-reduction methods and self-hypnosis. In recent years, because of top athletes discovering the wonderful benefits of total relaxation, chapters illustrating relaxation methods can often be found in how-to books in the sports section of bookstores and libraries.

There is nothing mystical about relaxation exercises, and you don't need to meditate under a waterfall or eat a diet of yams and lentils to do them. If your idea of relaxing is a mug of coffee and the Sunday paper, or sprawling on the sofa and watching a football game, you will be amazed to discover how the following relaxation exercises can lower you into a much deeper state of relaxation. You will also be surprised at how easy they are to do and how wonderful the physical and mental state of deep relaxation feels. In fact, you may find, as others have, that you will want to do them just for the pleasure of deep relaxation. But when you practice your mental imagery while deeply relaxed, you will find that you can better focus on the task and visualize the scene with greater clarity and realism.

Here are two relaxation methods that many people find easy to do.

- Blue Fog: Wear loose, comfortable clothes and sit in a comfortable, quiet place where you will not be disturbed. If you prefer, and you are not likely to fall asleep, lie on a sofa or bed and arrange pillows to help make yourself comfortable. Let your hands rest on your lower abdomen or in your lap if you are sitting.

    Close your eyes and allow your body to sink heavily

into your chair or bed. Breathe in slowly through your nose and draw the air deeply into your lower abdomen. The inhalation should take about six seconds; hold it for three seconds then exhale for about six seconds. The entire cycle will take about 15 seconds.

There is no strain involved in this. If you took only three seconds to inhale the first time, keep practicing until it takes you six seconds. Six seconds in, hold for three, and six seconds out. By the third day you should have the timing down without having to look at a clock.

After a few breaths you will begin to feel a mild calming effect throughout your body. It will sweep over you like a wave, and if you are normally tense and stressed, this new feeling will be strange to you. Don't worry about it; it just means you are beginning to relax.

To accentuate this pleasurable feeling, imagine your incoming breath as a cool, blue fog curling into your nostrils, tumbling and swirling down into your lungs, abdomen, thighs, and feet. At the completion of the six-second inhalation, visualize, as you hold your breath for three seconds, the blue fog tumbling throughout your body, cooling and calming you.

Now slowly exhale, imagining the blue fog reversing its course, swirling and tumbling up through your body and out your nostrils. But this time the fog is a deep red—the result of having collected fatigue, tension, anger, and frustration throughout your body. As you continue with the exercise, your exhalation will be less red until it's eventually as blue as when you inhale. As you repeat the breathing cycle, you will find yourself sinking deeper and deeper into a state of deep, cool relaxation.

- Progressive Relaxation: Like push-ups are to calisthenics, this progressive relaxation exercise is a classic one to bring on deep relaxation. It involves the progressive and systematic relaxation of all the major muscle groups: feet, calves, thighs, buttocks, abdomen, chest, arms, shoulders, neck, and face. Your goal is to tense and then release each major body part until you are completely bathed in total relaxation.

Assume a comfortable position on the floor, bed, or your favorite chair. The room should be quiet, comfortably heated, and your clothing should be loose and comfortable. Breathe in and out deeply a few times to get yourself settled into the position.

Start the exercise by thinking about your feet. See them and feel them in your mind, beginning with your toes, arches, and heels. Tense them as hard as you can, mentally and physically contracting every muscle fiber. Now, stop contracting and allow them to relax as you exhale the tension from them. Feel and enjoy the pleasurable, soothing sensations in your feet.

Move up to your calves, visualizing every inch for a moment before you tense them as hard as you can for 10 seconds. Relax and again feel the sensation that sweeps over the muscles. If your calves or any other muscles cramp during the tensing portion of the exercise, stop immediately and massage them.

After you have enjoyed the soothing relaxation in your calves, move on up to your thighs, buttocks, abdomen, chest, neck, and facial muscles. Repeat the procedure with each muscle group; awareness, contraction, and abrupt relaxation. If you have trouble relaxing, try segmenting your body even further: lower back, forearms, hands, and various parts of your face, in particular your jaw and forehead, where tension often causes pain.

Each body part should get about 10 seconds of tensing and about 10-15 seconds of relaxing before you advance to the next muscle group. Remember to breathe slowly and deeply as you go. You should be able to progressively relax your entire body in about 10 minutes.

Use one or both relaxation methods or research others. You will find that the more you practice, the easier deep relaxation is to achieve. Once there, practice your mental imagery repetitiously for 10-15 minutes.

One time I was dispatched to an abortion clinic on a report of a disturbance between two groups of people on opposing sides of the abortion issue. Other cars were dispatched as backup, but I got there before they did. There were about 150 very angry people waving signs, holding up bloody dolls, and shouting slogans at each other. I made a foolish move and got out of my car before my cover arrived and worked my way through the crowd up to the clinic door.

Both sides were trying to get into the clinic, but the folks inside had locked the doors and were peering anxiously out all the windows. Just as the crowd was getting really nasty, it occurred to me that I was caught right in the middle with no cover in sight. The protesters had been yelling at each other, but now they were turning on me and I was getting jostled back and forth as they pressed in tighter and tighter. One shouting man poked me with a sign and I pushed him back, which angered his side and caused the other half to cheer. Then someone from the cheering side rushed at me and I knocked him aside. A couple fights broke out in the middle of the crowd, and both sides started pushing each other. Several people shouted that they were going to move me out of the way and get in. I could hear sirens in the distance—the far-off distance—and I was feeling quite alone.

I have always practiced different types of relaxation exercises and I'm pretty good at bringing on a relaxed state. This wasn't the ideal setting, but as much as I could, I concentrated on deep inhalations and slow exhalations as I stood guard at the door. I told myself that I was getting calmer with each breath exchange and I mentally willed the tension from my body. Each time I exhaled, I would command my muscles to loosen and my body to feel lighter and lighter.

I only did this for a minute, but it worked. Although people were screaming at each other and at me, I became calmer and more in control of myself. I held my position and even calmed some people closest to me.

Mental Imagery Practice On Duty

Although you don't want to close your eyes on duty and get deeply relaxed for mental imagery practice, you can still do it to a limited extent in your police car or at your busy coffee stop. You will not go into a deep state of relaxation first, but superficially go through scenarios in your mind while you stay alert to everything going on around you. Is this as effective as when you first get deeply relaxed? No. But it will go a long way toward preparing you for a real event.

Try this. Park across the street from a convenience store and look at the setting. Now, with your eyes still open, imagine that you have just pulled onto the lot and parked two spaces from the door. Superimpose a thief coming out the door, a gun clutched in his hand. See yourself draw your weapon and take cover behind the hood of your car. Hear yourself order him to stop. See the man raise his weapon toward you, and see yourself firing rounds into his chest.

While you are sitting in your coffee stop, look at the two men eating at the counter. Imagine that they begin to argue, oblivious to your presence. See yourself slide out of your booth and approach them with the intention of settling their dispute. But before you get to them, the man on the left pulls a gun and points it at his buddy. See yourself draw your weapon and call out for him to drop his. See him swing his gun in your direction and see yourself sidestep and fire into his chest.

This entire exercise will take you 10-15 seconds, and no one in the restaurant, not even the two men at the counter, has the slightest inkling that you just went through a shooting while they were dining peacefully.

Is this practice sick? Is it so mystical and weird that you can only imagine David Carradine doing it on his TV program *Kung Fu?* Well, that is a judgment call. But there is one thing for certain: these types of incidents are common in police work. So if mentally rehearsing your response to them is thought of as strange by some people, so be it.

One officer worked a beat that had seven convenience stores, often called "stop and rob stores" in police vernacular. Since it was not uncommon for two or three of them to get held up during his evening shift, the officer used mental imagery to help smooth his response. He would park across the street and plan his approach in the event he was dispatched to an "in progress" call. He would create several scenarios about how it might go down, then imagine his response to each. At home, he would sit in a quiet place, close his eyes, and mentally bring forth a clear image of his response to the many variations. He found that the exercises helped him respond smoothly and with experience, although the previous experiences had taken place only in his mind.

There is only a remote chance that you will ever experience a real situation the exact way you visualized it. But then it can also be argued that on the street you would never stand motionless and fire at a static paper target, as you have done so often at the firing range. Nonetheless, both training methods are important and have proven to be sound and beneficial ways to train, especially when combined with other training.

Some of my fellow officers deal with the possibility of deadly force encounters by mostly ignoring the whole issue. I decided to think not "if" I got into a shooting but "when." I knew it would probably be sudden and unexpected, and that I might get shot or stabbed. So I started rehearsing those possibilities in my mind.

One night I found myself suddenly face-to-face with an angry man aiming a hunting rifle at me. As I looked down the barrel of that rifle, whose round would probably penetrate my body armor, a thought that I had rehearsed popped into my mind: "Just because you're shot doesn't mean you're dead or even down." I felt calmed and reassured by that thought and, even as I was anticipating bullets hitting me, I pulled my gun and began to fire.

I killed him before he got off a shot.

PHASE THREE: APPLICATION AND FOLLOW-THROUGH

If you have done your homework in the Conceptualizing the Stressors and Skills Acquisition and Rehearsal sections, you are more likely to do well in a deadly force encounter.

You could be a police officer for a hundred years and still

never master everything there is to know about law enforcement. The world of police work is always changing, and situations that evolve on the street are just too strange to ever be predictable. That is one thing that makes police work interesting and challenging, and most police officers wouldn't have it any other way.

The constant change means there is always something new to learn. The term "follow-through" means that you allow yourself to analyze and critique your performance in a positive and constructive way so you can further improve your skill level. First though, you need to clean up any psychological damage done to you or your family so you don't drag the incident around forever. You want that event to be fully processed, digested, gleaned for information, and put behind you as you move on with your career and your life. Chapter 10 ("Traumatic Incident Debriefings") will give you tips on how this can be accomplished.

This may take time and energy, but it will be well worth it.

HOW TO CONTROL FEAR

Here is a list of just a few things you can do to help diminish and control fear.

- Stay up-to-date on police tactics in all areas of your job and train regularly in them.
- Develop confidence backed by real skill. Know that your techniques will work when you need them. The more competent you believe you are, the less likely you are to feel overwhelmed by fear.
- Practice mental imagery of high-risk situations at least once a week.
- Learn what the physiological responses are to the fight-or-flight and understand that it will happen to you no matter how brave you are.
- Understand and totally accept the possibility that you may have to one day use deadly force.

- Review your past high-risk situations to determine what was done well and what needs to be improved.
- Constantly strive to improve your observation and assessment skills.
- Trust your instincts.
- Develop a powerful will to survive no matter what the situation.
- Maintain a high level of physical fitness.
- Be knowledgeable of crime trends and criminals in your city, your precinct, and on your beat.
- Stay mentally positive.
- Make sure you and your family get psychological debriefings for all traumatic events.

The Four R's of Deadly Force Training

6

Training is worthless unless it prepares you mentally, physically, and emotionally for what you will encounter on the street. The main objective in training police officers for deadly force encounters is to prepare them to make split-second decisions in extreme life-or-death situations. A member of a French SWAT team summed up the objective of training this way: "It is better to perform reasonably well under extreme circumstances than extremely well under reasonable circumstances."

Most police officers are bright, highly motivated individuals with good athletic ability who can easily acquire knowledge and motor skills for firearms and defensive tactics training. But this is not enough. They must be able to automatically choose the right combination of skills under extreme stress and a high arousal state. So how do we prepare officers for this challenge?

The Four Rs of deadly force training summarize general training principles that will help to achieve this goal.

- Realism
- Repetition
- Review of Performance
- Responsibility

REALISM

The Real World

I had been in two shootings when I went to firearms training at our annual in-service training. The instructor put me out in the open and told me to stand in one spot. A target, 25 yards away and suspended on a wire, began moving to my left, then to my right. I was told to fire four rounds as it passed each way.

During the first pass I emptied one magazine, did a combat reload, and emptied a second magazine. The instructor ran up to me and shouted, "What the hell are you doing?" I got angry and told him that first he put me out in the open, then tells me to not move, and not to go to cover. Then he tells me to stop firing at a moving target. I told him he was programming me for failure and I wasn't going to put up with it. I told him that as long as that target was up and moving, I was putting lead in it. Two creeps had already tried to kill me for real and I know you don't have time to think about what you're doing under those circumstances. I was not going to practice any techniques that might get me killed if it ever happened to me again.

The more realistic your training is, the more effective it's going to be. With deadly force encounters, realistic training needs to include two basic elements: dynamism, and enough stress to induce a high arousal state.

Dynamism means having to make fast choices in a rapidly changing situation. Deadly force encounters are usually sudden, dynamic situations where you often have to play catch up, that is, respond to the suspect's threats. Your training, therefore, should require you to respond to sudden and unexpected threats rather than just shoot at a stationary target. While target shooting is necessary to develop and maintain shooting skills, it alone does not have the dynamic element required to make deadly force training as effective as it can be.

It's also important for you to have the experience of performing under the cognitive, perceptual, physical, and emotional changes brought on by the high arousal states of extreme stress. This will better prepare you to cope effectively with those sensations and compensate for them when your life or someone else's is on the line. It will give you experience, practice, and something to think about in terms of your ability to manage fear when the real thing presents itself. "The more we sweat in training, the less we bleed in battle," goes an old military adage, meaning that realistic, demanding training will help keep you alive when the lead is flying.

Therefore, you want to practice deadly force training that instills fear and forces you to make fast choices in response to a rapidly changing situation. Such training might include simunitions training, firearms training simulators, live-fire houses, and mental rehearsal of realistic scenarios.

REPETITION

The second R of deadly force training will help you automatically choose the most effective behavior under the sudden conditions and high-arousal states that characterize most deadly force encounters. The vast majority of officers who have been in such incidents say they gave little or no conscious thought to most of their behavior and that they reacted as they were trained to do.

It takes a certain amount of mental and physical repetition for behavior to become automatic. Great athletes spend as much or more time mentally rehearsing as they do physically rehearsing because they know both are important.

When you were first learning how to drive, you held the steering wheel in a death grip as you stripped gears in your brain thinking about all the different things you had to do to keep control of the vehicle. You had to control the speed, know when and where to stop, be conscious of the subtleties of steering, watch out for other cars, and watch for traffic signals and pedestrians, all while the person in the other seat was yelling at you. But now you routinely drive from here to there, often not remembering anything about the trip because your mind was thinking about other things, or you were yakking on the car phone and eating a burger. It's a result of repetitious practice that you can do this without giving the effort much thought.

Though we are exposed to plenty of driving practice in our daily lives, deadly force encounters are not part of our daily existence, not even for police officers. But with proper training, you can condition yourself to respond like a well-oiled machine. But to get there, you need to first provide yourself with high-repetition, mental and physical rehearsal.

The KISS (Keep It Simple, Stupid) principle is also helpful in this context. The more complex a motor skill behavior is, the more likely it is to be forgotten or bungled under extreme stress. So what this means is, don't needlessly complicate your motor skills. KISS does not mean, however, to limit tactical options.

REVIEW OF PERFORMANCE

The third R of deadly force training allows you to evaluate the effectiveness of your response. If you are not getting feedback, you will not learn from the experience. The more immediate and realistic the feedback, the more effective it is. Let's return to the example of learning how to drive a car.

How did you learn to steer? Your instructor talked to you about the subtle nuances of steering, but when you got behind the wheel for the first time, you no doubt oversteered. As you headed toward a telephone pole, the sight of the pole gave you immediate, reality-based feedback that you were screwing up. Then when you jerked the wheel back the other way and headed toward the drainage ditch, you again received valuable feedback and you quickly corrected your action. Though the instructor gave you good advice, it was the response of the car and your immediate evaluation of your actions in relation to the response that taught you the most.

One of the benefits of reality-based dynamic training, such as simunitions training and firearms training simulators, is that they give you immediate feedback as to the effectiveness of your behavior. In simunitions training, you are highly motivated to do well so that the bad guy doesn't shoot you, another officer, or an innocent person. Firearms training simulators give you quick feedback about your reaction time and shot placement. The ones that are interactive give immediate feedback how the bad guy reacts to what you do or don't do.

Another good way to review performance is to do tactical critiques of actual incidents. This can be a formal debriefing done with a tactical expert or as an informal discussion with other officers during a coffee break. You can also seek out officers or supervisors who have strong tactical skills and discuss scenarios with them. Remember, the more scenarios you have discussed, thought about, and rehearsed in your head, the more information you will have to draw upon. Getting feedback about what works and what doesn't is invaluable to your learning. More on tactical debriefings later.

RESPONSIBILITY

The fourth R of deadly force training is about attitude, the one key factor that ties everything together.

There are three entities that are responsible for deadly force encounters and the aftermath.

Community Responsibility

All of us who live in our community, be it our neighborhood or our nation, are collectively responsible for all the problems associated with violent behavior and what we as a community choose to do about it. Many people lose sight of this and start blaming the individual officer for the entire deadly force encounter.

As an individual officer, you are not responsible for the community's inability or unwillingness to come up with effective programs to deal with such issues as domestic violence, chronically violent career criminals released from jail too early, violent juvenile delinquents whose parents can't find help for them, or desperate relatives of violent, mentally ill people who can't get care. But these are the kinds of festering social problems that can explode into a deadly force encounter, and it's the police officer who is the last line of defense.

Law Enforcement Agency Responsibility

The second entity responsible for deadly force encounters is the law enforcement agency. The agency is responsible for screening, testing, and selecting people who will make good officers, then providing them with good training.

The agency is responsible for taking care of an officer involved in a deadly shooting by backing him up, treating him fairly, and making sure he and his family receive high-quality debriefings and psychological care.

The agency is responsible for training its supervisors and managers and encouraging them to be strong, effective, and compassionate leaders who have the technical and people skills necessary to lead their troops through difficult situations.

The agency is responsible for recognizing the importance of peer-support by encouraging the development of peer-support teams and giving them access to high-quality training and clinical supervision from mental health professionals.

The agency is responsible for developing a positive and proactive approach toward the community by educating them about the realities of police work (especially deadly force encounters) and developing a partnership with them to help solve crime problems.

Officer Responsibility

The third entity is you, the police officer. When you are staring down the barrel of a bad guy's gun, only you, and any fellow officers who might be at the scene, are going to save lives. At that moment it won't matter how insensitive and irresponsible the community or your agency might have been to your need for training. All that will matter is how well you are prepared to protect your life and the lives of others.

Virtually any officer who has been in a deadly force encounter will tell you that afterward he took his training and preparation more seriously. If the in-service training was good, he participated 100 percent, but if it was poor or nonexistent, he complained and sought outside training on his own.

You are responsible for how you treat each other. Only you and your fellow officers can make the decision to provide the kind of peer support and respect that can help officers and their family members recover from the aftermath of a traumatic event. If your agency does not provide training and clinical supervision for peer support teams, you and your union should explore resources on your own.

You are responsible for your personal recovery and your family's after a traumatic event. Educate yourself about the possible psychological damage that can result and find trustworthy and competent mental health professionals to help negotiate the recovery process.

You also need to educate yourself about your legal rights and responsibilities to make sure that you legally survive the aftermath. Don't leave this up to your agency. They may back you up, but then again, they may not. You need to protect yourself.

Part Two

Beyond
the
Headlines

7

The following are not "war stories" but the personal anecdotes of nine officers who have used deadly force at least once in their careers, some a number of times. We call this chapter "Beyond The Headlines" because, as you will quickly see, there is much more to their encounters than what was reported in the media or gossiped about in police locker rooms.

Those whose stories appear here were willing to relive their experiences for one primary reason: they wanted to help other officers. For some, bringing up those sights and sounds again was difficult, but they did it anyway.

Without any prompting from us, the officers revealed their human side: their vulnerabilities, their weaknesses, and their strengths. They talked with love and concern about how their traumatic incident effected their spouses, their children, their parents, and their fellow officers. Not one of them swaggered or showed an attitude of "I'm cool because I've killed someone." All were unpretentious about their experiences because they have clearly grown in the aftermath to a place of strength and humility.

Their stories are told here without colorful adjectives, adverbs, or dramatic flair. They are dramatic enough without embellishment.

THE BACKYARD

"The tree I was lying behind had three trunks coming out of the ground, all of them about four inches in diameter. Now the guy's rounds were dropping lower and lower toward me. They were cutting through the limbs over my head and pieces of branches were falling all around me."

It began with a routine tavern fight. There was a 30-year-old black male assaulting patrons, dispatch said. A female officer arrived first and was told by the bartender that the guy had left and was probably heading toward his house down the street. It was a hot July evening, about 7:30.

Radio transmissions between cars and dispatch were routine for a few minutes, then the female officer's voice burst over the airwaves: the man, she shouted, had just stepped out on his porch, fired a rifle into the air, then stepped back inside.

Since the house is located in a high-crime area, officers who worked the area were experienced and knew immediately what to do. First, they quickly set up a perimeter so that all four sides of the house could be watched, then supervisors arrived and established a command post.

"I was just finishing a shoplifting call at a nearby shopping mall," says Ted Higa, *"and I was listening to all the radio traffic. I cleared my call and thought I would just write my report, eat my sandwich, and take routine calls while the other cars were tied up on the barricaded man."*

But it wasn't meant to be. A sergeant came on the radio and told Higa that he wanted him to establish a perimeter at the rear of the house. *"The bad guy's house was on 16th Avenue, so I went to 17th directly behind it, parked, and worked my way into the guy's backyard. It was a small yard that offered no cover and concealment. I tried to go into a small shed but it was overgrown with berry vines. So I moved over to a wooden fence and got behind it. It wasn't much for cover [solid protection against bullets] but it did conceal me."*

A few moments later the man stepped out on the back porch. *"He had a rifle and pointed it in the air and fired a round,*

then went back inside. I could hear him ranting and raving and literally stomping his feet as he walked from room to room. Then he
went out the front door. An officer came on the air and said the man
came out the front door with the rifle. Then the guy went back inside
again, stomped and cursed his way through the house, came out on
the back porch, and again fired a round into the air. He did this every
ten minutes or so."

Higa was lying on his stomach, his revolver trained on the
man each time he came out the door. He radioed the sergeant
and told him he could take a shot, but the sergeant said no
because the man wasn't shooting directly at anyone. "I didn't
want to shoot, but I wanted the sergeant to know I could.

"At first the guy was shooting straight up but as time went on
he began to lower the rifle. I moved over to a small tree that had
three, four-inch thick trunks. It wasn't much but it offered more
cover than the fence. Besides, I couldn't see well from the fence and
I wanted to be in position to keep my eye on the door and the windows. A few minutes later an officer crawled over to me and gave me
a shotgun, then crawled back to his place of cover since there wasn't
enough room for both of us."

The officers at the scene would subsequently learn that the
suspect, who had a long history of mental illness, had been
living in the house with another man and his elderly mother.

The man continued to stomp from the front door to the rear
door and shout obscenities. "He would always shut the door when
he would go back inside. So when he came out, I would first see the
doorknob turn, then the door slowly open. He would push open the
screen door, come out on the porch, look around, and fire a round."

The Hostage Negotiation Team was called, but SWAT
wouldn't be called for several hours. This has since changed at
this agency so that now both teams are called simultaneously.

"We just waited," Higa says. "But the guy's rounds were getting lower each time he fired. They were cutting through the limbs
over my head and pieces of branches were falling all around me. The
Hostage Negotiation Team contacted the man over the phone a few
times; once they thought they heard a female voice. From my position, I'd hear the phone ring inside the house, then it would stop

*when the guy picked it up. A moment later he would go off scream-
ing profanities, then come out on the porch and fire a round. The
guy was really agitated and it was clear that the negotiations
weren't working."*

Two members of the Hostage Negotiation Team positioned themselves near the garage about an hour and a half
after the incident began. Since the suspect was no longer
answering the phone, they decided to talk to him over a bull-
horn. The suspect responded by coming out on the porch and
firing toward it.

*"As darkness fell a cool breeze picked up, and it was turning into
a beautiful summer evening," Higa recalls. "The balmy feeling of the
night and the sound of rustling leaves sticks in my memory. I
remember thinking that it would be a great night for a barbecue and
a beer."*

Instead Higa was forced to lie hour after hour in the same
place where he had relieved himself earlier. He was in the line
of fire of an armed, mentally disturbed man as daylight
turned to night. He was cursed with a portable radio that had
a volume control either too loud or off. *"I was missing a lot of
transmissions while I was behind that tree. I would either shut the
radio off or I would mute the speaker by pressing my palm against it
as I held the shotgun with my other hand."*

After the incident was over, Higa noted a dim light bulb
over the door, though he doesn't remember it being on earlier.
*"It was now very dark in the backyard and there were lots of con-
fusing shadows. I didn't want a flashlight since that would show the
suspect where I was."*

A while later, officers drove a police car into the neighboring yard with hopes of using its headlights and spotlight to
illuminate the backdoor. But the fence was in the way. The
only things the spotlight lit up were the top of the suspect's
house and Higa's position. They turned it off after 15 minutes.

*"Then things got really quiet for a couple hours. The suspect
would periodically turn lights off in the house, then turn them back
on again."*

After four hours had passed, an officer from the front of

the house told radio that he saw the suspect upstairs and he had changed into a dark sweatshirt. This set into motion several thoughts in Higa's mind. *"I was thinking that the guy was aggressive and that he had already shot at the police. When I heard that he had changed into dark clothing, I'm thinking that he probably wants to go outside into the dark."*

A moment later the suspect stepped out the front door and fired yet another round. The sergeant asked over the radio where the man was shooting and someone replied that he was shooting low.

"If he comes out again," the sergeant said, *"shoot at his legs."*

Higa heard another rifle shot from the front of the house. *"Then I heard two more shots, bigger reports than what the man's rifle made. A couple seconds passed and an officer came on the radio and said the guy had gone back inside. Then someone said there was movement toward the back door. I had the barrel of my shotgun resting on the top of the fence and I was aiming at the door, leg height. I heard the door open then I saw the screen door swing out."*

A hunched backed figure came out the door and into the darkness of the porch. Higa didn't want the suspect to get into the yard because that would put him between the officers. This is called a crossfire, a potentially deadly situation where officers' bullets could hit each other.

"I made a decision to take the shot." Higa squeezed the trigger and the shotgun exploded. He had never fired a shotgun at night so he was startled by the fire that burst from the end of the barrel and the sparks that sprayed into the night like the 4th of July.

"I heard a female voice moan as the figure fell back inside the door," Higa says. *"I knew immediately I'd screwed up."*

He got on the radio and said, *"We got someone down in the back. I don't think it's the suspect."*

There was a pregnant pause on the radio and Higa felt a rush of anxiety in the silence. Behind him in the dark a police officer uttered two words. "Oh shit."

"My anxiety level just took off. I stayed at my position for a while, then someone came and relieved me. I slowly walked over

behind the garage and sat in a squat. It was as if I were out of breath. I just sat there trying to collect myself. A sergeant came over and I told him what had happened, then I talked with the SWAT sergeant about where the body was."

Higa and the other involved officers were eventually relieved from their positions and sent to the command post a block away. Meanwhile, SWAT entered the house and found a 70-year-old woman bleeding profusely in the doorway. She had been struck in the legs with shotgun pellets, one of which nicked a major artery in her thigh. They carried her out and placed her in a waiting ambulance.

SWAT found the dead suspect lying near the front door, his neck torn open from a shotgun slug fired by an officer in front of the house when the man had last come out the front door. Because of poor lighting, the officers had been unaware that one of the two shots had hit him.

While Higa and the others waited at the command post, Higa overheard a detective ask someone, "Do they know the woman is dead?"

The words struck Higa with the force of a speeding truck. *"Hearing that completely deflated me,"* he said. *"My practical side knew what had happened, but my emotional side was deflated. I knew everything was going to be focused on me and, though I was with my friends, I suddenly felt so absolutely alone, so isolated."*

Everyone directly involved went to detectives to write reports. *"I remember thinking that this has to be one goddamn good report, one that was totally accurate about what had happened. I was not only thinking about the poor woman, but about my personal liability and losing my job."* Then the chief showed up.

"I spent about 15 minutes with the chief and told her what had happened, that all my actions were in good faith. Then I just started crying. She didn't say too much."

Although Higa was not new to police work, he was a recent transfer to the agency and knew only a few people. When the police chaplain showed him a list of peer-support officers (officers who had been involved in traumatic incidents and trained in counseling), he recognized only one name, a training officer from his academy. *"I chose him and when he showed up later, I found that his presence really calmed me emotionally."*

Being interviewed by the detectives was a disconcerting experience for Higa. *"It was very uncomfortable having my Miranda Rights read to me. It put a heavy, dark cloud over me and just enhanced my sense of loneliness."*

As he left the interview, he found his girlfriend waiting for him. She drove him back to his precinct and went on home since his car was there. He changed clothes and turned down an invitation to go to a police bar with the officer who had killed the suspect. *"I just wanted to go home. It was sunrise now and I was exhausted."*

His drive home was a long one and he felt an overwhelming sense of disbelief. *"I tried to listen to the radio but my mind kept going back to the house. I don't remember talking to my girlfriend when I got home, other than to tell her I was going to bed. I slept for a couple hours then woke up and just lay there in total disbelief. Outside my window, I could hear the normal summer sounds of lawn mowers, birds, and kids playing."*

Higa stayed at home the entire weekend. While he found comfort in the calls from his friends and the chief, he just wanted to be left alone. Monday, he went to police headquarters to see the chief. *"I went into the chief's conference room where there was a long, shiny table. She sat at one end and the assistant chiefs sat along the sides. No one spoke. When the chief left to take a phone call, I just sat there in this silent room filled with silent chiefs. When she returned, she told me I was going to be assigned to Personnel until after all the court proceedings."*

When Higa went to Personnel and met the contact person, the officer coldly told him that he was too busy and would see him in an hour. The officer's abruptness added to Higa's feeling of isolation.

Higa was subsequently assigned to a desk job in another unit. He recalls that the job and even the desk, which was joking called "the penalty box," was one reserved for officers who have gotten into trouble and were waiting for a decision to be made on their fate. He remained there until after the grand jury, which took two months to conclude.

"One day while I was working in the office, the sergeant [the sergeant who kept telling him at the scene not to shoot] came to see me. He was upset because the grand jury was considering charging him with negligent homicide. He had been in the race riots of the 60s and he knew the African-American community in which my shooting occurred was already upset about another police-related death two months earlier. I think these factors made his decisions conservative that night."

Time passed slowly for Higa as he waited for the grand jury to make a decision. Then one day one of the district attorney's investigators, a retired police officer, came to his home. He told Higa that all officers had been cleared of any wrongdoing.

Next came the civil rights investigation and eventually that too cleared the officers. Though those grueling days were over and the hurdles had finally been passed, Higa's personal trial was just beginning.

Commentary

"I've always tried to be a good troop."

That quotation from Sergeant Higa pretty much sums him up. When he was interviewed for this book, he came prepared with a large, three-ring binder that contained all the reports and other paperwork from his shooting, all neatly organized for quick reference to make sure he got everything correct. In many ways, Higa is every agency's ideal officer: his wiry body moves with an athlete's bounce, he is hard-working, extremely conscientious, and a team player. He is a quiet and thoughtful man, more focused on seeing that things get done right than on grabbing personal recognition for his devotion to his profession. He was all business as he described his shooting, and his eyes and voice conveyed an earnest sincerity that speak for a man who values achievement and integrity. His wife has jokingly said more than once, "Sometimes I get sick of hearing everyone tell me what a nice guy my husband is."

After years of working hard to earn the respect of his command staff and fellow officers for being a "good troop," Higa saw it all crumbling away that fateful night. This shooting could have devastated his career, but due to his determination to turn a negative into a positive, both he and his agency are better for it.

After the shooting, he felt shunned and rejected by the agency he was still devoted to, and he felt badly about being assigned to the penalty box as if he was a problem officer. This demoralizing turn of events was made more bearable by a friend in that division who gave him work to do and offered friendship and support.

Some of his peers made remarks that were painful to this conscientious man, such as "Are you going to shoot another old lady today?" or the detective he overheard saying, "He's fucked, they're going to hang him out to dry." Fortunately, he also had peers who were supportive and helpful as he struggled to survive the aftermath.

Higa suffered from post-traumatic stress disorder after his shooting, but he didn't know what was wrong since no one had told him what to expect. He got counseling shortly afterwards but said, "The counselor just sat there and looked at me. Between him not talking and me not being a very talkative person to begin with, we just sat there staring at each other." He felt like he had the "Mark of Cain" on him, as if everyone on the street recognized him as "That Cop Who Killed The Old Lady." When he was off-duty, he stayed at home most of the time to avoid being recognized, which is a common feeling among police officers after a shooting. While this is mostly an irrational fear, Higa actually ran into a member of his grand jury the very first time he ventured tentatively out to a grocery store months later. Sure enough, the man recognized him.

Higa had daily intrusive thoughts about the shooting for years. He called them "the devils in my head," and it bothered him that he could not control his thoughts and make them go away. He became more withdrawn from his girlfriend (now his wife) and children, which wreaked havoc on his family life. He and his wife began arguing over nothing and he began avoiding her, even moving out for a week in an attempt to ignore the shooting. He just wanted to forget it and get back to a normal life, but he didn't know how and there was no one to guide him.

The couple was baffled about what was going wrong with their relationship. As he became increasingly withdrawn, his worried wife followed him around the house in an attempt to be of help, which irritated him and made him withdraw even more. Subsequently, they separated for a year and nearly became a statistic: another police family destroyed by a traumatic event that reverberated long after the shooting was over.

Higa missed her and persuaded her to reconcile, but they continued to struggle for several more years, still confused about what was wrong. Their marriage finally started getting better after they attended seminars on post-traumatic stress for police officers and began learning how Higa's reactions were *normal reactions to an abnormal event*. This led them to seek counseling with a police psychologist who helped them make sense of how profoundly the shooting had affected the whole family. Finally, the healing process had begun and it continues to this day.

Years after the event, the officer who gave Higa the shotgun that night in the backyard covered him on a call near the location of the shooting. The officer apologized for not calling afterward and said he had wanted to but didn't know what to say. The officer said he had learned much about peer support since then. Higa pointed out they had all learned a lot since then about tactics, training, and helping officers with the emotional aftermath.

Another reminder of the event for Higa came years later when a violent suspect, who was either mentally ill or high on drugs, was put into a holding cell. Later, when Higa and another officer entered the cell, they found that the man had plugged up the toilet, smeared feces on the walls, and was enthusiastically masturbating. "I remember thinking that this guy could wind up in a confrontation with the police just like the one I was in," Higa says. As in many cities, the mentally ill in Higa's area have few resources and are left to wander the streets, where the police become the agents of last resort in a complex social problem.

Higa said that the shooting prompted him to apply to his agency's training division so he could devote himself to helping other officers get the tactical, mental, and emotional skills they need to survive a deadly force encounter. He became active in his agency's peer-trauma support team and worked with the family-trauma support team, especially after he saw how the aftermath of the shooting tore his family apart.

He said that his own training as a rookie had been a negative experience. He perceived the trainers as mostly "just screwing with us and making us look bad" by giving them unrealistic scenarios they couldn't possibly win and by demeaning and humiliating them with gratuitous criticism and ridicule. It was more like hazing than training, he said. While some people would just take this experience and dump it downhill onto the next group of hapless trainees, this is not Sergeant Higa's way. Instead, he worked diligently for years to make training more professional, positive, and skill enhancing. He succeeded in his mission and, as a result, has earned the respect in his agency as one of their best trainers.

Sergeant Higa said it's hard for anyone who has not been through a shooting or other traumatic event to really understand the impact it can have. "You just have to go through it to be really enlightened," he said. "But I urge all police officers to start preparing now to survive, even if it seems unreal to you." And after watching his family nearly destroyed, he urges officers not to ignore their families and the tremendous impact these events can have on them. He says to find a good psychologist, seek out peer support, and urges the command staff to take care of their troops.

Though Sergeant Higa felt alone and abandoned after his shooting, he did not desert his agency. He just worked harder to make it a better place for everyone.

That is what a good troop does.

THE TRAFFIC STOP

It was a quiet, lazy Sunday and Officer Dan Foster was cruising along a main thoroughfare chatting with his wife on his cellular phone. As they discussed where they were going to go for dinner after work, Foster's eyes were watching a sedan directly in front of him. It was an old beater, with two males in the front seat and one in the back.

Though he continued talking on the phone, there was something about the car that held his attention. Police officers are always looking for things that don't quite fit, things that are out of the norm. There was nothing glaringly suspicious about the two-door car, just some little things, like the slight weaving within the lane, the way the riders kept looking around, and the way the guy in the back seat looked around nervously.

Then the car pulled to the curb and the occupants began talking to a young woman on the sidewalk. Were they just talking or were they harassing her? Although it was a high prostitution area, the young woman was clearly not a working girl. Then he remembered a suspect description that dispatch had put out earlier about beer nappers, thieves who dash into a store, grab a case of beer, and run out without paying. The car and its occupants loosely fit the description. He decided to check them out.

He said good-bye to his wife, switched on his overhead lights, and gave dispatch his location as he pulled to the curb behind the car. Foster walked up to the driver's side and asked the driver to step out and move back to the front of the police car. *"As I patted him down, I found a pocket knife and a box cutter. I knew from my box-boy days that box cutters are dangerous weapons. Then during our conversation, the guy implied that he and his buddies had stolen the beer. I handcuffed him and placed him in the backseat of my car."*

Foster, a police officer for two years, routinely handled such situations by himself and didn't feel he needed cover at this point. He spoke over the radio with the officer who had taken the beer napping call and asked him to come by to look at the suspects.

"*I went up and got the front passenger out before the other officer got there,*" Foster says. "*I shut the door and moved the guy back to the front of my car and handcuffed him. I saw that the third guy was moving around in the backseat of the suspect car, moving as if he were going to get out. I yelled at him to stay in the car.*" [It's considered good control tactics when extracting multiple suspects from a car to keep everyone contained and remove them one at a time.]

But the man ignored Foster's order and pushed the front seat forward; clearly he was going to get out. "*I pushed my handcuffed guy against the police car and drew my gun. I pointed it at the guy who was nearly all the way out of the car now, and told him to stay. But he kept coming out, saying, 'Go ahead and put a bullet in my head.'*"

Not wanting to fight two men, Foster holstered his weapon and threw the handcuffed man to the ground. "*When I looked back toward the car, the guy was all the way out and advancing toward me with an enraged look on his face. I was parked pretty close behind the suspect car so the guy was only about two arm-lengths away. I remember thinking that I was probably going to have to fight him. A second later he was on me and I felt a sharp pain in my shoulder. I pushed him away and into the back of the suspect's car but he rebounded off it; that's when I saw the knife in his hand. I stepped back and again went for my gun, but I had to struggle for a moment because my coat was in the way. When I finally got it, I brought it out firing. We were about ten feet apart and I didn't take time to find a sight picture* [raise the gun high enough to look down the barrel].*"

Time slowed for Foster as the action unfolded frame by frame. Only the suspect existed in his mind and eyes as he fired. "*I kept telling myself that I was going to win and live.*" When it was over, he thought he had fired only once, but six of his seven shots had hit the suspect.

Foster's shoulder ached from the stab wound. A moment later the first officer arrived and asked what had happened. "*The man stabbed me and I shot him,*" Foster replied, simply.

An ambulance and more officers arrived. Foster became aware that his second prisoner was still on the ground, so he and another officer picked him up and placed him into a police car. Foster helped handcuff the shot suspect [it's policy in most police agencies to handcuff shot prisoners since many officers have been injured and killed by suspects they thought were dead]. They rolled him over and found the knife lying underneath.

"I didn't feel anything when I touched the guy or saw him close up, other than anger because he had disobeyed me."

While some agencies routinely take an officer's weapon at the scene after he's been involved in a deadly shooting, Foster was allowed to keep his. Another officer, who had once been in a shooting, had him check his weapon, put in a fresh magazine and make sure there was a round in the chamber. *"This small act restored me back to normalcy. It made me feel that I was a fully functioning police officer again."*

Ambulance personnel tended to the suspect's wounds, then went to check Foster's shoulder while still wearing the same bloody gloves. Foster verbally jumped the medics and made it clear that he wasn't going to be touched with the suspect's blood. They donned clean ones, checked his shoulder, and advised him to go to the hospital. *"I'd advise all officers to always go to the hospital and be checked out after an incident such as this, since you may be injured and not know it."* Foster called the police union attorney on the way to the hospital.

At the hospital, Foster felt uncomfortable with the swarm of attention. *"Everyone was there: the chief, other superiors, lots of officers, the chaplain, and my wife. They were all totally focused on me and I thought they were making too big a deal out of the incident. I told the union attorney what had happened and he said he'd meet me later at the detectives' office."*

"My sergeant drove me from the hospital to the detectives' office. He just asked me how many rounds I'd shot. He was very soothing, reaffirming, and good to me. He's a good-hearted man."

Foster was left in a small, comfortable room where people

came in and spoke to him for a moment, then left. A lieutenant friend, who was a veteran of a shooting, came in and Foster was comforted by his words.

"There wasn't an officer-involved shooting policy in place then so I wanted my attorney present before I talked. A significant part of that evening turned out to be my refusal to give my statement to detectives right away. I spoke with the union attorney twice and he said he was comfortable with my story. But I told him I didn't want to say anything to detectives until I'd met with my own attorney."

When the union attorney went to the investigation team and told them Foster wanted his attorney present, the detectives called the Captain of Detectives at home. Eventually, two detectives took Foster into an interview room.

"They said they wanted me to talk about what had happened. I asked if I was under arrest and, if I wasn't, was I free to go. One of them went out and made another call. I know they wanted to do a good job but I was standing in their way. Since no one was there to look out for my interests, I had to do it."

Much to the frustration of the detectives and the district attorney's office, Foster left the police station without being interviewed and went home to sleep. He got up a few hours later and went to see his attorney, then returned home and slept some more. A few hours later, he returned to the detectives' office with his attorney and gave a statement.

The shooting was subsequently found justified. Foster's situation with detectives was one of several recent shootings in his police agency that helped establish a shooting policy that provides officers with certain legal rights. *"There were a lot of people there that night to see me,"* he says. *"But none of them were powerful enough to help me. I was my own power. I was in control by refusing to talk until I had representation."*

Since Foster's shooting happened on a main street in his city, he was asked how he feels today when he drives by it. *"I've talked about it so much in classroom presentations and driven by it so often that it doesn't bother me. Shortly after the shooting, I drove out and parked there and thought about what happened that day. But I don't think much about the location any more."*

When asked what he thought about his gun after the shooting, he said that he likes it a lot more. *"I still have it,"* he says. *"But I carry something different now just because it's a better duty gun."*

Commentary

Officer Foster is a young officer who could have come right out of central casting in Hollywood. He is tall, with all-American good looks, clean-cut, good manners, earnestly charming, and has a friendly attitude that makes him approachable. He tackles life with intense curiosity and a strong tendency to analyze and philosophize about it. He has a dogged determination to maintain an optimistic and positive attitude, a determination that can be sorely tested in the sometimes cynical and negative world of law enforcement. As a remarkably open person, he is willing to talk about his own feelings and about topics that others are sometimes uncomfortable talking about. With his mischievous sense of humor, he often suggests, when he is with a group of officers, that they all have a group hug. He then watches with amusement as they all begin backing away.

These qualities were sorely tested when Foster got involved in his shooting. His preparation to emotionally survive the event actually began before it ever happened. He had decided to quit drinking when it became apparent to him that he was using it to cope with certain emotions that he needed to face more directly. He joined his agency's peer-alcohol recovery support team and, with characteristic openness, talked about his problem as casually as others might talk about a sprained ankle. Sometimes he even wore a polo shirt advertising the logo of his alcohol recovery team. He says he is grateful that he was no longer numbing his emotions with alcohol when he got into his shooting because he knows it would have interfered with his ability to recover.

Officer Foster immediately recognized one important fact as he sat in detectives after his shooting. Seeing the chaos swirling around him, he asked himself, "Who, among all these people, is here to protect me and my family?" He quickly realized that there was no one other than himself. Foster may be earnest, optimistic, and positive, but he isn't naive; he is an exceptionally bright man and a quick study. As he sat there that night, he recalled what other officers had experienced after their shootings. He wisely decided to take a proactive stance toward his own post-shooting survival and refused to give a statement until he had a chance to sleep and talk to his attorney. Of course this caused a furor with his agency's brass and the district attorney's office, which was a problem he didn't need at a time when he was feeling shaken and vulnerable. But his dogged insistence to stick to his guns not only protected him, it also caused positive changes in his agency's post-shooting protocols. Now the process goes more smoothly for everyone.

Foster also took a proactive stance toward his own recovery. He found a counselor and started long-term psychotherapy to deal with his feelings about the shooting and his rough childhood.

As they so often do, the media made much of the man he shot. He was just a poor misunderstood young man, they said, and he had suffered much as a child. While Foster feels no animosity toward the suspect, he does not have much sympathy for the "abuse excuse" either. Foster also suffered abuse as a child, but in response, he chose a positive path for his life rather than the negative one the suspect chose. The conscious choices both men made ultimately brought them to that fateful moment on the street. Out of sheer determination and a positive approach to life, Foster won that moment and he feels good about it.

He also came to realize that the shooting helped him clarify the meaning and purpose in his own suffering as a child. Rather than inflicting his own pain on others, he has transformed his suffering into something positive, a dedication to do everything he can to protect, help, and save others.

Besides counseling, Foster took other proactive steps to ensure that his shooting was transformed into a positive force in his life. It was a year later, when he and his wife were attending workshops on post-shooting trauma, that he volunteered to receive an Eye Movement Desensitization Reprocessing (EMDR) treatment from leading police psychologist, Dr. Roger Solomon. This one EMDR session was a major turning point in his recovery, as it allowed him to gain powerful insights into how the shooting had tapped into his feelings of vulnerability and mortality.

As a member of the peer-trauma support team, Foster has frequently shared his experiences and insights in presentations to law enforcement personnel. He is a talented and charismatic speaker who takes major risks in front of his peers, but often keeps his audiences spellbound with his remarkable openness and willingness to talk about sensitive and controversial topics.

Foster's brush with death and his dealing with the complicated aftermath has brought him closer to his family, more in touch with his feelings, and more determined than ever to be the positive, optimistic, all-American role model. Interestingly, it has also connected him more intimately to the warrior role that has led him to join his agency's SWAT team.

He said he has not yet persuaded the team to adopt a group hug as part of their training routine, but he's working on it.

SLEEPER HOLD

While sometimes it's called a choke hold, this technique causes a constriction of blood to the brain. It's done by wrapping the arm around the subject's head with the elbow directly under the chin. Then, squeezing like a big nutcracker, the forearm presses against one side of the neck and the biceps muscle presses against the other. Unconsciousness can occur in as little as four seconds.

Judo students, who are athletic and in good physical condition, do it to each other routinely in practice and competition without a problem. Although there may be a few law enforcement agencies that still use the technique to control violent subjects who are mentally deranged, under the influence of drugs and alcohol, physically powerful, and impervious to pain, most agencies have banned its use in the past few years.

This is because on rare occasions, some people under the above conditions never wake up.

Officers Craig Dean and Roger Lane had just left the precinct when they got their first call: a shoplifter at a nearby 7-11.

"We were close so we were the first car to arrive," Dean says. *"As we pulled onto the parking lot, we could see that there were two things going on. At the right corner of the building, a guy who was obviously the store clerk was wrestling with someone on the ground, later identified as a shoplifter. At the opposite corner, there was a small crowd of people arguing with a huge black man."*

The officers scrambled out of their car and rushed over to help the clerk. They pulled the men apart and put the shoplifter in the back of the police car.

But before they could talk to the clerk, the ruckus at the other corner grew more heated.

"When we looked back over at the group of people, we saw the black guy hit another man in the chest," Dean says. *"We learned later that he had been holding back several bystanders who wanted to go help the clerk. He wanted it to be fair fight between the clerk and his assailant. The clerk wound up with a broken arm and several bite wounds."* The black man, later identified as John Lewis, stood six-feet seven inches and weighed 275 pounds, making him seven inches taller and 90 pounds heavier than Officer Dean.

The officers went over to stop the confrontation before it got worse. Officer Lane approached Lewis from the front as Dean came up from behind. Lane placed his hands on the man's chest to keep him from moving toward the crowd but the officer was promptly pushed away. Lewis was enraged, loud, and aggressive, and now he had assaulted a police officer. He was not obeying the officer's commands and he was clearly becoming more violent. He had to be controlled before he hurt someone, but he was definitely too large for normal police control techniques, like wrist locks and finger holds.

"I put my hands on his shoulders from behind to bend him back and break his balance," Dean says. *"I pressed my foot behind his knee and wrapped my arm around his head as he dropped into a seated position, with me kneeling behind him. I applied pressure to each side of his neck but the guy kept fighting, pushing my partner and others away. It took about 15 seconds before he weakened and fell over on his side."*

Dean and Lane quickly handcuffed the suspect, then stood to catch their breath. Normally, a person rendered unconscious by the sleeper hold will regain consciousness in 15 to 30 seconds.

"We could see that Lewis wasn't coming around and we could hear a noise coming from his throat," Dean says. *"We called for an ambulance but another officer who just arrived at the scene canceled it in the confusion, believing that it had been called for the store clerk."*

Since Dean and Lane were at the far end of the lot busy tending to Lewis, who still had not come around, they were unaware the ambulance had been canceled. *"We took the man's handcuffs off and began CPR. A third officer thought he felt a pulse, but looking back on it now, I'm not so sure he did."*

When it became apparent that an ambulance wasn't coming, Lane ran across the street to another ambulance company that was coincidentally located on the corner. He returned with medics, who immediately slipped an oxygen mask over Lewis' head as Dean continued chest compressions.

"I had a feeling the guy wasn't going to make it," Dean says. *"But I thought if he did, he would probably have brain damage. I felt bad about what was happening, but not real bad because I hadn't done anything wrong."*

After an ambulance had taken Lewis away, Dean went to detectives and wrote his reports (officers involved in deadly force encounters in this agency no longer have to write their own reports). When his detail sergeant called the hospital to check on the suspect's condition, Dean recalls that he got a "funny look" on his face. The sergeant lowered the receiver, looked over at Dean, and said that the man had just died.

A few minutes later, the mayor came to the detective's office and asked what had happened. Then, in one of many inappropriate moves that this mayor was known for, he asked Dean to demonstrate the sleeper hold on him. Dean stalled long enough until the chief distracted the mayor and led him off.

A member from the agency's peer-support team arrived. *"I didn't know the guy,"* Dean says. *"I didn't talk to him about the incident because I didn't feel a need to. In fact, I went home after my interview, got some sleep and went back to work the next night. I was fine working the shift and handled my calls as usual."*

Then the media began to run with the story. The second day was bigger than the first, and the third day got even bigger. The only photo of Lewis used by the media was an old one of him as a young recruit in his army uniform, professionally posed against a sky of fluffy, white clouds. *"Every day things just snowballed,"* Dean says of the public outcry. *"The second night, my partner and I were told to report to the chief the next day."*

The chief was supportive of the officers behind closed doors but not supportive of them in public. The incident was quickly made into a racial one and there was great protest from the black community. There were rallies in the town center, marches to city hall, and much discussion in community centers and on local television.

The chief immediately banned the use of the sleeper hold, a move that enraged many officers who felt that a valuable tool had been taken away from them for political reasons, leaving them vulnerable and without means to deal with violent subjects who couldn't be controlled using normal techniques. In protest, two officers at a precinct had T-shirts printed that read "Don't Choke 'Em, Smoke 'Em," implying that since they no longer had the sleeper hold they would have to use their firearm. The two officers began selling the shirts the same day as the suspect's funeral, an unfortunate move that pushed an already enraged community over the top.

"The public outcry and the media hoopla were incredible," Dean

says. *"It seemed like it went on for weeks."* But just when things couldn't get worse . . . *"It was decided that there would be a public inquest, a fact-finding hearing where the district attorney asks questions of everyone involved, without cross examination by other attorneys. It was thought that this would help heal the community."*

But it didn't. It made things worse. Dean says: *"The courtroom was filled with anti-police types, which made the atmosphere extremely tense. We were allowed to carry our weapons and we had armed escorts to and from the courtroom."*

The inquest lasted for several days and when it was over they found that the death was criminally negligent, but placed no specific blame.

"Even after the finding, which didn't carry any legal weight, I still thought I had done everything correctly. My feelings hadn't changed but I was worried that I would lose my job, that we would be made political scapegoats. My partner and I were assigned to a desk job for six weeks. I tried to stay as active as I could, so I ran a lot to relieve the stress."

Dean received lots of letters during those stressful weeks. He says they were all supportive and positive, though he thinks his agency kept the negative ones from him. He wrote every person back, even those who wrote positive letters-to-the-editor in the local newspaper.

"All my fellow officers were supportive and so were the assistant chiefs. But there was one black officer who said he thought I should be imprisoned. He said this in the hallway in court one day in front of other officers, and there was almost a fight when one of them defended what I had done."

Six weeks after the incident the grand jury convened and, after two days of witnesses' testimony, they returned with no indictment on the officers. The suspect's father filed a lawsuit, eventually collecting several hundred thousand dollars when the city settled with him out of court.

"We got word that the father took the money and paid someone to do a hit on me, but an investigation never disclosed any details and the threat eventually went away."

Dean and Lane were sent to another precinct, miles away

from the community where the incident occurred. Although the media uproar eventually died, Dean was often recognized in public. *"For about two years, defense attorneys would bring up the incident in court. Some judges let them and some would not. I'd also get threats from black people in my new precinct. I even had to get my home alarmed for my family's safety."*

Dean says he got a few insensitive comments from officers, though he never let on that their words bothered him. The worst came from a fellow SWAT member who, as a way of introducing the team to someone, would give their names and how many people each had killed.

"When he got to me, he said, 'This is the guy with the most awesome kill of all. He did it with his bare hands.' I thought that was a really stupid comment."

Commentary

If the Rock of Gibraltar was a human being, it would be like Craig Dean. His solid build and reserved air of quiet confidence give the impression that he could weather any storm simply by enduring it and outlasting it. That ability was put to the test when he found himself in the middle of a controversy that raged as intensely as any hurricane.

But he is not a man to be remotely interested in becoming embroiled in controversy. He accurately describes himself as a subdued, quiet person with no interest in publicity, flashy assignments, or self-promotion. All he wants is to put in an honest day's work and go home at the end of his shift. Instead, this very private man found himself living through a bizarre political circus, such as:

- The Mayor asking Dean to demonstrate a choke hold on him
- Private meetings with his chief, who would say one thing and then do another
- Being called a "murderer"
- Needing armed escorts when he went to the public inquest
- Receiving death threats
- Hostile and insensitive comments and behavior by peers and the public

- News crews following him
- Fear of criminal indictment and imprisonment
- Rumors of the dead suspect's father using the city's settlement money to hire an assassin to kill him

For two years afterward, Dean was jabbed by attorneys and public alike. His life was suddenly upside down and turned into something straight out of a supermarket tabloid. All this because he had been doing his job, using a restraint technique that his city approved of, trained him in, and wanted him to use instead of his baton or gun. In the end, the city decided that the restraint was too dangerous, though that was not Dean's fault. Nonetheless, he came perilously close to becoming a political human sacrifice, a fear shared by many police officers.

Perhaps the most amazing part of this strange tale is Dean's remarkable lack of anger, cynicism, or bitterness. He said that although he regrets the accidental death of the suspect, he has never had any bad feelings about being involved in an incident where someone died. Dean believes he was just doing his job as he was trained and sees "nothing mystical" about having killed a man, as some uninitiated officers see it. He said he fully expected to be criminally indicted after the media got hold of the event, but accepted the storm of controversy as "just part of the job."

Dean has the same matter-of-fact attitude toward bogus citizen complaints and the civil litigation that plagues officers in our lawsuit-happy society: "It's just the price of doing business and you can't worry too much about it or allow it to stop you from doing your job."

Dean said that he survived the awful events that summer by just "sucking it up," staying busy when he was off duty, exercising a lot, talking to people he trusted, and trying to stay as positive as possible. He appreciated all the citizens who wrote positive letters of support to him, to his agency, and to his hometown newspaper. In his usual diligent, polite fashion, he wrote them all thank-you notes.

Dean was required to see a psychologist for one session before he returned to work but was not offered (and fortunately didn't seem to need) long-term counseling. But he did seek out a police psychologist on his own years later to get a few specific questions answered about his feelings and reactions. He said it was worth it just to be told that all his reactions were normal.

Dean does not feel offended by the stupid and sometimes hostile comments made by his peers and the public. He does not believe any of them meant their comments in a malicious way and he does not take them personally. He chose to just let them roll off his back, like rain streaming down a rock and disappearing into the ground.

Though his chief was ready to sell him down the river for political gain, Dean still feels loyalty toward his agency. "That's just how I was raised. My parents were honest, hardworking people with good values. I was raised to be loyal and to always do my best. Besides, most people in my agency were OK. But in spite of this incident and the problems within my agency, I think I have a good job and I have always been steadfast in doing it well. I don't like to complain. I try to be a calm, steady person."

Dean has remained remarkably unaffected and untainted by his perilous adventure into the Twilight Zone. How has he managed to bounce back so intact? Part of it is just him: a Rock of Gibraltar determined to quietly endure any storm.

His following advice may help others achieve their own "piece of the rock."

- Stay busy and involved in life
- Exercise and stay physically fit
- Rely on peers, family, and friends for support
- Don't turn to alcohol
- Face life realistically
- Don't take other people's negativity personally
- Get a debriefing and seek counseling
- Don't whine

THE INTRUDER AND THE LITTLE BOY

"As long as I live, I will never forget the little boy's voice when he called out his name to us," says Officer Will Joiner. *"It was so sweet, but so full of sheer terror."*

A few minutes earlier, Joiner, a 12-year veteran of a major city police department, had been parked side-by-side with another police car driven by Patrick Clancy. Joiner had been telling him about how his father was dying of cancer, and that over the past several weeks he had been using his sick and vacation time to care for him. Joiner had reluctantly returned to work this night because he had no time left to take off. The dispatcher interrupted their conversation.

A man, five-feet ten to six feet tall, wearing a denim jacket and a flannel shirt was breaking into a house. The time was 3:18 A.M.

Other officers arrived first and learned from the complainant that the suspect was gone. But a police dog picked up the scent and followed it to a house one block away, where officers found a rear basement window broken. They surrounded the house and waited several minutes for the suspect to come out. When he didn't emerge, they knocked on the front door.

Owner Jonathan Simpson answered and officers told him they believed there was a burglar in his home and that he and his family should leave. Simpson ran up the stairs, awakened his wife and then went to awaken his youngest son. When his wife went into 12-year-old Jeremy's room, she discovered a man, later identified as Albert North, lying under the covers in her son's bed. He was holding a 12-inch knife to the boy's throat.

"I'm going to kill him if you don't back off," North mumbled.

The parents ran into the younger boy's room and closed the door as the officers backed down the short hallway away from Jeremy's room and down a short staircase.

North began to scream incoherently, though the officers

could make out one chilling part of it: "I'm going to kill him . . . I'm going to kill him . . . I'm going to kill him."

"My heart was beating so hard," Joiner says, who was positioned at the bottom of the stairs. He and Clancy had arrived a few seconds earlier and had been briefed about what was going on. "The guy just kept screaming and screaming." Another officer later said the screams were like something an animal would make.

A minute later, two officers outside spotted North through a second-story window. What they saw was his upper body as he stabbed downward with a large knife. The officers fired through the window, one shot each, but the glass deflected the rounds.

"I was confused at first," Joiner says. "I couldn't figure out where the shots came from. Then I could hear North crawling on the floor up there, screaming something about us trying to kill him. What were we going to do now? We kept yelling at the guy not to hurt the boy.

"Officer Thompson, who was with Clancy and me, called out to the boy and asked his name." The reply and tone of the child's voice are now permanently burned into Joiner's memory.

"He called back, 'Jeremy.' It was so sweet, but so full of sheer terror. I felt so powerless. Here I am so highly trained, college educated, and armed. But I felt so damn powerless. I love children and for a moment I thought of my own; I have three. I wondered what the Simpsons must be thinking and I thought what must be going through Jeremy's mind. He must be wondering why we haven't saved him yet. I felt so worthless.

"North screamed that he had just cut him, and was going to finish him off. Then he started to count down from five: 'Five . . . four . . . three . . . two . . . ' We heard Jeremy cry out and we all thought he was being cut.

"I charged up the stairs, Clancy and Thompson on my right. We moved down the narrow, dark hall, which was barely illuminated by filtered light from a downstairs hallway, and into Jeremy's bedroom. We could make out North, seated on the edge of the bed, holding Jeremy between his legs in a one-arm choke hold. The boy was completely shielding North's body, and the way he was holding the knife at the boy's throat made it look as if the knife was sticking in his neck.

"With his arm up and wrapped around the little boy's neck like a chicken wing, I had a perfect shot. I decided to do it. My eyes, already straining in the dim light, zoomed right in on his flannel shirt, like I was looking through binoculars. I double tapped twice [fired two rounds, paused, fired two more] into his chest. As bizarre as it sounds, I could actually see the rounds going in. I could see his shirt flap around and I could see the rounds going into his chest. Then when I pulled back, I could hear other shots going off. This confused me because I thought I was the only one firing. But my partners were also shooting, round after round.

"When I looked back at the bed, North was riddled with holes. But Jeremy was slumped over, too."

The little boy had been hit.

"It was like I suddenly stepped into the Twilight Zone. I couldn't speak other than to say, 'Oh my God!' It was so surreal. This had to be a bad dream; I must have stepped outside reality for a moment. Then someone shook me physically. All that had lasted only a moment."

For the next few minutes the room turned to organized bedlam as officers fought to save the 12-year-old's life. There were screams for an ambulance, screams for towels, screams for CPR. The officers kept shouting for Jeremy to hang in there. Joiner said that he remembers hearing "hang in there" repeated over and over. Someone applied pressure with a towel to Jeremy's head wounds and Joiner did mouth to mouth. When he felt Jeremy exhale, he was convinced the boy was going to be OK.

"As we were carrying him out on a gurney to the ambulance, someone again told Jeremy to 'hang in there.' In response, the little boy reached up, pulled off his oxygen mask and said, 'OK'. With all that doctors can do nowadays, we felt good that he was going to make it."

Four hours later when all involved officers were in the detective office, word came from the hospital that Jeremy had died.

"I thought my world had turned upside down," Joiner said. *"It was like someone had just sucked all the wind out of me and my heart had come out with it. I felt so sick, I was so overwhelmed with*

anxiety . . . it's so hard to describe the feeling. I've never felt it before. It was horrible."

Five days later, Joiner's father passed away.

"Since I had to make funeral arrangements the same day as the grand jury, I was excused from testifying. This made me feel really uncomfortable, like I was being made special. And that made me feel guilty."

Although there was the inevitable media circus for days and weeks afterwards, the general tone in the city was that the incident was a terrible, unfortunate tragedy, rather than a police foul up. *"I got unprecedented support from my peers,"* Joiner says. *"And I got cards and letters from people I hardly knew. I live in a really tight community outside the city and my neighbors and friends gave me lots of support."*

Joiner took a year off work, feeling that he needed to get completely away from the police world. *"It seemed that officers looked differently at me because I needed to take time off, and I felt guilty the other two officers weren't doing it. I felt self-conscious and feared I'd be labeled a sissy since it wasn't the typical macho thing to do. But all those feelings were unfounded because I got lots of support from my peers.*

"But it was still a hard decision to make because by virtue of my taking the time off and the others not taking it off, the natural assumption would be that it was my rounds that killed Jeremy [It was never officially determined whose rounds hit Jeremy]. *I still live with that and it haunts me. I'm never going to go out and say that it wasn't me, that it was one of the other officers. I consider myself one of those who fired; I'm an equal part of the tragedy."*

While Joiner got lots of support from friends and other officers, he didn't get it from his wife. He is quick to admit that part of the problem may have been his doing, but he is still bitter. *"You know, we think we are doing our family a favor by keeping all the bad things from them, but we aren't. After my first year with the agency, she stopped asking me about the job and I stopped telling her things. So when the shooting happened, she was there for me, but only at first. When she got over it, she thought I should be over it too. To this day I'm not sure she realizes how pro-*

foundly this experience has affected me and how it continues to affect me. Although I have taken steps to move on, I will never get over it.

"Then after I'd been off for eight months, she asked me, 'Don't you feel like you're on welfare? Shouldn't you get back to work?' Those words knocked me on my rear. I felt cheated that I couldn't lean on her. It's like she thought she had given me enough sympathy. I loved her before, but I'm not sure if I love her now."

About this time Joiner's wife came down with cancer. Although he spent time with her at the hospital and took care of her during various surgical procedures, he was drained of emotion. There was no more for him to give. *"I felt so guilty about this. I knew that I was not as attentive to her needs as I would have if I were leading a normal life. But I just couldn't do anything about it. I loved her, but there was no more of me to give.*

"I did get a big therapeutic relief interacting with my three kids and from thinking about my father. He was a great man."

Joiner returned to work 12 months later, first to the street for six months then to a desk job. Although the incident sparked several procedural changes and training methods in the police agency, he feels that the brass considers all the officers involved in the shooting as "just a dirty little secret." He is resentful that they have tucked it away. For example, when they presented him with an award, 2 1/2 years after the incident, it was done behind closed doors. *"I would just as soon not to have received it,"* Joiner said.

Three years have passed now and Joiner is planning to go back to the street. *"Some people ask me if I'm sure that's what I want to do. Some of those who ask are really concerned about me, others are just being idiotic because they think I have lingering issues about the incident, that I'm used up. They fail to consider that I'm mature, responsible, and quite capable of doing the job."*

When he thinks about returning to the street, he thinks about getting into another shooting. *"I have this sense that something is going to happen. It's not a fear or anxiety. It's just a matter-of-fact feeling that someone is going to make me shoot them."*

There is never a day that passes that the horror of that

night does not dance across his mind. Sometimes it's one more repetitious replay, other times it's an odd thought. *"You know, sometimes I think that if Jeremy wouldn't have died, I would have been a hero. I have a sense that I got cheated out of that. Then I feel like a piece of shit because that selfish thought even crossed my mind."*

Joiner would like new officers to realize that they can fall short of their goals no matter how hard they try. *"You can give it your best and fully expect that you are going to come out on top. Police probably feel that more than anyone. But I want young officers to know that shit happens and that things may not turn out the way they want them to. Prepare for that. Know that some things are beyond our control."*

Now halfway through his career, Joiner remembers high points of which he is especially proud. *"You know,"* he says thoughtfully, sadly. *"I've done lots of good things during my years in law enforcement, saved lives, caught bad guys, murderers, returned runaways to their parents. I've done lots of good. But in spite of all these things, it's this shooting that I'm going to be remembered for."*

Commentary

Officer Joiner is a large, powerful man with intense eyes, strong opinions, and an emphatic voice that belie the man inside who cares deeply about others. This man lived through one of every cop's worst nightmares: the killing of an innocent hostage by the very people who were trying to save him. While Joiner's life will never be the same, he has worked hard to come to terms with the event and to find the road back to the profession he loves. His first step toward recovery was having the courage to take a much needed year off work to allow the psychological wounds to begin healing. As is true for most police officers who recover from traumatic events, the key for Joiner was his relationship with others, especially his father, his children, his peers, and his civilian friends.

Many people who have lived through traumatic events say that one of their major insights was that their key to happiness was those people in their lives whom they cared about. Without connections to others, their lives would be empty and meaningless and they would find themselves adrift when disaster struck.

Officer Joiner became active in his agency's peer-support team and he has since extended a helping hand to other officers in the same way that his fellow officers helped him. He was grateful that he had maintained a close network of civilian friends in the small community where he lives, especially when they closed around him in a protective and loving circle while he struggled through the aftermath. Although his father was not physically present, Joiner's spiritual connection to the memory of the mentor he loved and admired was a strong source of comfort. These relationships were invaluable to him during the year he took to heal from all the personal losses he experienced when Jeremy died.

Like many officers, he found all the relationships in his life sorely tested in the wake of tragedy. As a result, he was faced with having to find a new relationship with himself, his wife, and his agency, and with finding meaning and purpose in his work. This became his full-time job for the year he was away from the daily demands of patrol work. Although it's a job that will never really have an end for Officer Joiner, he is engaging it with his characteristic intensity and passion.

THE WOMAN

No one knows how long the 52-year-old woman had been living in her pickup camper with her two cats, but she had been parked in front of the old house for more than five months. Neighbors said later that her behavior had always been strange, even a little violent, and the police had been called a couple of times to talk to her. Occasionally she had become verbally abusive with them, but she had not been overtly threatening or dangerous.

This afternoon she was annoying the man next door while he was trying to work on a car in his driveway. He called the police non-emergency line and reported that the strange woman had been sitting in her truck for hours, chain smoking, rocking back and forth, and staring at him.

Many 9-1-1 operators would have told the man to just deal with the situation the best way he could since it hardly seemed a situation to tie up a police car for. But for some reason, this operator sent the call to the dispatcher.

Partners Steve Mayer and Nancy Waller went into service at 6:00 P.M. and immediately got a radio call. They handled the call, then stopped at a convenience store and bought a couple of mega-sized soft drinks to sip throughout the hot August evening. They had just taken a cool sip when dispatch gave them their second call.

See the man at 1544 North Henderson. Says a woman next door keeps staring at him from her truck.

They accepted the radio call, probably with a smile and a thought that it was going to be one of those long, hot summer evenings where anything could happen and usually did.

Although Nancy Waller had been with the agency for only six months, she had nearly five years experience as an officer in a gang-infested area of Los Angeles. She liked being a police officer but had grown weary of seeing fellow officers injured and killed in the daily gang and drug wars in the City of the Angels. She decided to move to a mid-sized city where police work would be quieter. Steve, a four-year veteran, was her training coach, and they had been together for several months.

As they approached the address, they saw the pickup camper and, standing about 20 feet away in his driveway, the man who had called the police.

The man explained that the woman's truck had been parked next door for several months. He had attempted to get along with her and had even worked on her truck in the past, but he quit when she became verbally abusive. Today she just kept staring at him and rocking back and forth. And, oh yes, one time she had told him she didn't like the police.

They walked over to the truck and Officer Mayer began

talking to the woman through the window. She immediately became hostile, rolled up the window, and refused to talk any further.

It was Officer Waller's turn to try. The woman was still hostile, but at least she listened as Waller suggested a few places where she could move her truck. *"I was trying to impress my coach as to how I could help the woman."* But the woman suddenly began babbling about the end of the world and cussing Waller out. *"Don't try your psychological bullshit on me,"* the woman said once.

"She would be OK for a while," Waller said, *"then she'd rock back and forth and talked nonsense some more. We were working hard trying to solve her problems and find some resources that could help her. Eventually she agreed to move her truck, but only if Sharon, the woman who owned the property, told her to move. Apparently Sharon had been paid $20 for rent five months earlier, but it was unclear if the payment was for one day, 30 days, or forever."*

Waller and her partner retreated a few feet away so that the sight of their uniforms wouldn't agitate the woman more as Sharon talked with her. After a few minutes, Waller heard the woman in the truck say loudly, "OK, I'm going to leave. Take care of my cats." The two women spoke quietly for a few more moments, and then, just as Waller thought everything was going to be worked out, Sharon threw her arms in the air and walked away.

Waller asked what had upset her. *"I just can't talk to her anymore,"* she said before going back inside her house. As it turned out, the woman had told Sharon that she wanted the police to kill her, but Sharon withheld this information from the officers. Waller learned of this two days later from watching a news show about the incident.

As Sharon was walking away, Officer Waller again went over to the truck. But the woman rolled up the window and refused to talk. By now, Waller and Mayer had been there for almost an hour, with no progress to show for their efforts. But inside the truck, the woman was getting progressively more agitated by the minute, chain smoking and violently flailing around. Then she began growling.

Now what? Waller and Mayer went into the neighbor's garage to talk. *"Steve thought that maybe the best approach was to write the woman a note since she wasn't talking to us. He wrote that we were going to leave and that we would be back in an hour to check and see if she was still here. He signed it, 'Thank you very much. The Police' and slipped it under her windshield wiper."*

The officers began walking back to their police car. Waller says: *"We could hear her getting louder inside the truck, so we moved around to the far side of our car as a precautionary measure. We were only about 15 yards from where she was, but there was a grassy knoll that prevented us from seeing her. We could hear her though, yelling and screaming and fumbling around. Both of us were thinking that she might burst out of the truck any second."*

Waller could see the complainant still standing in his driveway. *"He was looking toward the woman, then toward us; he had a frightened look on his face. With my fingers I made a gesture like a gun, and the guy nodded yes then ducked behind his car."* Something was about to happen.

A moment later the woman ran over the crest of the grassy knoll toward the officers, her arm extended, her hand holding a pistol, its barrel pointing directly at them. Waller and Mayer ducked beside the trunk of the police car and shouted at the woman to put down her gun as they drew their own weapons. Mayer jabbed the button on his lapel mike and called for backup.

The woman kept coming.

"We both fired," Waller says. *"I fired once and Mayer fired three times. I know because all three of his ejected shells hit me in the face."* Earlier in the call the officers had set their big soft drinks on the trunk of the police car, so when Waller knelt and fired, she had to shoot between the two cups.

As three of the four rounds smacked into her, the woman dropped the gun and fell to the grass. For a moment she thrashed back and forth as the officers shouted at her to stay away from the gun. When she stopped moving, they advanced cautiously, Waller covered her at gunpoint while her partner applied the handcuffs. Waller retrieved a compress from the police car and applied direct pressure to the wound in the woman's side, the most serious of the three hits.

Within seconds the scene was crowded with uniforms, detectives, and medics. *"I was concerned about contamination of the crime scene, holding onto the witnesses, and not losing sight of the woman's gun. At one point, while I was doing first aid, a sergeant kept asking me questions about what had happened."*

A few minutes later, two uniform officers, both of whom had been in police-involved shootings, moved Waller and Mayer away from the crowd and acted as a buffer to keep people away from them.

"Later, one of the officers drove me back to the precinct so I could change clothes," Waller says. *"He kept talking about his shooting and how it had made him unable to sleep and had given him diarrhea for six months. I didn't talk about my shooting at all."*

At the precinct, she changed clothes and spoke with a union representative. *"He told me that the woman had died on the way to the hospital. I was concerned what the procedure was going to be because I was new and still thinking about how rough the process was in L.A., but the union representative laid it out and I felt better about what to expect."*

The same officer who had given her a ride to the precinct drove her to the main station to talk to detectives. *"Again the officer kept talking about his shooting, how miserable he had been afterwards, how he had vomited. I didn't really want to hear it now and I didn't think those things were going to happen to me, anyway."*

She met her personal attorney at the detectives office but it was hard for them to talk because they were continually interrupted by the brass and the police department's media officer. Then someone told her about the suspect's gun. It wasn't a real gun, they said. It was a replica.

"My first thought was that we were going to catch it in the media. They were already going after an officer who two days earlier had killed a mentally disturbed woman who had ran at him with

a knife in a grocery store. Now this. But my partner said, 'Well, we thought it was real.' He was right. How could we possibly have known it was a replica?"

Waller went home, deciding she would not give a statement to the detectives until the next day. She was glad she did it that way.

"I didn't sleep well that night. I just kept replaying the incident over and over. But the more I did, the more I could remember. The next day when I went back in to talk, I was able to give a more complete account of what had happened."

Waller took a month off work. *"I was pretty stressed out about the grand jury, although it turned out to be pretty easy. I talked to them for ten minutes and they asked me a few questions. The witnesses were all very supportive of what we did.*

"I replayed the shooting over and over in my mind before the grand jury took place, and even for a while afterwards. I was beginning to wonder if I would be thinking about it all the time. Now [1 1/2 years later] I hardly think about it at all. I've even forgotten people's names and many details."

Waller and Mayer worked briefly together afterwards. *"One of our first calls was on a woman reported as mentally disturbed. We both just looked at each other; it was a strange feeling. Although we had been aggressive, hard-charging officers before, we deliberately slowed things down for a while, then we slowly built back up again."*

Since Waller was new to the city, she relied on support from her old friends in California where she had been an officer. *"My family lives here in the same state, less than an hour away. They took it well for the most part, especially my grandmother who is quite a character. She just shrugged and said, 'Hey, you had to do it, kid. You had no choice. I saw her picture on TV. The woman looked nuts'."*

Commentary

Nancy Waller is a young woman who has already seen multiple deaths in her career. While officers must quickly become accustomed to seeing dead bodies, it's harder to get used to seeing friends and co-workers die. After losing two of them to line-of-duty deaths in Los Angeles, she figured that was enough and moved to a smaller city looking for a safer work environment. Little did she know she would wind up in a shooting before she had passed her new agency's probationary period.

Given all that she has seen, you might expect Waller to have a hard edge, but you would be wrong. Her tall, slender frame sits relaxed in the chair, her speech low-keyed, her smile quick and easy, and her eyes clear and untroubled. She talks about her shooting in a matter-of-fact manner and even finds dark humor in the event, an essential survival tool for all emergency services personnel. This type of humor can sound callous, cynical, and uncaring to the uninitiated, but without it officers would quickly drown in a sea of sorrow, frustration, and anger. That is why police officers and other emergency services personnel quickly learn to edit their speech when they are around "civilians," people who have little understanding of what they are up against on the streets and in emergency rooms.

The shooting itself was straightforward: after an hour of hostile and uncooperative behavior during which Waller and Mayer showed patience and compassion, the suspect charged them with a gun and refused all commands to stop and drop the weapon. She was brought down only a few feet away from the officers.

Fortunately, the aftermath of her shooting went smoothly. There were plenty of witnesses to corroborate the officers' testimony of what happened, and the grand jury did not indict. The media didn't make a circus of the event and there have been no civil litigation or federal charges. Waller and Mayer received good peer support, had access to professional counseling, legal representation, and union representation, took adequate time off, and were treated fairly by their agency. All these factors allowed them to fully recover from this event, which is exactly as it should be.

But the shooting was still a bump in the road. As often happens, Waller had difficulty sleeping and was intensely preoccupied with the incident for about a month afterward. But she found her relationship with others, especially her family and peers, to be a key factor in her recovery.

Today, Waller reports that she has not been personally changed in any major way because of the shooting. It has made her more aware of the importance of training and she takes it even more seriously now than before. Like all good officers, she has tried to learn everything she can from her incident to help herself and others in the future. For instance, she remembers that it didn't occur to her to use her gun sights, which is a common occurrence since shootings often happen suddenly and last only a few seconds. Waller said that she is studying this problem so she can add components to her own firearms training to make her a better instinctive shooter and more reliably use her sights in sudden, high-stress situations.

Like most police officers, Waller and Mayer are unassuming, down-to-earth people who don't fit the "Starsky and Hutch" image that is all too often portrayed on TV. Their compassionate interaction with the mentally disturbed woman is typical of what is routine for officers who at times face a daily barrage of verbal and physical hostility from people they interact with.

Waller has never expected to be thanked for what she does, nor does she make a big deal of the risks she faces. She will just keep going about her job in her unassuming way, taking it in her long, easy stride.

THE SUICIDAL MAN

It was a chilly January day and Dan Sanchez had 30 minutes left of his shift on his Friday. He had just issued a traffic citation to a motorist he caught pushing his car to 50 MPH in a posted 35 and was pleasantly surprised when the man didn't argue but actually admitted that he had been speeding. Pleasant, hassle-free traffic stops are one in a thousand, so Dan was feeling good. Still, he was looking forward to the end of his shift and the start of his weekend.

A few minutes later, dispatch gave a hot call to a neighboring patrol car and Dan quickly volunteered to back him up. Dispatch said that at 352 N. Argyle, there was a 24-year-old white male, suicidal, on drugs, and threatening with a gun. The complainant was the man's mother.

The address was located in a large, kind of cul-de-sac, with houses on the outside of the looping street and a half dozen houses in the middle. Dan parked his patrol car at its entrance to wait for the other police car to arrive. The address was about halfway around the loop, just out of sight on the other side of the houses in the middle of the block.

Sanchez recalls: *"Dispatch had just updated the call that the man was leaving in a Mazda RX 7 when I saw the car come around the loop and stop just a few feet away from my car."*

Normally, an officer will position his patrol car so that it provides him with some degree of safety from passing traffic and provide him with good cover should the motorist come out shooting. But the odd pattern of the street and the sudden appearance of the subject put Sanchez in a vulnerable position. He remained in his patrol car for a moment, thinking that there might be a pursuit. Instead, the man got out of his car and walked toward him. Sanchez got out quickly, his eyes alert for the gun that dispatch had mentioned. *"I told him to put his hands on the hood, then get down onto his knees."*

The man complied but stayed down for only a few seconds before he pulled himself up and moved toward Sanchez. *"I told him to stop but he just kept coming toward me. He kept saying, 'Do it . . . Do it . . . Do it.'"*

The man stopped and looked at Sanchez for a moment. An odd expression spread across his face, which Sanchez describes as a sardonic smirk. Then he thrust his hand inside his coat. *"As he withdrew his hand,"* Sanchez says, *"I shot him."*

Much to Sanchez's surprise, the man acted as if nothing had happened, though later it was learned that the shot had completely devastated his humerus, the long bone of the upper arm, and the arm had been left dangling by strips of skin. Sanchez says: *"He just twisted his upper body a little, no more than if you would have given him a slight shove. But his facial expression didn't change and he started coming at me again. I had heard about suspects who would get shot and just keep coming, but I didn't really believe it. I thought it was just scare tactics on the part of the instructors. But I was now faced with proof that they were right. The man seemed like a monster to me."*

Sanchez thought about going for his shotgun, but there wasn't enough time. He began backing up, moving along the length of the police car, then beyond it, but still the man came. Sanchez turned and ran but each time he looked back, the man was there, coming at him. It was like a scene in B-grade horror movie, except this was very real.

"The other officer, Bill Johns, stopped a block behind my car and got out. I moved to the passenger door but when I saw that the man was focusing his attention on Johns, who was backing toward the rear of the car, I moved toward the back, too." Both officers had moved a few feet beyond the car as the man continued to move aggressively toward them.

Johns radioed to dispatch, *"He's running at us!"*

"Does the subject still have the gun?" dispatch asked. But the officers were too busy to answer.

The man stopped by the trunk of the police car and looked at the two officers, who were standing less than 10 feet away and a couple of arm length's from each other. Sanchez describes their position as a triangle: He and Johns were the base and the man stood at the triangle's apex. A moment passed, then the man plunged his hand into his jacket.

Police officers learn in their training about the principle of action/reaction. When someone has to react to another's action, the reaction is always going to be slower. While some members of the press and many naive citizens think that an officer should see an assailant's gun or even be shot at before he shoots, the reality is that by then it may be too late. The process of the officer seeing, recognizing, and reacting takes longer than it takes an assailant to get off one or more shots.

The man had previously been ordered to his knees but he had come out of the position and charged Officer Dan

Sanchez, repeatedly saying, "Do it." When he made a sudden, overt action of reaching for his weapon under his jacket, he was shot in the arm. But still he charged the officer, refusing all commands to stop. When a second officer arrived, he charged that officer, too. Then when he faced both of them, he again reached under his coat, where ninety-nine out of a hundred people conceal their weapons.

The officers fired. Sanchez's first shot hit the man in the neck, his second hit the back of the police car. John's rounds struck the man's chest and chin. Bleeding profusely, the man crumpled to the pavement.

Sanchez radioed to dispatch, *"Code Zero! Code Zero!"* meaning an officer is in peril and to send all available backup.

"It wasn't until he fell that I noticed several fresh cuts on his wrist," Sanchez says. *"I uttered, 'Oh shit' and I heard Johns say, 'Oh God!' I had this powerful feeling that this wasn't over, that something was definitely going to come of this."*

The voice of the dispatcher penetrated the moment. "What is the situation there?"

Sanchez keyed his mike and simply replied, "He's down."

Within minutes, the scene was crowded with officers, supervisors, and medics. Sanchez and Johns were placed in separate cars and whisked away to the police station. Though Sanchez thought the man was dead, he learned later that the mortally wounded man somehow managed to revive himself and fight with the medics. At one point, he grabbed his shattered arm with his good hand and wielded it like a club, hitting the medics with his own arm as they tried to tend to him in the ambulance. He continued to fight in the emergency room, pulling the tubes and needles from his body. When examining the man's body later, the medical examiner found the words "HELP ME" carved into his leg.

Officer Sanchez returned to the police station and was ordered to write a report, though he didn't feel he was in any shape to write a decent one. But he dutifully tried anyway. *"A sergeant came and took my gun,"* Sanchez says. *"I was glad to get rid of it. Later, when I got it back, it felt tainted. I was happy when*

I eventually switched to a different one."

Before Sanchez had finished his report, which he says was practically incoherent, he was called to be interviewed by detectives. *"Right in the middle of the interview, a uniform sergeant came into the room and asked if I had ever seen a gun at the scene. I told him no, but that the guy had been reaching for one. Then the detective started arguing with the sergeant about interrupting the interview. The detective asked the sergeant if he really wanted to do this now and the sergeant said no, but he didn't want people looking for something that didn't exist."*

Although the initial information given by dispatch was that the man was threatening with a gun, unknown to Sanchez and Johns, he had left the house without it. *"I felt bad and hurt that there was no gun. I wondered how the grand jury was going to look at it."*

Sanchez was released to go home at ten o'clock that night. But before he left, he was told that the man had died. *"I went into the rest room for a while. I looked in the mirror and didn't recognize myself. I was grayish looking."*

A sergeant drove Sanchez to the sergeant's home, where the two of them and a third officer had a couple of drinks. Sanchez was amazed that the alcohol did not effect him. *"The drinks were strong but I couldn't feel them. Later, the officer took me home, where I saw on the news the scene and the chalked outline of the guy's body."*

Sanchez slept fitfully that night and in the morning he had an odd sense of being in the middle of a dream. He got up and began to go through the motions of getting ready to go to work. *"It didn't dawn on me not to go in,"* he says. But a knock at the door changed his plans. *"A captain came in and asked how I was doing. He told me that I needed to get an attorney. This surprised me and I asked if the city was supplying one. The captain told me no, that they only give you one if the case is civil.*

"I was on my own. The phone book is full of attorneys, but I had no idea how to choose a good one. I had never imagined myself being in this position and was totally unprepared for it. Finally, a fellow officer who was a third-year law student hooked me up with a friend of his. He heard Bill's story and mine and said that though they were

slightly different, they were close enough. He thought the difference made them sound believable."

For the next few days, Sanchez experienced a variety of reactions to his encounter. Newspaper reporters called him but he didn't call back. Without factual details, the reporters filled the blanks, most of which were wrong. Among his fellow officers, most treated him OK, though a few of them did a little Monday morning quarterbacking, saying he should have shot the man more the first time. One officer even appeared envious that Sanchez had been in a shooting and he hadn't. Then Sanchez experienced the beginning of what was to become a nightmare with his administration. Sanchez says: *"The administration felt uncomfortable because they had made a few mistakes. For example, they discovered the rounds we were carrying didn't do everything they were supposed to. They even asked Bill Johns and me what we thought had gone wrong."*

In spite of a "witness," an elderly man who lived near the scene and falsely claimed that the officers had fired dozens of rounds into the suspect, the grand jury came back with "no true bill," meaning they were exonerated of any wrong doing.

Sanchez returned to work but was given a desk and not allowed to wear his uniform. *"I felt terrible not being allowed to wear it,"* he says. *"The administration wanted to keep me out of the public eye. I felt embarrassed and humiliated. It was as if they were ashamed of me."*

He was ordered to see a psychologist for a fitness for duty evaluation. *"The administration didn't like the results, so they referred me to another one. I was eventually cleared to go back on the road."*

Two years later, Sanchez found himself in the middle of a civil suit. Though the deceased had a history of violence, was a known drug user, and had tested positively for methamphetamine, his family painted a picture of him in court as an angel. *"They brought in a couple of paid police experts, one an ex-chief out of San Francisco and the other an officer from back East. They told the court that the shooting should have gone down differently. This was a very anxious time for me."*

The civil trial lasted for three long weeks. Sanchez felt emotionally devastated as the plaintiff's attorney did everything he could to paint the two officers as incompetent cowards. Nothing in Sanchez's training or experience had prepared him for this type of event. At one point in the proceedings, Sanchez had to look at a mannequin dressed in the man's clothes, with trajectory rods sticking in it showing where the officer's bullet had entered. *"There was no preparation for seeing that thing. We came back from lunch one day and there it was, positioned just like when the guy was coming at us. This really bothered me."*

At the end of three weeks, the jury cleared the officers. *"After the civil trial,"* Sanchez says, *"I had lots of anger and I was suffering from stomach and intestinal problems. For a while I was aggressive and abrasive with people, then I went into a period of just avoiding everything. I was torn between hesitating to back up another officer and my feelings of loyalty toward the other guys. I didn't want them to experience that feeling of isolation I felt when I first faced the guy."*

Sanchez switched to the graveyard shift. *"There's no brass around that time of night and the calls are mostly alarms and hot situations. Working late night allowed me to avoid reminders of the incident."*

As so often happens after a high-profile incident, the public was often thoughtless or just outright cruel. *"Citizens would get out of their car on a traffic stop, raise their hands and say to the officers, 'don't shoot me.' When they did it to me, they didn't know I had been the one."*

Once, Sanchez went to a house to a serve a warrant. *"The guy had only one leg and was lying naked on a waterbed. When I told him to get dressed, he reached down and opened a drawer under the bed. I could see the butt of a gun and I yelled at him. He jerked his hands up in the air and shouted that it was only a BB gun.*

"I couldn't believe it. Could you see that in the news? I shoot some one-legged, naked man as he lay in his bed." Dan began to have serious doubts about ever being able to shoot anyone again.

Commentary

Dan Sanchez has expressive, dark brown eyes that are an accurate reflection of a man with quiet, but deep, feelings and a strong sense of spirituality. On that fateful day, when he felt like he was being chased by a monster from a nightmare, he had a premonition that the nightmare was just beginning—and he was right. This nightmare lasted for another 11 years and ended in the destruction of his career as a police officer. Along the way, he also lost relationships, sleep, peace of mind, and self-respect. Tormented by post-traumatic stress disorder, he felt lost and confused about what was happening to him. He felt rejected and unsupported by the command staff at his agency. Although others noticed that he was struggling, no one had anything to offer him that showed a clear path to recovery. Today, his eyes are still haunted when he talks about the shooting and its aftermath. The relationship between Sanchez and his girlfriend didn't survive the shooting and the civil trial. Neither of them was equipped to deal with the external pressure and the powerful emotions evoked by these events. Consequently, the relationship ended badly, leaving Sanchez with guilt about the pain he had caused her.

A deeply religious man, he felt guilt and shame about having taken a human life and he didn't receive any religious counseling to help him resolve this conflict. Emotionally scarred by a devastating civil trial and afraid of being thrown to the wolves by his agency, he became more fearful of being placed into a situation where he would have to shoot someone again.

Sanchez's sense of fear did not come from fear for his own safety. He had always loved being a police officer, and he never felt unusual anxiety about the physical dangers it presented. His fear arose from how people would perceive and treat him after it was over. He knew from experience that even if he did nothing wrong, there was still no guarantee he would not somehow be punished. He appreciated the support of some of his peers, but there was much they could not protect him from.

In spite of his torment, Sanchez managed to do positive

things that helped keep him going. After he and his girlfriend separated, he became blessed by finding a woman who eventually became his wife and best friend. Their close, loving relationship became a sanctuary for him that provided stability and allowed him a safe place to stay in touch with his feelings and maintain his ability to be closely connected to others. His wife is a cheerful, down-to-earth, and outgoing person who offsets her husband's tendency to want to withdraw and isolate himself from others. He instinctively knew that isolating himself was not healthy and he was grateful for his wife's easy sociability with others.

Sanchez had begun drinking heavily to numb his feelings, and he was putting on weight from lack of exercise and poor eating habits. Realizing that his health was failing, he quit abusing alcohol and began jogging, finding it so helpful that he started competing in "fun run" races. Now, his slim, fit physique and the spring in his step speak to the success of his running program and his determination to keep his body healthy even when his psyche is troubled.

As time went on, the shooting continued to haunt him no matter what he did. He was tormented almost daily by nightmares and intrusive thoughts, while his fear of facing the aftermath of another shooting began to turn to dread.

Hope was finally restored to Sanchez eleven years after the shooting when he and his wife attended a seminar on the impact of traumatic events on officers and family members. The police chaplain, who was coordinating the seminar, noticed how troubled Sanchez was. The chaplain, who was from an outside agency, and members from that agency's peer-support team volunteered to follow-up with him after the seminar. Sanchez was used to being disappointed and didn't expect anything useful to come of it. So when they kept their promise by arranging a meeting with him and Bill Johns, he was pleasantly surprised and grateful that they cared enough to go out of their way to extend a helping hand. The chaplain was quick to see that Sanchez was suffering from chronic post-traumatic stress disorder and referred him to a local police psychologist for treatment.

When Sanchez followed through on the chaplain's suggestion, his journey to recovery began. It was a painful beginning, however, especially when the psychologist pointed out that Sanchez's dread of getting into another shooting had reached the point where she believed he should not be out on the street. The doctor urged him to voluntarily remove himself from the street and request a limited duty position. Sanchez knew she was right and did it. From that day forward he didn't carry a gun, and he relieved that he finally didn't have to face that demon any longer.

But he was still worried because he knew that his agency had a track record of being punitive toward employees they perceived as a "problem." Unfortunately, that turned out to be true and Sanchez wound up in a protracted legal battle with his agency over the way they handled his case. Their harsh treatment of him ended any hope that he would ever fully recover to the point where he could return to the street, and today he is no longer a police officer.

Although Sanchez was disturbed over how his agency reacted to his request for limited duty, his primary concern was finding relief from the daily haunting of the shooting and its aftermath. The psychologist, noticing Sanchez's deeply held religious faith and his guilt over having violated "Thou shalt not kill," encouraged him to seek out a member of the clergy with whom he would feel comfortable discussing the shooting. Sanchez found a priest who had been a tank commander during World War II and had experience talking with soldiers and police officers. Sanchez met with him twice and found the sessions to be an important step in his journey toward finding peace and absolution from guilt.

Sanchez is a sensitive man who has always cared about others. He decided he wanted to contact his previous girlfriend from years ago and apologize for how the shooting and its aftermath had destroyed their relationship and caused them both so much pain. She appreciated his thoughtfulness and he hoped it would help them both put positive closure to something that had ended negatively. He also worked steadily with the psychologist and gradually came to terms with the shooting, himself, and the end of a career he had loved. He became more relaxed, the haunting images of the shooting and the civil trial began to fade, and his self-esteem was restored. The haunted, hunted look in his expressive eyes began to soften and he started looking forward to the future.

Not long after Sanchez realized that his law enforcement career was over forever, he was sitting in his living room planning to take his wife away for the weekend for her birthday. He knew that she had always wanted an expensive, special-edition hymnal book for church. He wanted to buy it as a surprise but he didn't know where in their budget he could take the money without her noticing.

Then he realized that he was sitting on it: his duty gun was hidden under the cushions of the couch. He sold it and used the money to buy the hymnal book.

The instrument of death he used to carry every day had been transformed into a symbol of spirituality and the gratitude he felt for the love and support of his wife. It was another important step in Sanchez's journey toward peace, redemption, and a new life.

ONE OFFICER, FOUR DRAGONS

Even if the sky were falling, there are some officers who would never get hit by a chunk. On the other hand, some officers are always right at ground zero. The first group may be thought of as slackers by their peers because they purposely avoid hot situations; the second group is thought of as adrenaline junkies because they race from hot call to hot call. Most agencies have both types.

But there are also those officers who, by no deliberate action on their part, are victims of fate. "Even when I decide to lay low for a while and drive around in an avoidance mode," one officer said, "wild and crazy situations still have a way of finding me."

An officer with the opposite problem said this: "I always want to get into some shit, but it's always going down in the next beat over or clear across town."

Patrick Clancy admits he is an adrenaline junkie and says he often races to hot calls so he can be part of the action. But there have been many occasions when the action seemed to single him out, even when he wasn't seeking it. In the past seven of his 13 years as a street officer, Clancy has been involved in four shootings.

"In my first shooting," Clancy says, "I was working in the neighborhood where I had grown up. I knew the people and I had a good feeling patrolling there. I was working the graveyard shift and I got a call on a man threatening with a straight razor. The police car in the adjacent beat got the cover and actually got there before I did and began chasing the guy on foot."

Just as Clancy got into the area, he heard the officer on the radio give his location and realized the foot chase was coming toward him. A moment later the suspect burst out of the dark with the officer in pursuit a short distance behind. The officer shouted something as Clancy scrambled out of the car, but he couldn't decipher what it was.

"I chased the guy toward a railing on the far side of the street. I use to play football so I gave the guy a forearm slam and he went down. When I told him to stay there, I expected him to do exactly that, but he began to get up."

It was then that Clancy understood what the officer was warning him about: the man still had the straight razor in his hand. The other officer struck the suspect several time with his nightstick, but the methamphetamines the suspect had consumed earlier made him impervious to pain.

"The guy was fighting hard because of the meth," Clancy says. "When I saw that razor coming toward me, I backed up and drew my weapon. I didn't think about drawing my gun at all; it was just suddenly in my hand. Three times I shouted at him to stop, but he didn't. He just kept coming at me with that razor."

From three feet away, Clancy shot him, twice in the head

and twice in the body. *"My response was definitely an automatic reaction. There was no thinking; I just reacted."*

At first, Clancy stood in shock. *"I couldn't believe this was happening. I thought, 'Oh shit. I wished this wouldn't have happened.' I kept thinking that this is my turf, I'm the cop and this doesn't happen here."*

When Clancy looked down at the wounded suspect, he noticed a tattoo on his arm, an image that has remained in his mind. *"It was a picture of two hands handcuffed together, with the words, 'Mother Tried.' One of my rounds had struck his biceps and blood was trickling toward that tattoo."*

A few moments later the scene was a crowded with uniforms, detectives, medics, and lots of strobing blue and red lights. In police vernacular, they say, "The whole world arrived."

"The other cops started to control me," Clancy says. *"They took my gun from me and the detectives drew chalk marks around my feet where I had been standing. Those chalk marks stuck in my mind for a long time because I'd seen it done so often to dead bodies. Then they put me in a car and I felt caged. I wanted to walk off the adrenaline. I wanted out of my uniform because I was sweaty and I wanted to take a shower. I would have given a million dollars for a shower.*

"And I kept asking myself if I did right."

When Clancy got to the detectives' office, they told him that the man might die and that he should prepare for that possibility. *"They treated me with more courtesy than they did at the scene, but I was left with this feeling that I was a small part of what had happened."*

Although Clancy wasn't offered union or legal representation, the interview went fine and he was eventually released to go home the next afternoon. His wife was on a trip, which made his home quiet and empty. *"I sat there and smoked like you wouldn't believe, and I don't smoke. I wanted to be around people; I wanted to go to work and be around cops."*

Clancy didn't sleep for three days. He sat, smoked, and paced the floor. He asked himself many "what if" questions. *"I was really glad my wife and kids weren't at home since I was such a basket case."*

When Clancy's wife did return home, he found it uncomfortable. *"She tried to do the right thing, but it was always the wrong thing. When she tried to get close to me, I wanted space. When she gave me space, I wanted her closer. I had a lot of guilt about what she was going through. Both her and my denial system had been ruined. She was having dreams about seeing me covered with a white sheet, and when she pulled it back she would see me under it."*

He suggests that officers call their spouses as soon after a shooting as they can. This way they know what happened before they see it on television. *"You don't need to go into the bloody details, but you do need to talk to them about what they are feeling. You need to discuss it with your kids, too. That way, when their friends see your name and picture in the media, they have a defense when some little asshole in school brings it up."*

The shooting happened on a Monday and Clancy went back to work the following Friday. *"I felt like I was in a fish bowl. Many officers believe they can pull the trigger, but in the back of their minds they wonder if they can. Then they look at a guy who has actually done it.*

"I wanted to tell them that it could happen to them and that they should take their training more seriously. You know, I used to put up with bullshit training, but now I expect the trainers to have their act together. If they don't, I push the bullshit button."

Clancy went to the hospital to check on the man he shot but was told by a nurse that he had died. Depressed, Clancy went to the precinct where he was told by the desk officer that the hospital had just called and said they had made a mistake. The man was still alive.

The suspect had slipped into a deep coma and doctors could not say when he would come out of it, if ever. Clancy had no choice but to go back to work, where he was haunted by the man's condition. *"All the time he was in the coma a part of me was always wondering when I would be told that he had died."*

Clancy waited for months, then years. Finally, four and a half years after the shooting, he got the dreaded call from his supervisor: the man had died.

That same night Clancy got into another shooting.

NOTE: Officer Clancy was involved in the incident, THE INTRUDER. This is his experience.

"My captain called me in the morning to tell me that my guy had died. I didn't want to stay at home; I wanted to be at work with my pals."

Later that night, Clancy and Officer Joiner were parked side-by-side talking when they received a call that a 12-year-old boy was being held hostage in his home.

"Just as we got to the house," Clancy said, *"we heard shots, causing me to think that the bad guy was shooting. But once we got inside, we learned that two officers outside the house had shot at the suspect through an upstairs window."*

The intruder was holding the boy in an upstairs bedroom while Clancy, Joiner, and another officer huddled on a landing a few steps below. *"The guy was screaming that he was going to kill the boy. There was no communicating with him and there was no discounting his threats. I knew this guy meant it.*

"Then one of the officers called out and asked the little boy his name. He answered 'Jeremy,' and the sound of his voice has stuck with me ever since."

A minute later, the man screamed that he was going to kill the boy and began counting down from five. They could hear a gasp and the sound of struggling. The three officers scurried up the stairs, down the hall, and into the dark room where the man sat on the bed, clutching the boy in front of him. He held a knife at the boy's throat.

"One of the officers shot but the man didn't react, and when his knife hand turned, I thought he was cutting the boy. There were a lot of shots, including mine, and the room filled with smoke." As the dense smoke cleared, Clancy saw that the man was down, mortally wounded.

But the little boy was slumped over, too. Somehow, he had been shot in the back of the head and blood was arcing from the wound.

"I can't put into words what I felt," Clancy says, still visibly

upset five years later. "I remember smashing my flashlight into a bedpost . . . I was just so tore up inside."

Clancy drew on every bit of his being to force himself into the adjacent bedroom where Jeremy's parents were huddled with their younger son, while Officer Joiner and an ambulance crew, which had staged out on the street, worked frantically on the injured boy. When he could be moved, officers helped the ambulance crew carry the gurney out of the house and into the ambulance.

"I was carrying the I-V bottle, and I remember hoping . . . I remember hoping with all my being that Jeremy was going to be OK."

Everyone involved in the incident went to the detectives' office and began waiting for the phone call from the hospital. As long minutes turned into hours, the officers were continually tortured with conflicting status reports on the boy's condition. One phone call would say he was going to be OK, then a few minutes later another call would say he was going to die.

"Everyone there was holding onto their denial," Clancy says of the tense atmosphere. "I was a union vice president and I knew I had to take care of the other officers. But I just couldn't. I was so worried about the boy, so . . . torn . . . so stunned."

Clancy had to get out of the office. Another officer drove him across town to the precinct so that he could take a shower and change into his street clothes. At the precinct, he ran into a friend—a fellow officer—and told him, perhaps more to convince himself, that the boy was going to make it. Clancy didn't know that the call had gone out to all the precincts as he had been driving to the precinct.

His friend broke the news: Jeremy had just died.

"I still hadn't been interviewed by detectives, but there was no way I could have talked to them right then. I had to slow things down. I went and talked to my attorney, I took a walk along the river, and I talked to some friends. I didn't go to get interviewed until eight o'clock that night. One of the district attorneys was upset and making threats because some officers weren't talking right away. We were just a piece of meat to him."

Clancy felt that he should see a psychologist and take

some time off, but two weeks later he saw a newspaper story where a precinct captain was quoted as saying that the three officers involved in the shooting were having psychological problems and were seeing a psychologist. Enraged that a confidentiality had been broken, Clancy returned to work.

"On my second day back we caught a guy after a long chase. I asked why he ran since all he had was a minor warrant. He just looked at me and said, 'At least you weren't out shooting a child.' He didn't know I had been involved but it still felt like a piece of steel had been run through my heart. I wanted a piece of him but I kept my cool and took him to booking."

"It was hard to work when I came back. One day I was talking to a young boy out on the street and he told me his name was Jeremy. I just froze; I couldn't respond. There was another officer there and he helped me out of it."

Clancy was seeing a psychologist but he found the experience a waste of time. *"Here I was after two shootings, gut shot so to speak from the second one, and the doctor wanted to work on my marriage. So I quit going. I went back to the police chaplain and asked to see a female psychologist, since I tended to guard my macho when I talked with male doctors.*

"I liked my new doctor and she helped me a lot. I had a lot of baggage from both shootings and I was under attack from the police department and the press. I just felt I was surrounded in a cloud of death and I kept asking what I had done to deserve this. In time I came to understand that I hadn't done anything, that these were just events that I happened to be part of. I began to realize that shit happens."

Clancy saw the psychologist regularly for seven months and progressively came to terms with the shootings. One day he and the doctor talked about how he had improved and they decided he didn't have to come in any more.

That night he got into a third shooting.

"That night I was feeling pretty good about my conversation with my psychologist and I'd just received word that I'd scored high on the sergeant's test. Early in the evening I had gotten into a big car

chase that had gone on for miles before we finally caught the guy. Later while I was doing the paperwork, I was thinking that the chase was a good way to end my career as a street officer."

Just as Clancy returned to patrol, a nearby patrol car was dispatched to a disturbance at a residential care center for the elderly. Clancy volunteered to be backup. *"There was a long driveway from the street to the front door where patients unloaded. I pulled up near the other police car, which had parked a ways from the door, and got out. Just as the officer started to tell me what was going on, a woman stepped out the front door and made a motion toward the inside. Then a guy stepped out the door with a shotgun."*

Clancy's reactions were instantaneous and he said later that he saw everything in slow motion. He backed toward cover and simultaneously drew his weapon. He yelled "gun" to warn the other officer as his eyes stayed glued on the suspect's large-barrel shotgun.

"I saw his gun's muzzle flash spread out in slow motion as he fired at the other officer. I began shooting back to give some suppression fire so the officer could get to cover. Then the guy turned toward me and fired. I remember how his muzzle flashed as I returned fire. A second later he jumped back inside and shut the door."

Clancy would learn hours later that one of his bullets passed through several walls and struck a patient inside the center, an 84-year-old man.

Clancy felt more in control of the situation because of his experience with his previous shootings. This time he wasn't thinking about himself but directing his attention outward to the situation. After laying suppression fire, he asked dispatch for SWAT, a hostage negotiation team, additional officers, and an ambulance to stand by. When the suspect fired a round out the back door of the center, Clancy asked radio to move the situation to a clear radio net.

"This time I'm not thinking 'Oh my God, I'm being shot at.' I was more in control. For a few seconds, though, I started thinking about my second shooting, but then I forced myself not to. I knew the covering officers would be experiencing some of the same distorted thinking patterns as I had in previous shootings. I knew they would

drive fast, have tunnel vision, and probably not hear things on the radio. Knowing this, I was careful to direct my cover in, telling them several times where they needed to go, and the safest way to come in."

Four hours later, a hostage negotiator talked the suspect out. He was a 26-year-old man having a fight with his 65-year-old girlfriend, the woman who ran the center. Although he was charged with two counts of attempted murder, he never saw inside a jail. A liberal judge, much to the outrage of a courtroom packed with police officers, sentenced the suspect to probation because he had the AIDS virus. Though Clancy was angry, he was more concerned the suspect would try to find his home. For several months he kept a careful watch from his rural country house.

The 84-year-old man recovered although he complained jokingly to Clancy shortly after the shooting, "I've been lying in bed trying to die and all you could do is wing me." The man's family, who had less of a sense of humor, subsequently filed a lawsuit.

Three years later, Clancy, now a sergeant, heard dispatch report that a man wearing military fatigues was firing an automatic weapon inside a downtown high-rise just two blocks away.

Before Clancy's third shooting, he had worked with his psychologist on reducing his need to rush into hot situations. It was not out of a need to be a hero but out of a desire to deliberately put himself into danger so other officers would not have to. He saw himself as a protector, a father figure. Having worked through the problem, he approached his fourth shooting only as an officer ready to do his part. Nonetheless, fate dictated that he was the closest car and the first one to arrive.

The 30-story high-rise contained businesses on the ground floor, a television affiliate in the basement, and condos on the upper floors. It was noon and the lunch crowd was out on the sidewalks.

"As I pulled up," Clancy says, *"a witness points out the guy. He was definitely armed and he was going into an insurance office on the ground floor. I could see him through the window and I saw him begin to take hostages."*

Clancy's three previous shootings and his training gave him a feeling of control. Still, a lunatic was firing rounds inside an office building in a crowded part of town; Clancy says his adrenaline was pumping.

"I immediately called SWAT and a Hostage Negotiation Team. The first two officers to arrive were veterans and experienced in shootings. We could see lots of shell casings on the floor inside the building's lobby. I knew we had to get inside there and hold the perimeter to prevent the guy from going elsewhere inside the build-ing. I also knew from previous situations that we didn't need lots of officers inside the perimeter, though that is where they always go first. I got on the radio and asked a sergeant to set up a perimeter outside and told him we would take care of the inside."

Once in the lobby area, Clancy and the two officers took positions behind a counter, a wall, and a desk. They could see the armed suspect inside the insurance office and the employ-ees lined up on the floor with their hands behind their heads.

As other officers arrived at the scene and took positions on the perimeter, they first found one wounded victim, then a second victim a few minutes later.

"I could see the guy from my position when he fired a shot. I was anticipating the round going through the big windows and I briefly closed my eyes to protect them as I saw the glass explode and pieces fly toward me. I was shocked when I looked up and found the glass damaged but unbroken.

"We didn't shoot back because there was lots of thick glass between him and us. The other officers and I whispered about how we were going to contain the guy and what action we would take if he came out."

The suspect released a burst from an AK-47 and the rounds exploded through the windows directly at the officers. No one was struck. Clancy stayed calm and informed radio they were receiving automatic fire. *"I wanted SWAT to know what kind of weapon the guy had."*

Later the officers would learn that the suspect had an AK-47, an SKS, a 12-gauge shotgun, a 9mm Glock, knives, and a thousand rounds of ammunition.

Outside, dozens of officers kept order to what could have

been chaos as police, FBI, ambulances, crowds, and throngs of media all jockeyed for position.

Inside, Clancy and the other two officers remained on the floor for two hours to prevent the suspect from going to the other floors. *"Throughout the ordeal, I consciously calmed my breathing. I would force myself out of tunnel vision by continually talking to the other officers. I would also glance down at the Saint Michael's ring my wife had given me. It helped to remind me to keep a winning attitude. All these things helped broadened my mental focus and helped me from having any blank memory spots.*

"I constantly took personal inventory to ensure I wasn't shaking, and I kept drying my palms. One time my stomach did a flip flop and I simply told myself what I was feeling. I said, 'There goes my stomach.' I believe I was able to stay rational and the other officers stayed in control during the long ordeal because of our training and our experience in other shootings."

SWAT and the Hostage Negotiation Team eventually got the suspect out without further injury to citizens and without injury to officers or the suspect.

Sergeant Clancy took a few days off and returned to work.

Commentary

Sergeant Clancy prides himself on being a traditional Irish-American police officer. His smiling blue eyes are full of humor and, in spite of his reputation as a tough street cop, he enjoys telling stories of how he charmed an angry suspect with humor and even got him to say thanks for persuading him to give up. He got to know the people in his district and, like many beat cops, he has been practicing community policing long before it became a politically correct buzzword. He's a devoted family man, likes people, likes to have fun, and has many friends.

He still remembers the shock he felt during his first shooting when the suspect ignored his badge and uniform and tried to kill him. Until then, he had thought that the authority of his badge, his Irish charm, and his goodwill toward all people would always protect him from having to shoot someone. He knew shootings could happen but he never believed they would happen to him. But when his denial was violently ripped away, he had to begin a long process toward self-discovery and adaptation, a process that would be challenged further by three more shootings.

Along the way, his journey was inspired by what has become one if his favorite quotes:

> "The credit belongs to the man who is actually in the arena—whose face is marred by dust, sweat, and blood who knows the great enthusiasms, the great devotions, and spends himself in a worthy cause, who at best if he wins knows the thrill of high achievement, and if he fails at least fails while daring greatly, so that his place shall never be with those cold and timid souls who know neither victory nor defeat."
>
> *Theodore Roosevelt*

In spite of the pain suffered by Clancy and his family, he was determined to not let it defeat him. At first he was poorly prepared for the psychological devastation to himself and his family. Since he had never been educated about the perceptual and memory distortions that can happen during a shooting, he became concerned when those things happened to him.

He felt bewildered, angry, and let down by a profession and a community that he loved. Some of his charm turned to irritability. He could have become another bitter, angry, burned-out cop, but his inherent love of life refused to allow it. His first step was to avoid the trap of denial and to admit to himself that these events had changed him forever and that he needed help making sense out of his experiences. He managed to find a psychologist who had expertise in the area of trauma and in the special concerns of police officers.

The doctor helped him understand that what he experienced during and after the shooting were normal reactions to an abnormal event. Besides helping him detoxify his own post-traumatic stress disorder, the psychologist helped him find other mental health professionals who could work with his wife individually and with them as a couple.

Clancy got involved in peer-support counseling. As a result, he became a strong advocate for getting training in his agency to better prepare officers mentally and emotionally for a deadly force encounter and its aftermath. He eventually became a trainer in these classes and a one-man counseling referral service, encouraging his friends and colleagues to get counseling whenever they were struggling with issues from their own incidents. Clancy worked to cultivate positive relationships with reporters as he educated them about the realities of police work. The more annoyed he became by insensitive administrators, the more tirelessly he worked to persuade his agency to give awards to officers who had put themselves on the line to keep the community safe.

Because of these efforts to help and train others, he became better prepared to face each subsequent shooting with a greater sense of control and understanding, both during and after the event.

Every time another dragon rears its ugly head, Sergeant Clancy has made a decision to face it and find a positive way to defeat it. His recovery process, which continues, has had many ups and downs over the years. His face is marred by more dust, sweat, and blood than he ever dreamed of, but he's still in the fight and the dragons remain defeated.

HOW MANY LIVES DO I HAVE?

"Pulling the trigger is the easy part. It's making the decision to shoot that's hard," says Tony Petterson, a 15-year veteran of street patrol. And he should know. Over the last five years, Tony has found himself in the middle of four shootings and countless "man with a gun" calls. After the gun smoke had settled from the last one and he had again emerged miraculously unscathed, he had to ask himself, *"How many more lives do I have?"*

Tony considers his first shooting as "no big deal," but it gave him both a sense of using deadly force and an understanding of how a police agency can be unsupportive when its officer's experience traumatic events.

"The radio call came out as, 'a man under the Lincoln Bridge shooting an automatic weapon,'" Tony says. Although the gun turned out to be a semiautomatic, its rapid fire made it sound like a machine gun. Nonetheless, there was a man under the bridge with a gun, and he was firing it. *"The first car to arrive saw the guy, and when the guy saw the officers, he ran down to the water."*

Tony and his partner went after the man and found him standing along the shore. Tony saw a gun, though his partner could not see it from where he was standing. *"I could see it in his waistband and I yelled at him to raise his hands. He looked at me but didn't do it. I was pointing my gun at him and telling him over and over to get his hands up. Since he was Hispanic, I thought maybe he didn't speak English, so I raised my one hand to indicate that I wanted him to raise his, but still he wouldn't do it."*

Most police agencies have a rule against warning shots, since bullets fired into the air must come back down. Any bullet not fired at a specific target can potentially hurt an innocent party. But the people who author the book of rules are rarely in a position to make life and death choices. Tony weighed all the elements in the standoff and made a decision.

"I moved my barrel off the guy and fired into a cement wall behind him. But still he wouldn't raise his hands. Instead, he did the sign of the cross and blew me a kiss. I knew what that meant and I knew what was coming."

The man's hand moved to his waist and he pulled out the gun. Backing for cover, Tony fired again, this time at the man. The round missed.

Unflinchingly, the suspect moved the gun toward Tony as if he were going to shoot, but at the last instant he tossed it into the river. Other officers jumped him, took him to the ground and applied the handcuffs. *"I was enraged at the guy. I pulled him to his feet, cussed him out, and slapped him."*

After all the paperwork and interviews, Tony took a few days off. When he returned, the job went on routinely, and after a while, he seldom thought about the incident. But six months later, a lieutenant came to the firing range where Tony was training and told the range officer to have him report to Personnel the next day. Tony had no idea why, never linking it to the shooting incident.

"When I got to Personnel, I was told to turn in my badge and I was relieved of duty for a couple of weeks while they finished investigating charges against me for firing a warning shot and slapping the guy."

When the investigation was over, Tony received a letter of reprimand and was reinstated to duty. He never got so much as a thanks for facing a man with a gun.

Two years later, Tony and his partner were on routine patrol when the police radio began dispatching a description of two bank robbery suspects and their car. Although the robbery occurred several miles from Tony's patrol area, the suspects had taken the freeway and were heading in his direction. Other officers followed the suspect car to an exit ramp, then to an underground parking lot.

Tony and his partner and other police units hurried to the scene. *"We pulled up alongside the large, L-shaped motel and could see the two suspects in a window slightly above us. They were holding their handguns in the air and kicking the screen out of the window. Then as they leaped to the ground, they fired about a half dozen rounds at us. If they had stayed right where they landed and shot, they would have filled our car with rounds."*

But instead they ran across the parking lot toward a busy, four-lane street. They ran out into the street, turned, and fired another half dozen rounds at Tony. *"I can still see the one guy's face as he looked back and shot."* He pursued and fired four rounds back, one round punching completely through a suspect's leg.

Later, Tony would learn that the suspects were former Marines who had committed 14 armed robberies. He says their movements had the polished look of good training. *"These guys looked like they had done this before. They knew how to run and shoot."*

Tony chased the suspects across the lot of a restaurant. *"Getting shot at was really making me angry. They ran alongside the restaurant and around the corner. I lost sight of them for a second, but just as I came around, I saw them firing several rounds at a police car that had just pulled onto the lot. They fired more rounds at me, then more at other officers."* The suspects fled across another street.

Tony routinely takes a shotgun out but he didn't have time to grab it when the suspects first started shooting at him and his partner. Another officer gave him one as they stood beside the restaurant. *"There was a hospital right there and I was concerned about the two suspects getting inside. I positioned myself by the door so they would have to go by me first, but one of them fired into a huge plate glass window, probably thinking that it would just blow out. But it didn't."*

One suspect desperately dived through the glass, but unlike in the movies where the director uses prop windows and the actor goes through uninjured, the suspect's head was sliced to ribbons. *"I went in right after the suspects did because I was still concerned about them hurting people or taking hostages. But I found both guys lying on the floor, one on top of the other. The guy on the bottom was severely cut and twitching badly."*

The suspect on top, who had been shot in the leg, gave up when he saw Tony and all the other officers pointing their weapons at him. Tony says: *"For a moment you could see he was thinking about what he should do, but when he saw all the shotguns he gave it up."*

When it was over and the hospital staff was placing the injured suspects on stretchers, Tony felt an intense wave of heat. *"I remember feeling hot. I unbuttoned my shirt, but that didn't cool me off enough, so I removed my vest. I was feeling a rush that was incredible.*

"You know," Tony says, shaking his head in disbelief, *"I must have lived a good life because none of those bullets hit me."*

All the involved officers went to the detectives' office. The experience there was uneventful for Tony and he is quick to say that he has been treated well by detectives in all of his shootings. All he wanted to do this day was to get home to his two children.

"I routinely parked my car out of the downtown area in the morning and rode the rest of the way in on the bus. One of the officers was going to take me to my car but I just wanted to go to my bus stop and ride back to my car as I always did. I wanted life to return to normal, as if I got off work and it was just another work day.

"When I got off the bus and began walking toward my car, I saw this gang member ahead of me walking my way. I don't know what he was up to but I remember thinking, 'don't even start.' He must have seen my face because he just veered off and walked away."

Tony was still on an adrenaline high when he got home and says he stayed high for about 24 hours. *"When my boys got home from grade school, I told them what had happened but they just took it in stride. They asked a couple of questions and I answered them honestly.*

"Then one of the boys asked, 'So, what's for dinner, dad?'"

Less than a year after Tony's running gun battle, he and several other officers were in a greasy spoon restaurant close to the border of four patrol districts. They had just gotten their breakfasts when dispatch informed all cars that county deputies were chasing a bank robbery suspect. While the chase was not happening in the city, the county shared several connecting streets with the city. The city officers' instincts told them to eat quickly.

A few moments later, an update from dispatch said the fleeing suspect car was coming into the city. The officers bolted to their cars, each heading in the direction of connecting streets.

"I was working by myself and I went up Garrison, the primary street that comes into town. But there was some confusion about which street the suspect was coming in on."

Partners Greggor and Thompson spotted the suspect car speeding toward them and watched it lose control at a corner, strike a car, then accelerate away. The officers gave chase, staying safely behind the holdup car as it blew through crowded intersections and played "chicken" with other police cars. Greggor and Thompson lost sight of it, but another police car found it and gave chase. That car lost it, too, then another police car found it and gave pursuit through the narrow, busy streets. Citizens on the sidewalks helped officers by pointing which way the car had gone.

"We were told by radio that the suspect had at least two guns and a police scanner," Tony says. *"I needed to be ready, so I took the shotgun out of the rack, chambered a round, and placed it across my lap. I didn't want to be caught by surprise like the last time and not have time to get it."*

As the chase continued for several more minutes, Tony jumped ahead to an intersection where he figured the suspect would cross. *"I parked my car out in the intersection when I saw the car coming. But I just knew the guy wouldn't stop, so I backed up just as the car sped by."* The chase continued.

"Now the guy was approaching an intersection where traffic had it jammed up. The guy tried to go around them on the right, in what he thought was a lane but was actually a parking strip, and he ended up stuck behind a parked car. I was thinking that we have to keep the guy contained and boxed in."

The other officers were thinking the same thing and they positioned their cars so the suspect car was unable to move away from the curb. Behind the suspect's car was a newly opened restaurant with a large picture window crowded with curious diners peering out. Seconds later they would scurry away to safety at the rear of the restaurant.

Tony scrambled out of his car with his shotgun, his thoughts still on keeping the suspect in one place to reduce danger to people on the sidewalk and in the businesses. In the second or two that it took him to get out and move within 10 feet of the suspect's door, the holdup man was out and moving slowly toward the rear fender. He held a Beretta along his thigh. *"The guy was looking at someone I couldn't see* [later determined to be another officer just out of Tony's sight] *and the guy kept repeating in a demanding voice, 'Just do it, just do it.' Then he looked at me and started backing up toward his open door. He brought his gun up to his head. Again he said, 'Just do it.'"*

Tony was standing between six to nine feet from the suspect. *"I wasn't thinking in terms of cover. I knew that we were here until someone shoots. I repeatedly told the guy that it was over."* Due to Tony's tunnel vision, he was not aware that Officer Greggor was to his left, pointing a shotgun at the man, and another officer was to the left of Greggor, pointing his handgun.

If the suspect heard Tony's order, he didn't show it. Witnesses later said that the suspect swung his Beretta toward Tony, but Tony only remembers the man's elbow dropping and his wrist bending. Tony fired.

"I saw the pellets hit, but on his right side," Tony says. *"Since I was standing in front of him, I couldn't understand how my shot hit him in the side. I looked down and saw that the spent shell hadn't fully ejected, so I shook it out and pumped another round in."*

Tony had not heard Greggor's shotgun explode or the other officer fire his handgun. *"My tunnel vision made everything smaller,"* Tony says. *"You could have been standing right next to me and I wouldn't have seen you."* It was Greggor's shotgun pellets that struck the suspect in his right side. Tony's pellets center punched the suspect's abdomen, though Tony had only seen Greggor's hits.

"I went up on the guy, who had slid down the side of his car into a seated position, and kicked his Beretta away. Another officer picked up the gun as two others pulled the guy over onto his stomach and handcuffed him."

Again Tony was hit with a rush of adrenaline, greater than any synthetic pill could create. *"I went to the car phone and punched in my home number. I got the recorder but I knew my boys were home, probably still sleeping. I screamed for someone to pick it up and I kept screaming until it awoke my boys downstairs. When they answered, I screamed at them what had just happened and that I wanted to see them. I just needed to hold them. When they asked how they would get to me, I told them that Greggor would come and get them."* Tony says the rush was so intense, so extraordinary, that it was almost like an out-of-body experience. The boys were not brought to the scene.

"I was worried about the shotgun and I got it and put the safety on. I went over to the suspect to see where my round hit and I was concerned about the restaurant window." It was then that Tony saw where his shot had struck. *"An officer put his arm around me but I shook it off and told him not to do that; I needed space."*

The precinct captain was on the scene when the shooting occurred and immediately ordered that the three officers be put into a police car and driven to detectives. Tony remembers seeing the fire department's medics working on the suspect as their car pulled away.

"I'm not sure what the hurry was to get us out of there," Tony says. *"But I know now that I will never let them take me away that quickly again. I needed to stay there and get grounded again; I needed to land. Getting pulled away so quickly didn't allow me to see the whole picture."*

In the detective's office, Tony was told to sit in a small room by himself. When his captain came in to talk to him, the detectives asked the captain to leave. *"They shut the door after he left and I didn't like that. I got up and opened it and a couple minutes later they tried to shut it again. I told them to leave it alone.*

"Although my attorney told me not to go back to the scene, I went back about three days later. I needed to be there to fill the gap of being pulled away so quickly. As I walked around the place, I had the feeling that people in the restaurant were wondering who I was. Then I thought they recognized me, though common sense would tell you they weren't the same people who'd been there the day of the shooting."

A few days later, a businessman in Tony's patrol district told him that the suspect had been an acquaintance of his and had been to his store. Tony recalled having a fleeting thought just before he fired that he had seen the man somewhere before. The businessman told Tony that he used to go to the shooting range with the man and that the suspect practiced shooting with a gun in each hand, firing simultaneously and with accuracy.

Tony says that he was treated fine by other officers. But a non-police friend called him a few days afterward and asked if he felt badly.

"For what?" Tom asked.

"For taking a human life," his friend replied.

"No," Tony said right back at him, probably remembering the man's gun moving toward him. *"I'd feel worse about running over an innocent squirrel than I do shooting someone who's trying to kill me."*

In Patrick Clancy's story, described in FOUR SHOOTINGS, Clancy and two other officers contained a heavily armed, mentally deranged man in a downtown 30-story highrise. Tony Petterson was one of those officers.

"My partner and I were at the precinct when the call came out that a man was firing an automatic weapon in a high-rise two blocks away. A moment later an officer, who just happened to be nearby, came on the radio and confirmed that the situation was real."

As Tony and his partner ran toward the building, other people passed them running away from it. As they neared, Tony saw Sergeant Patrick Clancy with his gun drawn and pointing toward an insurance office on the ground floor. "He's in there," Clancy said.

"For the next few moments our police instincts took over rather than our smarts," Tony says. *"I was suddenly on my belly, crawling toward the door, then through it. Clancy was right behind me. I saw rifle shells all over the floor and I saw a survival knife. When I saw the knife, I knew we were dealing with a nut. When I looked into the insurance office, I saw this woman looking around a cubical partition at me. I motioned for her get back."*

A third officer named Dobbs came into the lobby from another door. The three officers took cover in different places around the lobby. Their unspoken plan was that if the gunman left the insurance office and entered the lobby, they were not going to let him go to another level in the crowded building. Even if he came out with a hostage, he was not going any further.

Outside, dozens of officers were arriving and securing the

perimeter, evacuating office workers and children from a nursery. SWAT and hostage negotiators were setting up and a hoard of news media was descending. From an office across the street, a secretary could see into the insurance office. She told 9-1-1 that she could see people on their knees with their hands behind their heads and she could see a man in camouflage walking back and forth with a rifle on his shoulder.

"I was standing behind a marble pillar thinking that it would stop a bullet," Tony says. *"Then I heard a shot and a cracking noise by my ankle. I knew that sometimes you can get hit and not immediately feel it. I looked down to see if my ankle was still there and it was OK; the bullet had hit a metal frame by the door."*

Tony knew that the other officers were experienced and had been in shootings before, but he still wondered how they would react if the suspect came out. But before he could think about it too much . . .

"The guy fired a burst on full automatic, shattering windows in the lobby. One of the rounds struck a marble pillar across the room, which, judging by the size of the hole, convinced me that marble wasn't good cover after all. I looked down at my puny handgun and thought, 'Shit!'"

"When the shots set off several fire alarms, Patrick Clancy made a joke about not wanting to be inside the lobby anymore. Then one of the guys asked which one of us was going in after the guy. This was definitely a joke because none of us were going in."

Two citizens had been hit before the police arrived. They had been found on the street and in the basement and had been taken away by ambulance. Because smoke from the shots had activated the fire alarms, the elevators had shut down, preventing the gunman from getting to the upper floors.

SWAT went into action about 45 minutes after the three officers had set up in the lobby. One of their first tasks was to take over the inside perimeter and get the officers out. When done, they concentrated on negotiating with the gunman to release the hostages and to surrender. It took several hours, but the man finally gave up without further incident.

"Although I was no longer in the lobby, I stayed busy helping

SWAT. When the hostages began to exit, I at first couldn't find the woman I'd seen through the window. Finally, I saw her; she was the last to leave and she was OK."

When it was all over, two SWAT officers took Tony back inside and showed him the wall he had been standing behind. Some rounds had struck the other side but miraculously had not penetrated. *"My anxiety level went even higher when I saw those holes, and I didn't think it could get much higher. I began asking myself, how many lives do I have? I wondered if I needed to talk to a therapist, or God, or someone."*

As described in the Commentary, Tony did the right thing to come to terms with his shootings and, as a result, he is still working the street. But he knows that other officers and their specific situations are different, that some are unable to return to their duties. He says: *"Society should take care of officers who can't come back after killing someone; they've laid their lives on the line. People need to understand what police officers are doing for them. I get paid to come to work every day, not to get my ass shot off."*

Commentary

Tony Petterson bears a strong resemblance to Steven Seagal. His long, dark hair is pulled back into a neat pony tail and his deep brown eyes survey all that is going on around him. In many ways, Tony is also like the characters that Seagal plays on the silver screen: He is ready to play hardball if necessary and he's determined to win. His four shootings have taught him that his job is "not just to capture the suspect, but to survive the gunman." Like Seagal's characters, he does not suffer fools gladly, and his outspoken opinions don't always endear him to the brass. He is always ready to complain about injustice and will fight for the underdog. This has led him to be active in his union, fighting for the rights of officers to have a fair and safe work environment.

There are, however, some features about Tony that don't resemble Seagal. Unlike the laconic actor, Tony has an expressive face and is rarely at a loss for words. During this interview, the words flowed from him in a passionate stream and his face and hands provided lively support to his speech. Tony is not a loner but a family-oriented man, a single father to two teenaged sons. His frequent mention of them during the interview speaks of his fatherly devotion.

From the time he was a young boy, Tony has wanted to be a police officer. After 15 active years working the street, he still loves his profession. He said, "I couldn't not rush to a dangerous call. That's just not me." But after four shootings he wonders, "How many lives do I have left?"

What allows him to continue going back onto the streets in spite of this concern is the knowledge that he is "ready to play hardball" at a moment's notice, and he is determined to play it better than the suspect. Whenever he gets ready to leave the locker room at the beginning of his day, he looks into the mirror and says to himself, "This is how you are going to look at the end of your shift." This is a common ritual for police officers who have directly or vicariously had brushes with death on the street. He frequently rehearses scenarios in his mind and is always trying to improve his skills and strategies. What shakes him in one incident becomes a learning experience that helps keep him alive in the next.

He always strives to keep his skill level one step ahead of the suspect's, knowing that in at least two of his shootings he was competing for his and other lives against skilled gunmen who knew what they were doing. He also came to recognize that armed suspects are often desperate and therefore especially dangerous, and that anything can happen any time. He urges officers to be prepared, to always think ahead, and never be complacent.

Besides the survival skills and attitude that help him stay alive on the streets, Tony has also learned important lessons about what happens when the shooting ends. Although he has not developed post-traumatic stress disorder, he has seen some of his fellow officers suffer and he knows from personal experience how vulnerable people can feel in the wake of a traumatic event. He is supportive of debriefings, counseling, and peer-support, and adamant that any officer who has been hurt physically or psychologically deserves the best care and support that the agency, peers, and community have to offer. He sizzles with indignation when he talks about officers who have suffered because they did not get what they needed.

Tony has learned to pay attention to his own feelings and reactions and to quickly take care of them. He urges all officers to educate themselves about traumatic events. He says, "Officers need to be assertive about taking care of themselves afterward. They should do what they want and tell others what they need." For Tony this included not wanting to make any decisions for a few days after his second shooting. When he got home, about all his sons had to say was "What's for dinner, Dad?" He realized he did not want to make that decision or any other decision yet, so he said, "I already had to make a life and death decision that day. That's enough for a while. I told my friends and family that if they wanted to do me a favor, they could make all the decisions for a few days."

Another important lesson Tony learned was the importance of his family and friends. Right after he had shot and killed the armed bank robber, he felt an overwhelming urge to contact his children. He called his kids from the scene and told them to get down there right away so he could see them and hold them. He knows this was an irrational request, but this powerful need to make contact is common for officers and family members after a traumatic event. For instance, officers with children will often feel an irresistible urge to see and hold their children after a shift where they have witnessed death or injury to a child. It's not unusual for officers to go in and look at their kids sleeping 10 times in one night after experiencing or witnessing an ugly event. Tony has tried to educate his sons about police work and encourages them to ask questions and talk about their feelings so they will be prepared to handle it when they see their Dad's name and picture in the media. Tony's preparation has paid off because so far his kids have taken it in stride.

Steven Seagal always survives the action in the movies. Tony knows this is not guaranteed in real life, but he has taken charge in his usual emphatic and strong-willed manner to make sure the odds are greatly in his favor. Tony has also made a rule for himself: his last words to his kids when he goes to work are "I love you" and he leaves them positive and loving notes. That way those words will be the last message they got from their father in the event that one day he does not make it home.

THE RIDER

"Since we were working this kind of job, David and I had talked about what we would do if we ever got robbed. We discussed different ways we would disengage from the suspect, like toss him our wallets, back away to a place of cover, do something to get away from him."

While police work has always been dangerous, most veteran officers agree that there was more violence toward police officers in the early '70s, a fact that can be easily supported by statistics. Much of it was a result of poor training, a lack of portable radios, and just a looser way of doing police work. In addition, there was still a great hatred of police officers left over from the turbulent '60s.

When Lee Brandon and David Moody began working together as undercover vice officers, they had both been on the job for more than three years. Not only did they become good partners but they quickly became close friends. They worked in a unit called Drugs and Vice, concentrating mostly on vice activity, such as prostitution, pimping, and gambling. They worked hard at their job and were responsible for half the unit's statistics.

"It was 1974, and they were violent times for police officers," Lee Brandon says. *"There were lots of police-related shootings that year in our agency. In fact, two months earlier we had witnessed a fellow officer die in the street."*

The two vice officers always hit the streets in their "muscle car" around 8:00 P.M. and would cruise the usual spots to see if any prostitutes were working. On this night, they made a pass by a rundown burger joint in a poor part of town, a place infamous for its prostitution, drug dealers, fights, and shootings. *"There were three prostitutes standing out front as we pulled to the curb. If we had seen them in time, I would have dropped Dave off and tried to make a deal by myself since prostitutes generally don't like to get into a car with two guys. We tried to get them to come over to us but they refused."*

The officers decided to give up on them and began to pull away from the curb. *"Just as we pulled away,"* Brandon says, *"a guy called out to us to stop, then ran up to our car. He had a big Fedora hat, fancy clothes, and looked like a pimp. He asked if we wanted to buy drugs and we said no, we wanted whores."*

The man told the officers that he knew where there were two women and that he would show them where they were. *"We let the man get into the backseat of our two-door car, then I drove around for about 10 minutes while he felt us out. First I showed him a business card that said I owned a tow company, then he wanted to see some money. We thought that was a little odd because dopers always want to see your money, but it's rare for a pimp to want see it. I showed him a wad of fake money that in the dark he thought was real. Then Dave showed him a $5 bill wrapped around a wad of paper in a money clip. The guy believed that was real too, so he gave me directions to the house where the women were."*

From the backseat, the pimp directed the officers to a dark, shabby residential area where Lee remembered investigating several taxi cab robberies when he was working uniform. The officers were feeling uncomfortable with the situation and were about to curtail the deal when they noticed two scantily clad women standing on a porch. "That's it," the man said, and Lee pulled the car to the curb.

"As soon as I pulled over," Lee said, *"the guy reached between the bucket seats and yanked the keys out of the ignition. I figured he was looking for a tag or something that indicated it was a police car. There wasn't one, but I still didn't want him to have my keys. So I twisted around to get them; that's when I saw his revolver.*

"The guy started screaming that it was a robbery and that he wasn't fooling. As odd as it seems, it was at that moment that I

*noticed that his clothes weren't as nice as I'd first thought. They
were shabby and I could see that he looked more like a junkie than a
pimp.* " He told Lee to grip his steering wheel with both hands.

Brandon's mind was racing as he tried to figure out what
to do. When situations had gotten hot in the past, he had
flashed his badge. But he didn't think that would work on this
guy. *"I gave him my fake bundle of money; Dave gave him only the
$5 bill from the money clip."* But this irritated the man and he
demanded that Dave Moody give him the rest of the money.

Brandon was thinking how to disengage the driver's door.
"You have what you wanted," he told him as he cracked the driver's door. *"This set the guy off screeching in a high-pitched voice.
You know, I was in the infantry in Vietnam and had since been in
dangerous situations as a police officer, but this was the first time I
had really experienced fear. The guy put his revolver against the side
of Dave's head and I could see the bullets in its cylinder."*

Brandon knew he didn't dare open the door further since
that had set the man off a moment ago. *"The guy kept the gun
against Dave's head as he pulled Dave's white sport coat open and
patted him down for the money. I dropped my hands from the steering wheel, reached under my jacket, and slipped my 9mm out of my
shoulder holster. He was screaming so loud he didn't hear me release
the safety, but a moment later he noticed my hands were off the steering wheel."*

The man screamed at Brandon to get his hands back on the
steering wheel. Brandon complied, pinning the unholstered
semiauto under his arm, out of sight of the man in back. *"The
guy felt the handle of Dave's two-inch revolver and thought he'd
found the money. He cried out, 'I've got it!' and pulled back Dave's
sport jacket. As he bent forward and tried to pull out what was really a gun, I stuck my hand under my arm, grabbed my gun, and started to pull it out, careful to keep my wrist cocked so he couldn't see it."*

But something caught the guy's eye and he began moving
his gun from Dave Moody's head toward Brandon's.

A gunshot roared through the small car and a blinding
flash assaulted Brandon's eyes.

"I couldn't see and I was confused as to who fired the shot. But

I brought my gun up in my right hand and thrust it over my right shoulder and began firing it upside down in the direction of the guy." Brandon fired until his gun jammed, something he wasn't to recall until nearly a half year later. In one swift motion, he pushed the door open, cleared the jam, and rolled out of the car firing over his left shoulder.

"*The guy in the back was screaming 'I'm shot, I'm shot, I'm dying.' As I rolled out, I can remember thinking: I hope so.*"

The next few seconds were a confusion of trying to understand what had just happened and what was still going on. "*I looked back in the car and saw Dave sitting there with his white sports coat covered with blood. I jumped back in, banged into him, and asked if he was OK. He said yes, and asked if I was OK.*"

When the suspect had moved his gun from Dave Moody's head toward Brandon, Moody had pulled his revolver and fired over his shoulder. That was the mysterious shot that blinded him. The bullet, which was a 158-grain load, struck the suspect in the chin, traveled under the skin, and stopped less than midway to his ear; a nonfatal wound. Moody then rolled out of the car, looked back and saw his partner shooting over his shoulder. In the noise and confusion, Moody thought Brandon was engaged in a firefight and jumped back in the car. But then Brandon rolled out and fired additional rounds. When he stopped firing, he saw his partner inside the car covered with blood, so he jumped back in.

All this took place in less than 10 seconds, much of it unseen by each officer because of their total focus on their piece of the moment. Besides the gun jamming, Brandon would not recall some particulars of the encounter for several months.

"*We talked about what to do. There wasn't anyone out in the dark street and the hookers on the porch were gone. We didn't have portable radios so we decided that I would contain the scene and Dave would go knock on some doors to see if he could use someone's phone. The first one was answered by a little old lady who opened her door a crack and just peered out. What she saw was a blood soaked man who told her he was the police and needed to use her phone. She quickly shut the door, then opened it up again, probably after releasing the chain, and told him to come on in."*

Within a few minutes, police cars and an ambulance arrived. A medic got into the back, checked the suspect, and told Brandon that he could feel a pulse. The medic asked what he should do. *"I told him to take the guy to the hospital,"* Brandon says with a shrug, indicating the obvious. *"So the medic grabs the guy by the hair and drags him out of the car, onto a stretcher and they take him away. It was odd, but the ambulance people were as enraged as we were and they treated the guy like he was the scum of the earth."*

The shift sergeant drove Brandon and Moody to the detectives' office. Brandon felt uncomfortable when they took his gun from him and was concerned that the blood splatter on it would damage the metal [when someone is shot at close range, the weapon and the shooter are usually splattered with "blowback blood"]. They told Brandon that they just wanted to test fire it and they would get it back to him.

The two officers were told that the pimp had died shortly after arriving at the hospital.

The chief came in and Brandon told him what had happened. A moment later Brandon heard him tell the media officer to tell the press that it was a narcotics investigation. *"I realized then that the chief was more concerned about the politics of the shooting than about us. He was also concerned about the number of rounds fired. I told him I had fired seven and Dave had fired one. He said something about how many missed the guy, then asked me again why I had fired so many. I was starting to get mad so I told him I fired seven at the suspect and saved one for me and one for Dave. He just turned around and walked out of the room."*

Brandon got his gun back an hour later. After the officers were interviewed by detectives, they were left with nothing to do, nor did they know what was expected of them. No one gave them direction. So they went right back out on the street and returned to work.

The city's newspaper wrote a straightforward story of the incident without its usual editorializing. Even the mayor was quoted as saying something to the effect that this is what happens when crooks run around with guns. The two officers experienced a sort of celebrity status from their fellow officers, but neither was bothered by it.

An alternative newspaper did an investigation and found that the suspect's gun had been stolen eight years earlier and, coincidentally, the report had been taken by the Drug and Vice unit's captain. The story implied that the gun had been planted. Brandon says that the ridiculous article bothered him, but he decided to ignore it and get on with his life.

About a month after the incident, Brandon saw a report that was a compilation of his agency's intelligence unit and federal intelligence that said a hit man had been hired in San Francisco to kill him. The deceased and his family were of the Muslim faith, but it was unknown if the family or the mosque had hired the man. The report also said that the man had already left California and was on his way.

Brandon went to a deputy chief and asked if he could use an unmarked police car and a portable radio to take home until the threat had passed, but the chief said no. Though he was frustrated and concerned about his family's welfare, Brandon didn't give up looking for help. Since he lived outside the city in a nearby county, he asked the county sheriff for help, and they immediately supplied him with a car and a portable radio.

One night, the suspect's sister came to the Drug and Vice office. *"Dave didn't want to go out to the reception area and talk to her, so I did,"* Brandon says. *"I thought she would be rational but she wouldn't listen to my explanation about what happened that night. She said that we should have identified ourselves as police officers and not have shot him. When I tried to explain some more, she began screaming, then she attacked me. We had to eventually put her out of the office, and it made me take the threats even more seriously."*

Brandon moved his wife and two children out of their home and into his parent's house. Two weeks later he moved them to another location and continued to move from place to place for a half year. At one point the feds went to the mosque and told them that they knew what was going on and they knew who the man was. The feds said they wanted the situation to stop.

The man and the death plot eventually went away, and Brandon moved his family back into his home. *"But I slept poorly for two years after that,"* he says. *"I had continuous thoughts that someone was coming after me."*

Although Brandon was never significantly affected by the shooting incident, his partner began having problems about six months later. *"Dave was getting more and more froggy* [police vernacular for nervous and agitated]. *One night he wanted to take the rest of the shift off, so I did too. We went bar hopping and got pretty drunk. As we were staggering back to the police station in the middle of the night to call our wives, Dave verbally ripped into a guy sitting in a car at the curb. I asked Dave what he thought he was doing and pulled him away. I apologized to the guy in the car and told him I would take Dave home. But we'd only gone halfway down the block when the car roared up to us and two bare-chested guys jumped out. They said they only wanted Dave and one of the guys kicked him to the ground. I got into the fight and fought both of them for about ten minutes while Dave lay on the ground.*

"At one point I lost my gun. One of the guys picked it up and tried to shoot me in the stomach. But when he tried to chamber a round, there was already one in it and the gun jammed. When I told him we were police officers, he started to mellow. He mentioned some officer's name he knew, then gave me my gun back. Both guys got back in their car, drove off, and that was the last we saw of them."

Brandon went to the same deputy chief who had refused to let him have a police car and a radio, and asked to get help for Dave. *"At first he refused, so I told him that if Dave did something to get into trouble, I would go public with his refusal to help. Dave got help after that."*

More than 20 years have passed since the shooting, and today Lee Brandon and Dave Moody are high-ranking officers in their agency. At the time of their shooting, their agency didn't have a plan for helping officers after a traumatic incident, but within a year after their shooting, Brandon and Moody helped establish a peer-support group of officers experienced in traumatic incidents. The program is still in place to this day and, in fact, the agency is considered one of the more progressive in offering programs to help officers prevent psychological trauma and for helping them after deadly incidents.

Commentary

Captain Lee Brandon is a tall, imposing man. He could easily be intimidating if he wanted to, but his relaxed demeanor and gracious manners quickly put you at ease. His intelligence shines through as he thoughtfully analyzes his experiences. He tells his story in the precise, measured manner of a person accustomed to the command task of explaining missions and instructions to others. His concern for people comes through in his emphasis about how he, his partner, his family, and his fellow officers have been affected by the many traumatic incidents they have been exposed to.

Facing death and being responsible for others came early to Brandon during his tour as a captain in the Vietnam War. He credits his experience there with giving him the ability to have an objective view of humans killing each other. "I realized it wasn't personal, it was just business." This helped prepare him for the violent nature of police work in the early 1970s, when police officers were being murdered in greater numbers than today. Even so, it still shook him to witness a fellow officer dying on the street from a line-of-duty death. "It really drove home to me that we could be killed doing this."

Brandon said that he is by nature a cautious person who prefers not to take unnecessary risks. He believes that an ounce of prevention is worth a pound of cure. This led him to be a strong believer in discussing and rehearsing scenarios ahead of time so that he and his partner had a plan if things went wrong. He thinks this preparation was a major factor in surviving the ambush, and he urges all officers to discuss and rehearse scenarios ahead of time and to tactically debrief them afterwards.

The shooting was a profound learning experience for

Brandon, and the lessons he learned from it took years to fully understand and assimilate. The intense arousal and fear generated by the ambush caused major perceptual distortions and memory loss that were amazing to him. Although he was aware that he was experiencing tunnel vision during the incident and that his peripheral vision was disappearing, he was unable to stop it.

Even more amazing to him was how he forgot major elements of the event until months later. When he gave his statement to the detectives, he believed his story was complete and accurate. But three months later while driving home from work, additional memories of the event suddenly came flooding back. He remembered his gun had jammed between his first and second burst of shots and that when he had rolled out of the car, he cleared the jam before he got off his second shots. As he said, "Having your gun jam during a gun battle is something you wouldn't easily forget." Once he began remembering, other forgotten memories came back. He said he never would have believed this could happen if he had not experienced it himself (this is a common experience with trauma survivors). All this has made Brandon a strong supporter of training for officers, agencies, and investigators about what happens to officers during and after a traumatic incident.

There were many more lessons to be learned as the aftermath of the shooting unfolded over the coming months and years. Brandon and his partner didn't have a radio because "there weren't enough to go around." This insensitivity to their welfare continued when Brandon was refused a radio and car to help protect himself and his family from the death threats that followed, and later when his agency refused counseling for his partner, though he was obviously troubled by the incident. In the mid-70s there were no debriefings, no counseling, no organized peer-support, and no time off. Unfortunately, this situation still exists in too many agencies throughout the country.

The seriousness of this lack of help and support, like the memory loss of the event, had never occurred to Brandon until he personally experienced it. He said that watching his family suffer from the death threats and his partner suffer from the shooting disturbed him and made him feel impotent. He had trouble sleeping and became hypervigilant and unable to relax. Brandon was unable to return to normalcy until five years after the shooting.

But he is not the type of person to let feelings of impotency make him helpless. As usual, he went into action to make sure everyone was taken care of. When his own agency refused to help, he successfully enlisted the help of the local agency where he lived to help protect his family from death threats. He also enlisted federal agents to keep him updated on the activities of the assassin. When his agency refused to get help for his partner, he didn't take no for an answer and made sure he got the counseling that proved helpful to him.

A year after the event, the learning process was still going on, and this galvanized Brandon into even further action. As he discussed the shooting and its aftermath with his partner, they came to realize that in their agency half of all officers involved in shootings had either quit or taken a stress leave. They decided to do something about this unacceptable situation. They connected with their new police chaplain and together formed their agency's first peer-support team. Brandon says, "This was out of necessity; we were losing too many good officers."

Brandon was gratified to see how effective this program was and remained active in it until he was promoted to the command staff. He then bowed out due to concerns that officers might feel uncomfortable with a commander as a support person. But he remains willing to help anyone who requests his assistance.

He also came to realize the importance of taking time off after a traumatic event. After his gun was test fired and the blood wiped from it, it was returned to him the same evening. Then, due to poor supervision, he and his partner simply went back out onto the street and finished their shift. While this insensitivity and ignorance were common in the 1970s, Brandon is happy to report that today his agency appropriately gives officers three days paid leave after a shooting.

Fortunately for Brandon, he had to take six months off the street when his agency required him to go to school to meet their educational requirements. This occurred when he was still reeling from his shooting's aftermath and thinking about leaving his agency. He said the time off significantly helped him heal, and he now encourages officers and agencies to make this part of their post-shooting process.

Brandon also became a strong believer in educating and supporting officers' family members on the impact of traumatic events. He and his wife have been married for 29 years and he said he has tried from the beginning to prepare his family for the demands of being married to an officer. He believes this has helped them survive their six months in hiding from an assassin and the many other stressors his career has visited upon them. He gives much credit to his wife, whom he describes as a "strong person." His respect and affection are evident when he talks about her.

Brandon and Moody were on their own after their shooting. While their agency's strategy resulted in the career destruction of half of its officers involved in shootings, it did not destroy theirs. His thoughtful analysis of what was going on around him and his determination to find solutions rather than succumb to the problems led him to save himself, help his partner, and facilitate positive changes in his agency.

Brandon strongly encourages agencies to develop plans and programs to help officers and their family members heal from shootings and other traumatic events. Do it now, he urges, don't wait. As he would tell you: being thoughtful, planning, and taking care of others is what being a commander is all about.

THREE SHOOTINGS

It was St. Patrick's Day and Officer Bill Nordin was looking forward to a quiet shift and a cold, holiday beer after work. He had been on the street for an hour and was getting ready to stop for a cup of coffee when he got a radio call about a man beating a woman. He aimed his patrol car toward the address, thinking it was probably just another typical domestic squabble. But then dispatch updated the call to someone being stabbed. A moment later, the call was changed again: someone had been shot.

"I mentally upgraded the call to a man with a gun," says Nordin, who had been an officer for nearly eight years then, three of them on the SWAT team. *"The call was confused, but it was obvious that it was getting worse."*

Moments before Nordin had received the first call, the suspect had been driving in a quiet suburban neighborhood. When his car ran out of gas, he walked to a nearby apartment where he knew a pregnant woman. He was a big man, bearded, wearing a T-shirt, blue jeans, and a large knife on each hip. Disliked and feared by his relatives and people who knew him, he was known to be violent, an ex-boxer as good with his fists as he was with his knives. He had stabbed a man just the night before but had not been caught.

Once inside the apartment, he got mean. He began making threats to kill the woman, cut out her baby, and kill her other child who was in a nearby room. When he went to the refrigerator for a beer, the woman screamed for an upstairs neighbor. When the neighbor got there, the men began to fight and, as is often the case in knife attacks, it took a moment for the neighbor to realize he wasn't being punched but stabbed repeatedly. When the neighbor fled to call the police, the attacker ran down the street, then between two houses.

"I found the stabbed guy and he was able to give me a description of the suspect and the direction he had fled," Nordin says. *"Myself and several other officers began searching the neighborhood as neighbors gave us updates about where the guy was last seen.*

"A few moments later, I saw him between a couple of houses. I drew my .45 and told him to get his hands up but instead he drew a knife, said 'fuck you,' and came right at me. I fired two rounds but

there was no reaction from him other than to turn and run around the corner of the house. So I fired a round at the corner, hoping to keep the guy back away from it. I sliced wide around the corner, thinking the guy was either hit or had fled over the fence. All this went down in about three seconds."

But the bullet had not penetrated the corner and the suspect had not fled. Instead he was waiting, crouched like a wrestler. He lunged and Nordin fired four times. *"I couldn't back up because there was a fence behind me. The guy covered about three quarters of the distance before he fell at my feet.*

"I don't know how many rounds hit him and it was never determined due to the confusion of entrance and exit wounds. Since he was crouched and bent forward, one of the rounds hit his head, which was the fatal wound that stopped him. I sidestepped a little and reloaded my weapon while another officer covered him. He wanted to handcuff the suspect, but I told him to hold on a minute because we needed to slow things down."

The suspect gurgled for a few moments, turned gray, then died.

"As I looked down at him, I remember wanting a chew of tobacco. I thought about all the things that were going to happen now: the medical examiner was going to come, the photo guys, the brass. For a second I started asking myself if I had done right. Then I told myself, 'Yes, I had.'"

Within minutes the area was saturated with police officers, ambulance people, TV reporters, and neighbors. *"I was told to get into the back of a police car, as if I was under arrest, but I refused. Instead, I walked over to a cluster of officers and mingled with them, trying not to be noticed.*

"I was feeling this tremendous exhilaration. It was a real rush and I'd never felt anything like it. Hey, he tried to kill me, but I killed him first. Fuck him. Then when the ambulance people started working on him, I remember thinking that I didn't want them to save him."

The verbal exchange between Nordin and the suspect and the first three gunshots had been transmitted out over the radio. *"When I first confronted him, I was holding my portable radio in my non-gun hand. When I squeezed the trigger, I simulta-*

neously squeezed the radio mike. If I missed with those first two shots, which was never determined, it was because I was trying to hold onto the radio and use a two-handed grip on my weapon. During the two seconds it took me to get around the corner, I put the radio back into my belt holder and fired the second time with a good grip."

An officer from the agency's peer-support group—officers who had been involved in deadly force encounters—drove Nordin to the detectives' office. Nordin didn't know the man and would not talk to him about the shooting, though the officer kept encouraging him to.

"They told me in detectives not to talk to anyone about what had happened. I didn't like that at all. I'd just been in a shooting and I felt that I had to talk to someone. Later, an officer friend of mine came in. He had been in a shooting once and had been in a lot of firefights in Vietnam. He took me to another room and asked, 'What the hell happened?' This made me feel good because everyone had been telling me not to say anything. After I told him, he just hugged me. It felt really good to tell someone."

Whereas Nordin took comfort in having his friend present, he still had a sense of facing everything alone. He didn't have a union representative or an attorney to advise him. While he waited to be interviewed, various chiefs, assistance chiefs, and other supervisors came up and spoke with him or patted his back *"Coming up to me like that was pretty phony. Then they would gather in little clutches across the room where they probably talked about the city's liability."*

Nordin says that when he was finally interviewed, the detective, who he didn't know well, took him into an interview room. "If you fuck with me," the detective said, "I'll fuck with you."

"This set me back," Nordin says, *"because there was no conflict. I was telling the truth. I thought this was a little odd. Several years later, the detective said he didn't remember saying it. Maybe it had been his way of neutralizing our roles."*

Although in the next four years, Nordin would be involved in two more deadly shootings, this one has remained in the forefront of his mind. *"I was preoccupied with it for a while, which is natural, but I can't put it to rest because it keeps coming back to me in odd ways. Every few months I run into someone who, when they find out I'm a cop, tells me about the guy. They don't know I'm the one who killed him, it's just coincidental. Then from time to time I hear from the guy's family who wants to thank me for killing him.*

"Just recently the guy's grandmother even wanted me over for dinner."

One day, four years after Nordin's shooting, a man walked into small bank branch inside a large grocery store. He vaulted over the counter, took hostages, and ordered them to activate the alarm. He said he wanted the police there.

Coincidentally, there were officers at the store taking a shoplifting report when the call came over the radio. They immediately cleared the area around the bank and waited for SWAT.

Nordin, now an 11-year veteran, seven years with SWAT, was at home mowing his lawn when his beeper went off, indicating a SWAT call-up. As he raced to the scene, he received updates about what was happening in the bank. He met other SWAT members at the store and they quickly put on their equipment and planned their approach. They decided the best place to set up was in a long hallway that ran next to the small bank.

During the first two hours, the suspect released all but two female hostages from a back room. Then later he let one of the women out to use the rest room, telling her to return or he would kill the other woman who was eight months pregnant. SWAT would not let her go back, of course, though she attempted several times to sneak away and get back into the bank

A few minutes later, the suspect fired a round through the wall. Believing the hostage had been shot or would be shot, the SWAT team, led by Nordin and Miller, his partner, streamed out of the hallway, ran along the wall behind the teller windows, and stopped at a small door to the back room. They started to smash it in as Nordin pulled the pin on a flash bang, a grenade-like device used by SWAT that emits a tremendous bang and intense flash, typically used to distract suspects. But they were stopped by a soft, female voice from inside the room.

"I'm OK," the voice said.

"We froze at the door. Our element of surprise was gone because we had been too noisy on our approach. Later we learned that he was waiting for us inside the room, holding the woman in front of him, his arm wrapped around her neck, and his .357 pointed at the door. We backed out of the area the same way we had just approached. This time, however, Miller, another officer, and myself huddled in the manager's officer at the opposite end of the teller's row. A couple of other officers positioned themselves on the customer side of the teller windows where they thought they might have a shot at the small door, while the rest of the team returned to the hallway."

The suspect asked for a pizza and several music CDs, which were subsequently delivered on a cart and left outside the door. Later the suspect opened the small door and stepped out with the hostage in front of him. Although a SWAT officer near the counter could only see a small portion of the suspect's forehead, he made the difficult shot. The round was deflected by an inner-office mailbox so only a bullet fragment struck the suspect, causing a minor wound.

"The guy pulled the hostage back into the room and shouted for us to get back, that he was going to kill her. This was it, we had to move. We ran along the wall until we got to the open door and I threw the flash bang into the room. A second later we rushed in and saw the guy standing in sort of an alcove where the employees hung their coats. The flashbang probably startled him because the woman was beside him now and he was holding her with just one arm. We had our MP5s on semiauto; I fired into his face and Miller fired into his chest." Blood and brain chips sprayed across the walls. The suspect crumpled to the floor.

"I took a deep breath. After three hours it was finally over. I looked at the guy and thought: 'Yes, we're done. Are you happy, asshole?' Then someone from out in the teller area yelled 'Officer down.'"

The alcove in which the suspect was crouching was in the

same wall that extended behind the teller cages out in the bank. As Nordin and the other two SWAT officers made their entry through the door, the remaining team members were still running toward it along the outside wall. An MP5 round had passed through the suspect, through the wall, penetrating a SWAT officer's hip. A small piece of shrapnel struck another officer in the shoulder.

As always, officers, detectives, and ambulances crowded the scene within seconds. Nordin and all the other involved SWAT officers were taken to detectives where again Nordin didn't have an attorney, a union representative, or a peer-support person. *"It helped to have Miller with me because we had not only shared the experience but we both had been in shootings before. All the brass swarmed in again and were still as phony with their concern as in my previous shooting."*

Someone in detectives made an insensitive comment about the SWAT team shooting one of their own people. The officer who said it left and didn't learn until later the rage his words caused among the SWAT officers.

"During the following months, Miller and I talked about the shooting a lot. We both had entered that little room with the same mind-set: If we were going to die, we were going to die together, though we were going to do our best not to get the other killed."

Nordin's and Miller's wives are both officers with the same agency. The information released just minutes after the shooting was confused and Mrs. Nordin was told her husband had been shot. They sped to the hospital, where they saw the two wounded officers brought in on stretchers; Nordin was not one of them. Mrs. Nordin, though, was not convinced that her husband was OK until she went to detectives and saw him.

Nordin took almost a month off work. *"I had to process all the information and do a lot of thinking about it. Since I had the experience of the first shooting, I knew that the processing would take a while before I would eventually get through it."*

A few months later, Nordin went into the bank and asked how the woman was doing who had been taken hostage. He had not heard from her since the incident, not a thank you card nor a phone call. They told him she had delivered her baby shortly after the shooting and that both were doing fine. After a little more small talk, Nordin asked if he could cash a check, though he was not a customer of the bank.

They refused him.

The first night Nordin returned to work he realized he had come back too soon. *"I just knew I wasn't ready. My head wasn't in it yet, so I took another week off. My rule of thumb is to go back to work only when you know that you can handle another shooting."*

Two nights after he came back, he got into another one, his third shooting.

In Nordin's agency, SWAT is frequently used to do high-risk entries for search warrant cases. Because of their special skills and equipment, they are best qualified to smash in the door, contain the situation, and handcuff all the occupants before the drug unit or gang unit conducts their search.

"We knew this house was fortified, that there could be lots of people in it, and that they had two or three vicious dogs. We had a pretty good idea of the floor plan and we had fair intelligence about what was inside.

"When the raid started to go down, there were lots of things happening at the same time: a guy came out on a back patio and shouted 'police,' then went back inside; we broke a back window out so that we could cover a room where we knew there were stored weapons; our armored car hooked up to the front door to pull it open; and a SWAT guy fired a burst into one of the attack dogs.

"Miller and I and an officer named Torrence entered through an unlocked patio door. There were two couches in the living room, one occupied by a man and a woman, the other by just one man. We advanced on them, looking over our MP5s and shouting at them to get on the floor."

But in one swift motion, the man sitting by himself reached between a sofa cushion, pulled out a derringer, stood, and thrust the weapon over Nordin's barrel and into his face. *"I had seen the guy on the sofa, but my submachine gun blocked my view of his arm for the split second it took for him to sweep his gun hand up. I didn't see it until it was in my face.*

"There was a moment when I thought I was going to get shot in the face. But I fired first and the other two guys shot, too. The guy twisted as the rounds struck him, then he fell over a small table." The room filled with smoke and the couple on the other sofa screamed in panic and buried their faces in the cushions.

Torrence was shocked at how close he came to losing his friend. "I thought you were dead," he said repeatedly. "I thought you were dead."

"I told him to knock it off, which immediately snapped him out of it. I looked at the dead guy and, like in my first shooting, I wanted a chew of tobacco."

The SWAT team made a conscious effort to slow everything down. There were still people on the sofa that were potentially dangerous and the rest of the house had yet to be searched. When they entered the kitchen, they were momentarily startled by what they thought was a dead baby on the floor. It turned out to be a doll.

"A lieutenant wanted me to sit in the police car but I refused. I told him I wanted to see my wife because I didn't want the confusion for her like last time. Since she was working in a uniform car nearby, she came right to the scene and we were able to talk. Then I went downtown."

When Nordin and the other officers got to detectives, they got word that the detectives back at the scene could not locate the small gun. They did find a damaged butane lighter that they thought was probably what the SWAT officers had seen and reacted to. In fact, when they were photographing the living room, they shot a picture of a detective holding a lighter in his extended arm, reenacting what they thought the suspect had done.

The confusion over the suspect's gun was the result of a bizarre set of events. When the officers shot at the suspect, one or more rounds hit his hand, hurtling the derringer through the air and into a paper bag lying on the floor, which contained like-colored tools. Later, when a crime scene photographer looked inside, he thought it only contained tools, so he shoved it under a table with his foot. Several hours passed before someone examined the bag more thoroughly and found the gun. Although, the officers were later accused by the anti-police crowd of planting the gun in the bag, there was one piece of irrefutable evidence: the gun's trigger was covered with bloody tissue from the suspect's finger.

"*Our entire contact in detectives' office was adversarial,*" Nordin says. "*The detectives didn't want to be there, the medical examiner did a sloppy job, and the investigators at the scene did a poor job. But the other SWAT officers gave us tremendous support because most of them have been in shootings and many are on the peer-support team.*"

Nordin's wife asked him to "step out of line," meaning she wanted him not to be the first or second man on entries. "*She was right, and I did step out for a while. But now I'm back in the first two positions again.*"

Although it's not uncommon for Nordin's SWAT team to do several search warrant entries a week, and they routinely practice high-risk entries, Nordin shakes his head in wonder at the man who pointed a derringer at the no-nonsense officers whose faces were covered with black hoods and goggles, who were wearing camouflage fatigues, sidearms, and aiming deadly MP5 submachine guns at him.

"*A search warrant is different from a hostage situation,*" Nordin says. "*In a hostage situation you know the guy isn't going to give up, but on a warrant you don't know what people are going to do. You never know when someone will use deadly force on you. Judging the crime is not a gauge to determine when deadly force might be used against you.*"

Nordin is far from being a callous man, though he views his three shootings as a warrior whose fate has placed him in situations where he has had to use his skills, and ultimately deadly force. As so many officers have asked when examining the "why me" question, Nordin has thought about why he has been called on three times. "*There have been times when I've wondered if for some reason it's my destiny to shoot people for the police department.*"

While Nordin would rather not have been in any of the shootings, he has grown stronger from them and, with help and support from his family, his peers, and counseling, he has developed a healthy outlook on the encounters, his life, and police work. *"One time a drunk woman drove through a stop sign without stopping and I hit her car broadside. There was a little girl in the car and her injuries put her into a coma. I feel worse about that than any of those I've killed."*

When asked for advice on preparing for a deadly force encounter, Nordin listed these important points.

- Mentally prepare.
- Mentally go from a neutral state to a state of aggression.
- Know in your mind that you will shoot until the threat is down.
- Do all your homework before the shooting.
- Talk to the right people afterward.
- Feel good about surviving.

Commentary

Officer Nordin is an urban warrior. His muscular, compact frame moves with the efficient power that comes from years of martial arts training and knowledge that when the chips are down, every movement counts. If there is a package to be opened or a string to be cut, the knife he always carries suddenly appears in his hands as if by magic. His gestures are quick and fluid, the kind that could snatch a fly out of the air or respond instantly to any situation. Beneath his crew cut, his eyes take in everything with a matter-of-fact frankness that is direct but not hostile. If something bad happens, this is a man you want on your side.

As a full-time member of SWAT, he has chosen to use his many talents in a way that emphasizes the warrior role that officers sometimes are required to play. And he has done it well. All the suspects that Nordin has shot are precisely the type of criminal that we need warriors for. They were dangerous predators who thought nothing of taking two pregnant women hostage and threatening to kill them and an innocent child. One predator had so little regard for human life, including his own, that he tried to shoot Nordin in the face even when he was surrounded.

Not every criminal and street situation can be defused with negotiation and patience. Sometimes the criminal needs to be killed. Though this may sound harsh, keep in mind that even the suspect's family in Nordin's first situation are still thanking him to this day. When these predators are on a rampage, Nordin steps up to the line and puts his life squarely on it to save others. On more than one occasion he has looked death straight in the face with his steady, direct gaze, and said "Fuck you, I'm living. I'm going to win."

Based on the warrior stereotypes you see in movies and on TV, you might expect Nordin to be a cold and laconic man, maybe a man whose somber and reserved demeanor is a cover for a somewhat tortured soul. Nothing could be further from the truth. He is talkative, with a razor sharp wit and a stand-up comic's ability to see humor in just about every situation. His articulate, rapid-fire speech is full of quips and comments that flow effortlessly and keep everyone laughing when he's on a roll. When he sees his friends, he's just as likely to hug them as shake their hands.

Unlike his TV counterparts, Nordin says he needs to talk about his feelings when he's facing an emotional crisis. He seeks out family members, friends, and peers when he needs support. In turn, as a member of his agency's peer-support team, he frequently offers his help to others. He is an advocate of professional counseling and has been generous with his time in helping to train other officers to survive deadly force encounters. He is a gifted trainer who shares his own experiences and his considerable tactical expertise as part of his ongoing effort to help his fellow officers. He is a man who sees meaning and purpose in his work and his ability to help others on the street and in the classroom.

Nordin has not been tormented by his shootings. While he

had the usual temporary preoccupation with the events, he had the wisdom to protect himself by taking time away from the street until he worked through each incident. "You are ready to go back on the street when you are ready for the same thing or worse to happen on your first shift back," he says, giving perhaps the best answer to the question of how much time should you take off after a shooting. He should know, since his third shooting happened on his second night back after his second shooting.

Although Nordin feels good about surviving his deadly force encounters with dangerous predators, he has no illusions that the public or his agency really appreciates his commitment to his duty as a warrior. Any illusions he might have had were probably shattered when the bank branch, where he had laid his life on the line, later refused to cash his check.

Nordin knows how the media all too often distort incidents involving police officers to make them look vicious or incompetent. He also knows that no matter how well he performs, his agency has the potential to hang him out to dry if it becomes politically expedient. He believes that the public and his agency see SWAT as a pack of pit bull watchdogs—dangerous but necessary. Just keep them locked in the basement and out of sight until they are needed. He believes that few people really understand what they are up against out on the street. These realizations have been painful for a man who is a consummate professional, a man who takes his mission seriously.

So why does he keep doing it? Like most good soldiers, he does it because it needs to be done and because he can do it. His rewards come from being proud of a difficult job done well, and for the respect and friendship of his fellow team members, friends, and family.

Nordin said that the aftermath of his shootings was more stressful and discouraging than the actual events. But he is not bitter or even particularly angry about all the disillusionments he has experienced. He has processed them in the same direct, matter-of-fact way he deals with the other dangers he has faced. For him, it's all part of the price of doing business.

He puts it this way: "Face it, deal with it, learn from it, then move on."

Psychological Injuries

8

"Your body only gets assaulted once in a while but your brain gets assaulted every day."

Retired police sergeant

Before we discuss the aftermath of a shooting, we want to reiterate one important point. There are many other traumatic events besides police-involved shootings that can cause psychological injuries. Shootings comprise only a small percentage of ugly events that can leave an officer's emotions in turmoil. Any event that disturbs you should be debriefed.

Know that not everyone who sustains a psychological injury from an upsetting event will experience full-blown PTSD. But they may experience other emotional problems that don't meet the precise definition, and these can be equally painful.

The technicalities of the diagnosis are less important than the fact that you have sustained a psychological injury and it bothers you. Being bothered by an event is compared to wrenching your knee during a foot chase. You expect it to hurt until it heals. Similarly, if you wrench your psyche bad enough, it too gets injured and hurts until it heals. Whether the injury is mild or severe, it needs to be taken care of. Know that a psychological injury does not have to be catastrophic to warrant treatment.

Captain Young is with a large urban agency. He has seen many gruesome events in his 23-year career, but one in particular had always stuck with him:

Twenty years ago when I was a rookie, I was involved in a high-speed pursuit in which the speeds exceeded 100 miles per hour on a major freeway. The suspect had already rammed several police cars by the time the pursuit violently ended after he deliberately rammed a police car into a center divider, then careened into the patrol car in which I was a passenger with my coach.

Both cars were totally destroyed. I was not severely injured so I bailed out to help the officers in the other car. I tried in vain to get the horribly mangled body of a dead friend out of the police car. It shook me badly and I wondered if I really wanted to do stuff like this for the next 25 years of my life. Back then there were no debriefings other than going out and getting drunk.

Fortunately, one of the veteran coaches on the scene saw the pain in my eyes, took me under his wing, and did his own informal debriefing. He got me through the event and probably saved my career. I completely got over it except for one thing: every time I drove by the scene of the accident, I automatically replayed the damn thing in my head in living color. This went on for over 20 years. Nothing I ever did could stop that tape from playing. It wasn't freaking me out, but I could happily live without it.

Recently, I heard about a relatively new trauma treatment called EMDR that might stop the tape once and for all. It sounded goofy but I thought, "What have I got to lose by trying?" So I decided to go to a psychologist and get the treatment. During 15 minutes of EMDR, I vividly relived the event and even remembered parts of it I had forgotten until that moment. Somehow I felt differently afterward.

I didn't know what to think until the next time I drove by the accident scene. I was half a mile past it when it dawned on me that for the first time in 22 years, I hadn't played that damn tape. I was elated. That was two and a half years ago and the tape has never come back.

All it took was 15 minutes of treatment.

Captain Young is a cheerful, well-adjusted man who enjoys his career and his life. Though he is far from being disabled by his earlier trauma, he decided he didn't want to put up with this nagging pain every time he drove down that freeway.

If you have a wrenched psyche, be it mild of severe, do yourself a favor like he did. Get it taken care of. There is no guarantee that treatment will be 100 percent successful, but you owe it to yourself to try. The EMDR (Eye Movement Desensitization Reprocessing) that Captain Young referred to is one of many trauma treatment methods that mental health professionals have that can be effective in helping to heal psychological injuries.

THE AFTERMATH OF A SHOOTING

It's only one hour before the end of your shift. As you head for the call, you get additional information about possible shots fired. It seems quiet as you approach the house, that is until the front door bursts open and a woman covered with blood staggers out and falls down the front steps, landing at your feet. Behind her, an enraged, cursing man charges out and points a shotgun at your chest. Your gun, which has somehow found its way into your hand, thrusts forward. You see your muzzle flash in eerie silence as you pump round after round into the suspect, while at the same time you anticipate getting struck with a load of buckshot. You pray your vest will stop it.

After what seems like forever, the suspect collapses. You feel overwhelmed with relief, then with joy as you realize you are alive and uninjured. You also realize that soon the whole world will be there and that your life and your family's will be changed forever.

As we saw in Chapter 5, the physical changes that occur as a result of high arousal can cause strange perceptual and cognitive distortions that can make a shooting seem like something out of the Twilight Zone. This can be disturbing to an officer who is unaware that these are natural reactions.

After a shooting, there are a variety of reactions that officers may experience that are within the normal range. While they may be mild or severe, they should never be considered weird or an indication that the officer is weak.

In the minutes and hours immediately following a shooting, an officer may experience the following reactions, many of which are the result of natural chemicals and hormones introduced into one's system by the high-arousal state:

Physical

- trembling
- sweating
- chills
- nausea
- diarrhea
- hyperventilation
- dizziness
- urge to urinate
- jumpy, hyper
- thirsty

Emotional

- wide range of heightened emotions, including bouts of crying
- intensely preoccupied with the event, playing it over and over in your mind
- second-guessing yourself and others
- elated and happy to be alive
- fierce joy over having "won" a life-or-death fight
- angry, irritable, hypersensitive
- paranoid, fear of being judged by others
- self-conscious, concern about being recognized in public as a participant
- vulnerable, anxious, worried, scared
- sad, despondent, sense of loss
- numb, robot-like, unusually calm
- alone, alienated from others who "haven't been there" and "can't understand"
- confused, overwhelmed by the event and the aftermath

Cognitive

- dazed, disoriented
- difficulty concentrating
- memory impairment

It usually takes three or four days for your body to return to normal after a major adrenaline dump. During that time you are likely to be preoccupied with the event and experience some of the reactions listed above. This is why more and more agencies recommend a minimum of three days off after a major incident. Even if you are not traumatized, you may experience a sensation similar to a hangover as your body returns to normal.

During the first 24 hours after a shooting, it's common for you to feel hyper, more emotional than usual, and have disrupted sleep. This isn't just from the excitement of the shooting or the physical changes in your body caused by the adrenaline rush, but from all the hoopla that comes after the smoke clears. Within minutes the scene will be crowded with agency brass, investigators, the media, district attorneys, and a host of other officers all swirling around you. As adrenaline and other chemicals clear out of your system, you may feel tired and depressed and want to sleep. After three or four days of controlling your own schedule and taking care of yourself, you might be back to normal and ready for action. That is assuming that everything goes well, the hoopla dies down, and you are left alone to return to your normal routine.

Unfortunately, the event is rarely over after the last shot has been fired. You have to give statements, suffer through the media's slant, the public's outrage, the concerns and anxieties of your family and friends, your agency's response, the reactions of your peers, the fear of being judged by others, and any formal hearings, such as grand juries and shooting review boards. No matter how justified your actions, you are likely to be worried about being disciplined, criminally indicted, having to face a federal charge of civil rights violation, and being sued in civil court by anyone who hopes to make a buck off of you and the shooting.

Unfortunately, these things can drag on for weeks, months, even years, all the while interfering with your ability to bounce back from the event and return to your normal routine. Many officers have said that what happened after the shooting was more stressful than the shooting itself. Because of this, we strongly recommend that officers not return to the street until the investigation, the in-house review board, and the grand jury are completely over. Until this process is completed, you are likely to be preoccupied with it, which may keep your anxiety level from diminishing.

Post Traumatic Stress Disorder

The *Diagnostic and Statistical Manual - IV* (DSM-IV), published by the American Psychiatric Association, is the official manual used all over the country to define psychological injuries and mental disorders. In it, a traumatic event is described as "the person experienced, witnessed, or was confronted with an event or events that involved actual or threatened death or serious injury, or a threat to the physical integrity of self or others. The person's response involved intense fear, helplessness, or horror." Clearly we can see that officer involved shootings fit into this description.

Post traumatic stress disorder can be defined as a normal reaction to an abnormal event. While we don't consider broken bones normal, no one would be surprised if you got a couple after getting struck by a car. Similarly, PTSD is a bruised psyche that has experienced the psychological equivalent of being hit by a car.

Exposure to a traumatic event will not always result in PTSD, just as some people can get hit by that car and not receive a major injury. However, for those who do experience PTSD, it's defined by *DSM-IV* as having the following four components.

1. Exposure to a traumatic event.
2. Intrusive, persistent reliving of the trauma as character ized by at least one of the following symptoms.

- upsetting recollections
- nightmares
- feeling or acting as if the event were recurring
- psychological distress when reminded of the event
- physiological reactivity when reminded of the event

3. Avoidance of reminders of the event and numbing of general responsiveness as characterized by at least three of the following:
   - avoiding thoughts, feelings, and conversations that are reminders
   - avoiding activities, places, and people that are reminders
   - inability to recall important aspects of the event
   - reduced interest in or reduced participation in significant activities
   - feeling detached or estranged from others
   - restricted and reduced emotions
   - sense of foreshortened future

4. Persistent symptoms of increased arousal as characterized by at least two of the following symptoms:
   - difficulty falling or staying asleep
   - irritability and/or outbursts of anger
   - difficulty concentrating
   - hypervigilance (inability to relax, always feeling on guard)
   - exaggerated startle response

You don't have PTSD unless you are still experiencing the above symptoms more than a month after the event. If you experience anything the first month, it will be "acute stress disorder," meaning you are having a temporary reaction to a highly stressful and traumatic event. There is a reasonable chance that you will return to normal within a month. According to police psychologist Dr. Roger Solomon, about one-third of the officers involved in fatal shootings will have a mild reaction and will quickly return to normal. He estimates that another third will go on to have a moderate reaction and another third is likely to develop a severe reaction.

Even if you don't develop the exact symptoms of PTSD, a traumatic event can put you at risk for developing a whole host of other problems. A partial list of these potential problems would include alcohol abuse, social isolation, poor job performance, excessive absenteeism, disciplinary problems, depression, excessive anxiety, sexual problems, appetite disturbance, chronic physical illnesses, difficulty getting along with others, and what is generally described as a "bad attitude." We would encourage you to be alert to any negative change in yourself and your family members after a traumatic event and to seek treatment with a mental health professional if these changes persist for longer than a few weeks.

Some officers may develop what might be called "survivor mode functioning." This is often characterized by a strong need for control and denial of emotions. They might become too controlling and protective of themselves and others, much to the annoyance of family members and friends. They might become rigid, distrusting, and lose the ability to be "off-duty." Family members might feel as if they are being "interrogated" rather than having a normal conversation. The officers might become overly identified with the role of police officer and consistently work large amounts of overtime, while losing interest in activities outside police work. Since these problems can develop even without being involved in a deadly force encounter, it's imperative that officers seek more balance in their lives.

Problems With Your Relationships

Officers often report disturbances in their relationships after a shooting. These relationships are important to you, and if they remain unresolved they can cause long-term problems.

• Your relationship with yourself might suffer if you haven't been able to work your way through the almost inevitable second-guessing of your actions. This could lead to feelings of guilt and lowered self-esteem.

- Your relationship with your family members might suffer if they are unable or unwilling to understand what you have been through and don't provide the support and concern you need. They may become confused and upset over the event and/or changes in your behavior.
- Your relationship with other officers who were at the scene will suffer if you don't debrief the event between yourselves and work your way through any typical second-guessing of each other.
- Your relationship with your peers who were not present might suffer if you receive insensitive comments and second-guessing by them. You may feel alienated from those who haven't gone through what you are now experiencing.
- Your relationship with your agency might suffer if you are ignored by supervisors and command staff or left with the feeling that they will "hang you out to dry" if they decide it is politically expedient.
- Your relationship with the community might suffer if you find yourself savaged and second-guessed by the fact-distorting media, or if you are criticized and condemned by citizens who have no idea what you are up against.
- Your relationship with the justice system might suffer if you find yourself nit-picked and punished for the tiniest mistake.
- Your relationship with your entire career might suffer, possibly transforming you from a cop who loves his job to a disillusioned one who counts the days until retirement.

If you find that any of these relationships are disrupted, do what you can to repair them or find a way to live with them with some semblance of peace and acceptance. This may not be an easy task, but it will be a vital one to avoid becoming a bitter and unhappy person. Ask for help if you need it.

Why Do Some Officers Develop PTSD While Others Do Not?

According to noted psychologist Dr. Donald Meichenbaum, there are three factors that play a part in whether people develop serious psychological problems from a traumatic event.

1. Prior history of the individual. Individuals with prior unresolved traumas and problems may be more susceptible to psychological injury. Trauma can have a cumulative effect. More than one officer has sought treatment because he was convinced that if he saw another dead baby it would be the end of his career and maybe his sanity. Since dead babies are an occupational hazard, the only hope for these officers is to deal with all the past dead babies haunting them so they can face the next one unencumbered by unresolved grief and horror.

    One officer told us about getting into recovery from alcoholism before his shooting. He is convinced he could not have dealt with the event if he had still been drinking.

2. The severity of the trauma. Not all shootings are the same. An event is likely to be experienced as severely traumatizing when:

    *   it is sudden and unexpected
    *   the individual experiences vulnerability and loss of control
    *   the outcome of the event is bad
    *   the degree of injury, threat, and death to self and others is severe
    *   closely held beliefs are shattered (such as losing your sense of invincibility or witnessing the suffering of innocent people)

3. What happens to the individual afterward (the nature of the recovery environment). Of the three factors, this one is the most important for predicting whether you or your family will be traumatized by an event. For instance, if you were to suffer a serious heart attack, the speed in which you are transported to a hospital is

important to whether you live or die. If you were shot with a near-fatal round, again the speed of your treatment is critical. The same principle applies to psychological injury. No matter how horrible the event, you are more likely to bounce back if you get help as quickly as possible, such as in the following areas.

Peer-Support

After a shooting, you are likely to be worried what your fellow officers think and how they are going to act toward you. If they are supportive, it will be easier for you to get through the event and be reintegrated back into the "police family" when you return to duty.

Treatment by your Agency

You may think just seconds after your deadly force encounter: "Will I get into trouble for this?" It doesn't matter how clean and justified the event; you are likely to worry that your agency will hang you out to dry.

There are many agencies with command staff who are honest and care about their troops and who will treat them fairly even when there is pressure to make them a political sacrifice. Command staff who are fair and supportive, and who have educated themselves on how they and their agency should treat an officer after a shooting, will make a big difference in allowing the officer to calm down and get on with a quick recovery. Good leaders are worth their weight in gold.

Unfortunately, there are other agencies that are not so caring, and these are the ones with worried officers. Agencies that mistreat their officers through ignorance and a lack of caring, and that see them as being politically disposable, do much to traumatize them and their family members.

Support from Friends and Family

The ability of friends and family to support you through the aftermath of a shooting varies and it can be complicated by caring people who are also disturbed by your brush with death, and the whirlwind of events afterward. Traumatic events can bring families together or it can tear them apart.

Part Three

When the Shooting is Over

9

As was pointed out earlier, the single most important factor in recovery from traumatic events is the way in which the person is treated after the incident.

Once the gun smoke has cleared, you will be bombarded with consequences from an array of sources:peers who were at the scene and those who were not, the entire chain of command, detectives and other investigators, family members, friends, the public, the media, attorneys in various roles, and so on. All too often these consequences can be negative to the extent that you may feel like you are being treated like a criminal.

Deadly force encounters are dramatic, high-profile events and as such require special consideration by officers and agencies about how to deal with them. Police psychologists have seen the devastating consequences on officers when they have been subjected to inappropriate reactions and treatment after a deadly force encounter. The Psychological Services Section of the International Association of Chiefs of Police is a group of police psychologists from across the country. They have drawn upon their collective experience to formulate the following guidelines to help agencies and officers develop a response plan to deadly force encounters.

POLICE PSYCHOLOGICAL SERVICES SECTION
International Association of Chiefs of Police

**Administrative Guidelines for Dealing with
Officers Involved in On-Duty Shooting Situations**

*Adopted by the IACP Psychological Services Section at the
1988 Annual Section Meeting.*

In the past, officers involved in on-duty shootings were often subjected to a harsh administrative/ investigative/legal aftermath that compounded the stress of using deadly force. A "second injury" can be created by insensitively and impersonally dealing with an officer who has been involved in a critical incident.* Due partly to such treatment, many officers have left law enforcement prematurely, as victims.

To minimize emotional problems, the Police Psychological Services Section of IACP has adopted guidelines for dealing with officers involved in a shooting. The guidelines were first submitted to the section by the author in 1987 at the section meeting at the IACP conference in Toronto. After discussion and the making of some changes, the guidelines were preliminarily adopted. At the 1988 section meeting, they were approved as presented below.

The goals of these guidelines is to provide information on how to constructively support the officer(s) involved in a shooting in order to diminish emotional trauma. Extensive field experience has shown that following these guidelines reduces the probability of long-lasting emotional problems resulting from a shooting. However, these guidelines are not meant to be a rigid protocol. It is important to apply these guidelines in a flexible manner that is appropriate to the situation.

1.   At the scene, show concern. Give physical *and* mental first aid.

2.   Create a psychological break; get the officer away from the body and some distance from the scene. The officer should remain with a supportive peer or supervisor and return to the scene only if necessary. This break should be of a non-stimulant nature, with discretionary use of drinks with caffeine.

3.   Explain to the officer what will happen administratively during the next few hours and why, so he does not take the investigation as a personal attack.

4.   If the gun is taken as evidence, replace it immediately or when appropriate (with the officer being told it will be replaced). This guideline can be modified depending on how aggravated the circumstances are and how stressed the officer is, e.g., very depressed, agitated, suicidal, etc.

5.   The officer should be advised to consider retaining an attorney to watch out for his personal interests.

6.   The officer should have some recovery time before detailed interviewing begins. The officer should be in a secure setting, insulated from the press and curious officers.

7.   Totally isolating the officer breeds feelings of resentment and alienation. The officer can be with a supportive friend or a peer who has been through a similar experience. (To avoid legal complications, the situation should not be discussed prior to the preliminary investigation.) It is important to show concern and support to the officer during this time.

8.   If the officer is not injured, either he or the department should contact the family with a phone call or personal visit and let them know what happened before rumors from other sources reach them. If the officer is injured, a department member known to the family should pick them up and drive them to the hospital. Call friends, chaplains, etc., to make sure they have support.

9. Personal concern and support for the officer involved in the shooting, communicated face-to-face from a high-ranking administrator, goes a long way toward alleviating future emotional problems. The administrator does not have to comment on the situation or make any premature statements regarding legal or departmental resolution, but can show concern and empathy for the officer during this very stressful experience.

10. The officer should be given some *administrative leave* (not suspended with pay) to deal with the emotional impact. (Three days, more or less as the situation dictates, is usually sufficient.) Some officers, however, prefer light duty to leave. Depending on the situation and the officer's reactions, it may be best to keep him off the street temporarily and avoid the double-bind situation of the officer's going back to work and facing the possibility of another critical incident before the investigation, grand jury hearing, coroner's inquest, and district attorney's statement have been completed.

     All personnel at the scene (including dispatchers) should be screened for their reactions and given leave or the rest of the shift off, as necessary.

11. To defuse the stigma of seeking counseling, there should be a *mandatory* confidential debriefing with a licensed mental health professional, experienced with the law enforcement culture and trauma, prior to returning to duty. This debriefing should be held as soon after the incident as practical. Return to duty and/or follow-up sessions should be determined by the mental health professional.

     Everybody at the scene, including the dispatcher, should have a debriefing with the mental health professional within 72 hours. While this can be a group session, the officer(s) who did the shooting may or may not want to be included in the group debriefing, as actually doing the shooting creates different emotional issues. Follow-up sessions for other personnel involved in the shooting may be appropriate.

12. Opportunities for family counseling (spouse, children, significant others) should be made available.

13. If the officer's phone number is published, it may be advisable to have a friend or telephone answering machine screen phone calls, since there are sometimes threats to the officer and his family.

14. An administrator should tell the rest of the department (or the supervisor, the rest of the team) what happened so the officer does not get bombarded with questions and rumors are held in check. Screen for "vicarious thrill seekers."

15. Expedite the completion of administrative and criminal investigations and advisement of the outcomes to the officer.

16. Consider the officer's interests in preparing the media releases.

17. The option of talking to peers who have had a similar experience can be quite helpful to all personnel at the scene. Peer counselors are an asset in conducting group debriefings in conjunction with a mental health professional, and in providing follow-up support.

18. Allow a paced return to duty; that is, the officer can ride around with a fellow officer or perhaps work a different beat or shift.

To prevent such incidents in the first place, train all officers in critical incident reactions and what to expect personally, departmentally, and legally.

---

*Roger M. Solomon, "Post-Shooting Trauma," *The Police Chief*, October 1988, pp. 40-44.

TAKING TIME OFF AFTER A SHOOTING

A mistake officers often make after a shooting is to not take enough time to recover psychologically before returning to the street. These are some typical reasons they give.

- "I don't want my fellow officers to think I'm a wimp or that I'm just milking this to get some time off."
- "My supervisors and command staff made it clear they expect me back on duty after my mandatory three days off."
- "When you get thrown off the horse, you have to get right back in the saddle again or you might never want to get on again."
- "I really like my sergeant and don't want him to have to worry about staffing or paying other officers overtime to take my place."

SOLDIERS AND POLICE OFFICERS: THE COMBAT CONNECTION

Some people compare the experiences of combat soldiers (and Marines, Navy SEALs, and Air Force personnel like fighter/bomber pilots) to police officers and ask why soldiers don't experience PTSD at the rate police officers do. The truth is, however, that many soldiers do indeed suffer PTSD. In World War II it was called "shell shock," and the phenomena of PTSD was much in the press after the dust of Vietnam finally settled. Indeed, today there are still many Vietnam vets suffering from PTSD.

It is true that most combat soldiers can fight for long periods with little rest and continue to function effectively in a combat role. Many of them experience some level of PTSD and other problems but continue to fight anyway, just as many people have the capacity to continue to function despite suffering from physical and psychological ailments. When you are focused on physical survival and accomplishing the mission while engaged in intense mortal combat, you don't have the luxury of worrying about feeling healthy and happy. And just because soldiers continue to fight day after day and often routinely see their friends killed or wounded doesn't mean they aren't suffering. They may even numb their feelings (block them out) so they can stomach the violence (this is one of the symptoms of PTSD). Although this can help them function, it is nonetheless sometimes a serious impediment to their successful readjustment to civilian life. Just ask the families of vets suffering from PTSD.

Given this, one simply can't compare the life of a combat soldier with the life of a police officer. In a combat zone, the soldier has only one role to fill: that of a soldier. Police officers, on the other hand, are *not* in a combat zone all the time, and they are expected to move fluidly from one role to another, oftentimes on a daily basis. In a single day, the police officer may have to wrestle a mentally ill individual, help a homeless person find shelter for the night, act as a referee in a domestic squabble, issue a traffic ticket to an elderly woman, and survive a gun battle in a supermarket. Then he has to go home and live normally with his family. The combat soldier doesn't have to go home after a firefight and become a loving and patient parent to his children and be open to intimacy and communication with his spouse. He doesn't have to try to maintain friendships with civilians who have little understanding of what they are asking him to do for them. He is not expected to be unfailingly polite, effectively helpful, and compassionate to a wide variety of people and their complex social problems during his combat patrols.

The police officer has to maintain effective social and emotional connections with himself and an array of people and situations to function well. But the symptoms of PTSD will prevent him from doing that. The inability to establish and maintain these emotional connections is less of an immediate issue to the combat soldier, who is primarily focused on staying alive and killing the enemy. It will, however, become an issue for the soldier when he leaves the combat zone and tries to have a happy and fulfilling life back in "the world."

All this relates back to the different environments police officers and combat soldiers live and operate in. The soldier will not have to worry about facing an internal affairs investigation because he got cranky with a civilian or discharged his weapon. If he shoots someone in the line of duty, he is unlikely to face a criminal investigation, an inquest, or a grand jury, where people who weren't there will make judgments about whether or not he was justified in using deadly force. The soldier will not be subjected to intense and negative media scrutiny (although some Vietnam vets did have to face this to some extent). Nor will the soldier have to face the specter of a civil suit for just doing his job. Indeed, when the soldier does his job well—kills the enemy quickly and efficiently—he will likely be praised and might even receive a medal or a promotion, sometimes both. Conversely, the police officer will face intense scrutiny and possible discipline for even the slightest error in judgment, which in the case of the soldier is often overlooked or viewed as a learning point.

In summary, the soldier operates in an environment that totally supports and even praises his combat role, whereas the police officer operates in an environment that looks at any deviation from his role as "Officer Friendly" with suspicion and discomfort.

Actually, it's essential that soldiers returning from combat zones who are experiencing PTSD or other problems *also* be given time off, debriefings, and psychotherapy so they can recover from the trauma they carry with them out of the combat zone. Our failure to provide this is one reason why so many veterans have failed to successfully adjust to civilian life after the fighting ended.

Going back to full duty right after a shooting might show lots of grit and determination, but it's short on wisdom. All that will happen is that the healing will be delayed and the injury aggravated. No matter how well you take care of yourself, healing requires a certain amount of time, and you can't hurry it beyond a certain point.

Many agencies give officers at least three days paid

administrative leave after a shooting. This is a start, but it will not always be enough.

Stay Off the Street

Let's start with legal survival. In many jurisdictions you must undergo a review of your use of deadly force, such as a grand jury, an administrative shooting board, or an inquest. No matter who is doing the review(s), you must explain in a professional and compelling manner why you were justified in using deadly force. You need to be clear-headed and your memory must be at its best, though it's common for these interviews not to occur for days, weeks, or even longer after the shooting.

What might happen if you go back out on the street before your performance is reviewed? Anything, given the nature of police work. You could get into another shooting before the first one has been reviewed, or you could find yourself facing some other traumatic event that might leave you shaken and distracted. This would definitely not be in your best interest.

At the very least, you should stay off the street until your shooting has been fully reviewed and you have been cleared of wrongdoing. This may include being completely off work or on limited duty status off the street. *Remember, even if your shooting was legally justified, you can still be sued in civil court or be made to face federal charges.*

How Can You Tell When You Are Psychologically Ready To Go Back On The Street?

Once your shooting review is over, make sure you have been thoroughly debriefed and satisfied that you are not suffering from the symptoms of post-traumatic stress disorder, depression, or whatever. If you have doubts, your mental health professional can help you with this decision.

Officer Bill Nordin, who we saw in "Three Shootings," probably summed it up best when he said that you know you are ready to return to the street when you are prepared for the same thing or worse to happen five minutes into your first shift. He elaborated with, "I've been involved in three shootings over my 14-year career. After the first one, I went right back to work because that's what everyone did. No debriefings, no talking, just get back out there and prove to yourself and others that it didn't bother you. After my second shooting, I had come to realize that approach was a mistake. I decided to take care of myself regardless of what my agency or any of my fellow officers had to say.

"I didn't go right back out but instead took two weeks off. Afterwards, I was getting restless and eager to return to the work I love so much. So I went back. I walked into the locker room and I put on my uniform and my gun belt. But it felt wrong. I knew I wasn't ready to be on the street and I definitely wasn't ready to go out there and make life or death decisions. So I took off my uniform and told—not asked—my sergeant that I was going home. I didn't care what he thought. It was my life and I knew that I cared about it more than anyone else. I was going to protect it.

"So I took another week off and this time when I went back it felt right. I walked out of the locker room with my uniform and gun belt on and I knew I was ready. Then on my second shift back I got into my third shooting. Since I had allowed time to recover from the second shooting, I was ready to survive physically and psychologically. And I did. Today I'm doing fine with all three shootings and I'm still on full, active duty."

How Much Time Is Enough?

This will vary depending on you, the situation, and what happens to you after the shooting. It may take days, months, or even years before you are ready to go back. What is important is that you take care of yourself like Officer Nordin and not go back until you feel sharp, rested, recovered, and physically, emotionally, mentally, and spiritually prepared to confront a deadly threat. This decision is up to you, with assistance from the mental health professional you have hopefully seen for your debriefing.

If supervisors, command staff, peers, friends, and family members pressure you to "stop goofing off and get back on that horse," tell them to stop practicing psychology without a license.

Get a Debriefing

If your agency doesn't provide you with a debriefing with a mental health professional, we strongly encourage you to seek one out on your own. Even if you think you are doing fine, you or a family member could have some problems down the road. When you and your family are educated about possible trauma reactions by a mental health professional, you will be able to recognize them should they occur in the future. Additionally, by having had a debriefing, you will have someone you already know on standby should you need them.

10

Traumatic Incident Debriefings

I was involved in a complex, deadly force situation involving many officers. Several times I thought me or one of my fellow officers would be killed. We all performed well, and none of us got hurt. In spite of the positive outcome, I was really shook up afterward. No matter how hard I tried, I couldn't stop having vivid images about it over and over when I was awake and when I was asleep. I was hardly sleeping and I felt anxious, irritable, and angry all the time. My relationship with my wife was quickly going from fine to awful and there was no way I was in shape to go back to work.

The things that saved me were peer support, the command staff's encouragement to take off as much time as I needed, and the group and individual debriefings.

Shortly after the shooting, I wanted to go back out on the street although I knew I wasn't ready. I felt guilty taking time off and didn't want my fellow officers and the command staff to think I was goofing off. My precinct commander called and asked how I was doing. When I told him how I was struggling, he encouraged me to take as much time as I needed and said he would trust me and my psychologist to know when I should come back. His call and support lifted my guilt and allowed me to focus on getting better.

After the grand jury was over, everyone involved in the shooting assembled for a tactical debriefing. It was the first time I found out what had really happened apart from my own little piece of it.

Because of tunnel vision, loss of hearing, and other weird things I experienced, there was much I forgot or never knew until the debriefing. Hearing the full story helped me put closure on it and made me feel like I had learned important lessons that would help me for the next situation. It also made a big difference to all of us that there was a place to vent our emotions and to support each other without fear of being judged.

I was also given as many individual counseling sessions as I needed, about six in all. I saw a police psychologist who had specialized training in trauma debriefing and I was amazed how quickly it helped me regain my sanity and sense of control over the shooting and my emotions. My wife and I got marriage counseling that helped us recover as a family and deal with our new reality of the risks of my job. That was two years ago and I'm still doing fine. Without the support, the debriefings, and the time off, I think there's a good chance my career might have been over.

This officer was lucky enough to work for an agency that knew it was cheaper to give him adequate time off and skilled treatment than to lose a trained officer and have to hire and train a replacement. While some agencies have figured this out, others have not.

Much has been learned over the past 10 years about the effects of trauma and how to treat psychological injuries. Ignorance should no longer be an excuse to ignore psychological injuries and fail to provide care for their officers. Even if some agencies lack compassion, financial and liability considerations alone should dictate a wise investment in the kind of care the officer above was lucky enough to receive. As agencies become more aware of the potential for long-term psychological injury, they are increasingly using formal debriefings to treat officers before their problems become chronic ones.

WHAT IS A DEBRIEFING?

A debriefing is any discussion after an event that helps the participants come to terms with it and learn from it. Hopefully, it will help them gain closure so that the event will not continue to cause emotional distress. An informal debriefing can simply be a discussion that arises spontaneously after an event, while a formal debriefing takes the discussion one step further because it's organized and facilitated to ensure it helps everyone.

There are four types of formal debriefings that can be done after a traumatic incident.

- Individual Psychological Debriefing
- Group Psychological Debriefing
- Group Tactical Debriefing
- Incident Clarification

These types of debriefings are different from each other and all are valuable. Sometimes, when circumstances are appropriate, a debriefing may include all four. The following is a brief discussion of the logistics and purposes of each. These are suggestions only; the exact type used will depend on the circumstances and available resources.

The first three types are done with individuals involved in the incident.

Note: *It's important to remember that officers have significant others who may be affected by an event. It's strongly recommended that they also be offered the opportunity to receive individual and group psychological debriefings.*

Individual Debriefing

The involved officers (and family members, seperately or together as needed and desired) receive individual debriefings by a mental health professional (MHP) trained to do trauma debriefings with law enforcement personnel. They should be *mandatory* to remove the stigma of seeing a psychologist and because they are a vital part of the recovery process. They should be done within 72 hours.

The purpose of the debriefing is to educate the officers

and family members about trauma reactions, assess their psychological status, and make recommendations to the officer about recovery procedures, such as further counseling and time off. It also gives the officers and family members a familiar face to return to for further treatment if they should develop post-traumatic stress disorder. Although one session is mandatory, the officer and family members should be provided with as many additional voluntary sessions as needed to help recovery.

It's essential that debriefings be *confidential* (with the usual exceptions about imminent danger to self or others). They should not be used as a "fitness for duty" evaluation, and information is never given to the officer's agency, other than confirmation that he attended. However, MHPs can, with the officers' written permission, be an advocate for him to get additional time off or limited duty. If the agency is concerned about an officer's fitness for duty, the agency should send him to a different mental health professional for this evaluation.

These individual sessions are important since many officers will have feelings or issues about the event that they simply will not discuss in the presence of another officer, supervisor, or significant other, no matter how skillfully and positively group debriefings are conducted.

For those officers (and family members) who are suffering from post-traumatic stress reactions, individual psychological debriefings, with further treatment as needed, are usually effective in bringing significant relief. Additionally, debriefings can even protect an officer's career and benefit the agency by greatly reducing supervision problems that may occur when an officer has returned to duty not healed from a psychological injury.

If your agency does not provide an individual debriefing, seek one on your own. Many officers have health insurance that will pay for it. Find out what your insurance covers for "outpatient psychotherapy" and what type of mental health provider you must see for your insurance to pay.

It's usually inadvisable to try to go through the workers

compensation system to get them to pay for the debriefings. Often the compensation carrier will demand chart notes and reports and may even do their own investigation of the claim and the claimant. This obviously destroys the confidentiality, and officers often find the compensation system to be intrusive and upsetting.

If you are provided with a mandatory individual debriefing or want to get it on your own, research the following to be sure a debriefing is a situation you will be comfortable with:

- How confidential will the session be?
- What is the licensure of the MHP you are seeing?
- What are the laws in your state regarding legally privileged confidentiality of the sessions with the type of licensure the MHP has?
- What, if any, information will be provided to your agency?
- If you are using your health insurance, what information will be provided to the insurance agency?
- Request that the MHP not write down any of the details of the event in his notes.
- What would the MHP do if he received a subpoena for his notes or testimony?
- If the MHP works in a counseling center, find out who owns the notes. Is it the MHP or the center? If it's the center, who has access to them?
- If the MHP works for your agency, is it entitled to know what you have discussed?

There are some exceptions that usually apply to legally privileged confidentiality. The laws vary from state to state so you need to check locally. A typical exception would be if the MHP believes you are an imminent danger to yourself or others. If you file a worker's compensation or disability claim for stress or any emotional problem, it's possible all your medical records, including your visits to an MHP, could be open to the discovery process.

Remember, if you receive a mandatory individual debriefing, you are under no obligation to discuss the details of the event with an MHP. Make your own decision based on how comfortable and confident you feel as to how the MHP is prepared to deal with the sensitive legal issues involved.

Know What Training and Experience in Traumatic Debriefings the MHP Has

There have been major advances in the understanding and treatment of traumatic incidents. MHPs who have received specialized training are better equipped to give you the type of information and treatment that will help you make sense out of what you have experienced.

Know What Training and Experience the MHP Has Had with Police Officers

Police officers are most comfortable with MHPs who have learned about the unique problems and pressures they face daily.

Finding a MHP

Word of mouth is one way to find a MHP. Ask other officers and see if any names are mentioned regularly. Your agency or a neighboring agency may have resources, such as a chaplain's program or an Employee's Assistance Program, that may have a referral list of therapists trained to work with police officers.

Group Psychological Debriefing

The group psychological debriefing is a group discussion about the emotional impact of the incident on the officers and their family members. The goal is education and the mobilization of peer support. The purpose is prevention of psychological injury by helping to defuse the immediate reactions of officers and family members and give them basic support and education needed to start the recovery process.

Group debriefings are not treatment. Individuals experiencing psychological problems because of the shooting or any other reason should be treated by a qualified MHP, preferably a trauma expert with training and experience in working with law enforcement personnel.

The debriefing team is usually composed of a MHP and members of peer-support teams who have training in this area. No written notes or records are kept. All officers involved in the event are invited to attend and they can invite their family members (who may also benefit from a separate group debriefing of their own) and other involved individuals, such as dispatchers.

The participants are gently encouraged, but not required, to share their feelings to get support from each other and the peer-support teams. It's also a time to be educated about potential trauma reactions. Though the debriefing should be held within 72 hours, it can still be effective later.

The emphasis is on feelings, not tactics. A detailed examination of an event that is being investigated, such as a shooting, is usually not appropriate in this setting for several reasons:

- Peer discussions usually have no legally privileged confidentiality (see "Precautionary Note" below).
- In shootings and other legally sensitive events, investigators prefer that participants and witnesses not discuss the event among themselves until all interviews have been completed.
- Focusing on tactics detracts from the main purpose, which is emotional support and education.
- Officers may not be comfortable discussing the gory details in front of their family members or other officer's family members.
- An improper discussion of tactics without appropriate leadership can lead to failure to learn important tactical and legal lessons. MHPs usually don't have the technical expertise to facilitate tactical critiques and should not attempt to do so.

PRECAUTIONARY NOTE: There is usually no legally protected confidentiality in peer-support discussions. It's risky for participants in a legally sensitive event to discuss the details with anyone except those who have legally privileged confidentiality, such as attorneys and MHPs. Check the laws in your local area to find out which professions have it. Spouses are usually also afforded legally privileged confidentiality. Although the participants may agree to not reveal information discussed during the debriefing, they can be ordered by their department or subpoenaed by the courts to testify about what was said during the discussion.

When you are involved in a shooting, you are likely to have a powerful urge to discuss the details with others. The psychological benefit of this needs to be weighed against the legal risks.

If you are a peer-support person, you should consider the legal consequences of allowing a participant in a shooting to tell you details about the event.

So what can be discussed in a group psychological debriefing? Officers and family members can talk about the physical and emotional reactions they have experienced and how the shooting and its aftermath have affected them and their daily lives. It's important to find out that their reactions are normal and that they have acceptance and understanding from their peers about what they are going through. It's also an opportunity for peer-support to be mobilized and offered in whatever manner will be helpful. For example, if shooting participants need to testify before a grand jury, they will often find it comforting to be accompanied by peer-supporters to the court house. They can also be helpful in encouraging shooting participants to take time off or get professional counseling.

Group Tactical Debriefing
A group tactical debriefing is a tactical critique of the incident. Attendance is voluntary for anyone interested and should be conducted by involved officers and led by tactical

experts, such as supervisors, command staff, and training staff who have been trained to conduct a tactical debriefing in a positive and constructive manner. It may also be helpful to invite the radio dispatcher and the detectives who investigated the incident to provide additional information. This debriefing should have no written records. There is also value in having a MHP sit in on debriefings of particularly traumatic incidents to provide emotional support as needed.

Many agencies don't conduct tactical debriefings on shootings and other sensitive events because they are justifiably concerned that a plaintiff's attorney will try to use any information he can glean from them to hammer the agency and the officers in a civil suit. If an officer has concerns that his agency may hang him out to dry after a justified but politically controversial shooting, he should be understandably reluctant to participate in an honest tactical critique. Given these legal risks, it is inappropriate to make *any* type of debriefing mandatory that does not have legally privileged confidentiality. Officers and agencies have to weigh the training advantages afforded by a tactical debriefing against the legal risks and make their own decisions on how to best handle it.

Group tactical debriefings are valuable for several reasons:

- They are an invaluable learning and training tool for the entire agency. Lessons learned from one event can be used to help officers and agencies perform better during the next one.
- They will often be the only opportunity that involved officers, supervisors, and command staff have to find out what really happened. Each officer will have his or her own tunnel vision of the incident and will usually not be able see the whole picture without the group tactical debriefing. Survivors of all traumas usually have a strong need to find out exactly what happened because it's important to the psychological healing process.
- As the participants learn what happened and what other officers saw, heard, and thought, all second-guessing will

end or at least be minimized. When involved officers stop second-guessing each other, then second-guessing by officers who were not there will diminish.

Suggestions for Conducting Group Tactical Debriefings

The following suggestions can be helpful to make tactical debriefings positive, constructive learning experiences for all. Exact procedures will vary depending on the circumstances.

• Participation is voluntary. Most officers will want to participate if they believe it will be conducted in a positive and constructive manner.
• All the participants must agree about the confidentiality of the debriefing. This should be clarified before the debriefing begins.
• There are no written records. The participants should agree about how any tactical commendations will be passed on to other officers or agencies.
• The debriefing will focus on the present incident. Don't bring up prior incidents unless they are tactically relevant to the current discussion.
• The debriefing focuses on what can be learned by officers, supervisors, and command staff.
• Self-critiques are best. Most officers are willing to voluntarily examine their own tactics if they are heard in a positive and constructive environment.
• All supervisors and command staff at the scene who are participating in the debriefing are also critiqued. This could include their performance as supervisors and on-scene responders.
• Supervisors and command staff critique themselves first.
• Acknowledge and praise effective behavior at the scene.
• All suggestions for improvement are nonjudgmental; emphasize behavior, not individuals.
• The debriefing recognizes that there is often more than one way to effectively handle a situation.

- Group tactical debriefings are never used as part of any disciplinary procedure.

WARNING: There are many legal and political considerations that will affect the timing of a tactical critique or whether it's done at all. The same concerns mentioned earlier about the lack of legally privileged confidentiality in peer discussions should be considered. The benefits of a tactical critique need to be weighed against possible legal risks. At the very least, tactical critiques should not be done until all grand juries, shooting review boards, and other legal investigations are over and all officers have been cleared of any wrongdoing.

Incident Clarification

Incident clarification is a group discussion of the event to educate uninvolved officers the incident. While this type of debriefing may or may not require the participation of the involved officers, they can participate. This is typically conducted at the roll call following the event.

Invariably, there is curiosity, speculation, and second-guessing by personnel not involved. The more dramatic the incident, the more likely this is to happen. Since this is natural, the most constructive way to deal with it is to have a member of the command staff make presentations as to the facts to the rest of the agency. Preferably, this person was involved in the incident and present at the group tactical debriefing. If there was not a group tactical debriefing, the person doing the incident clarification needs to do his homework to ensure accurate reporting.

Incident clarification can be an effective way to reduce or end inaccurate rumors and destructive second-guessing that usually follows in the wake of an incident. It allows uninvolved personnel an opportunity to ask questions and air their concerns or feelings. This is helpful after a particularly traumatic incident that may emotionally affect personnel who were not at the scene. It also gives the command staff an opportunity to gage the reactions of their personnel and address their concerns.

* * * * *

All four debriefing types are not necessarily one-time events. Depending on the circumstances, there may be a need for more than one if the participants are still struggling to gain closure. Know that debriefings can be helpful any time, even months or years after an event.

All personnel who might be affected by the event should attend. For instance, officers who saw an officer-involved shooting but didn't shoot should be debriefed as fully as the shooters. Nonshooters should also be considered "involved officers" since they can be just as traumatized as the shooters.

NOTE: Remember that there are many events besides shootings that traumatize officers, such as fatal traffic accidents, incidents involving dead or injured children, suicides, death of a partner or close friend, fights, near shootings, and stabbings. Officers should be encouraged to seek a debriefing following any event that has emotionally affected them, no matter how trivial it may seem to others.

Psychologically Surviving the Aftermath of a Traumatic Event

11

There are four main areas of influence that can have an impact on how well and how quickly you recover from a traumatic event:

- making yourself stress resistant
- peer support
- good supervision and leadership
- mental health professionals

Each of these areas is important in different ways. Some of them, like making yourself stress resistant, are under your control, whereas others, like supervisors showing good leadership and supervision, are less under your control. To the extent that any one of them is lacking, the others become that much more important.

We encourage you to look at all of these areas and start thinking about them now. How can you take better care of yourself? What are you doing to encourage and participate in positive peer support in your organization? How well do you cope with bad supervision and what can you do about it? Who are the MHPs in your area you can trust and who can work well with you and your family?

When things are going smoothly, these questions may not

seem too urgent. But when a shooting suddenly turns your world upside down, they become most important. The following will give you something to think about in each of these areas.

MAKING YOURSELF STRESS RESISTANT

Making yourself stress resistant is under your control, and you should make it a priority. Besides preparing for a specific stressor, there are five areas you can consider that may help make you more stress resistant in general.

Healthy Lifestyle Choices

These are obvious things that you probably already know are good for you, such as regular exercise, eating healthily, getting sufficient sleep, going to the doctor, and drinking alcohol in moderation. The fact is this: a healthy body will bounce back faster from physical injury and it will give you an extra edge to cope with stress.

Social/Emotional Support Network of Friends, Peers, and Family

Humans are social creatures. Social isolation is unnatural and usually unhealthy. People who have social and emotional connections they can turn to in times of stress for support, comfort, feedback, and help will fare better than people who are alone or living inside a shell. Do you have people in your life with whom you have mutual trust, mutual concern for, and mutual willingness and ability to lend a helping hand and a caring heart? While some people need more social contact than others, the exact amount is less important than the quality of the relationships and the fact that you are getting your personal needs fulfilled.

An important part of recovery from a traumatic event is the reaching out to this social support network during the minutes, hours, days, weeks, and even months or years afterward as you struggle to make sense of what has happened and come to terms with how it has changed you and your life.

If you feel lonely and isolated, then do something about it. Sitting at home watching TV and feeling sorry for yourself won't cut it. Nor should you hang out in bars. Instead, consider some positive alternatives, such as joining an organization of people who have similar interests, hobbies, or religious beliefs, or do volunteer work centered around service to others. These activities get you out in the world and around positive people doing positive things. This also allows you to make a deposit in your "good karma account," something all of us can always use!

We would also encourage you to not limit your social contacts to police officers. This is a natural tendency, but one that will develop an unhealthy "us vs. them" mentality regarding anyone outside law enforcement. Officers work in such a different world than most other people that there is a tendency for them to associate only with those who understand them. It's up to you to learn how to get along with people from all walks of life and allow yourself to become friends with some of them. Doing so will make you more balanced and a better person.

Solving Your Own Problems

Life is often not fair, and all of us get shafted eventually. Those who bounce back the quickest are those who learn to take this reality in stride and who don't think of themselves as perpetual victims. When presented with an unpleasant or traumatic event, they are quick to ask, "What do I need to do to take care of myself?" They seek information, assistance, new coping strategies, whatever is necessary to turn a negative into a positive or, at the very least, a learning experience that will make them better, stronger, and wiser for the future.

This doesn't mean they don't get mad, sad, disgusted, and fed up, nor does it mean they will not develop psychological problems after being exposed to a horrible event. What it does mean is that they refuse to let adverse events or people destroy them, and they accept that it's their responsibility that this doesn't happen. They will take responsibility to educate themselves about the problem and see that it gets it taken care of. Psychologist Al Siebert wrote a book on this topic called *The Survivor Personality* (see References and Suggested Reading in the back of this book). It contains many good suggestions on how to avoid becoming a perpetual victim/whiner, how to be proactive, and how to thrive under pressure and stress.

A Spiritual Foundation That Provides Value, Meaning, and Purpose to Life

How do you find happiness, peace, fulfillment in a world so full of evil and craziness? This is a particularly important question for police officers and other emergency services workers who see so much of the ugly and traumatic side of life.

Let's define spirituality as some type of belief or feeling that allows you to feel meaningfully plugged into the web of life around you. It's something that is bigger than you, a core that you carry everywhere. Spirituality transcends any one situation and gives continuity to your existence and your values through time and across events. It's life enhancing, it encourages compassion and respect for others, and it allows you to feel grounded and positive in the face of adversity.

For many people, formal religion fills this need. For those who don't subscribe to a formal religious doctrine, spirituality can be a commitment to a deeply held value or set of values, such as "my purpose in life is to make sure the world is a better place for me having been here." However you achieve it, this sense of meaning and purpose will serve you well when faced with pain and trauma.

PEER SUPPORT

A common theme in the officers' stories throughout this book is the importance they place on the respect and support they get from fellow officers. You may have limited power over how your command staff treats you, how the public reacts, and even how your friends and family members cope with the ugly events you experience in your duties, but you do have power over how you treat each other. Only you can make the commitment to be there for other officers when the chips are down.

Many police officers involved in deadly force encounters have suffered from insensitive comments made by their peers. The police subculture is rarely a genteel society. It tends to be a bit rough around the edges and it pays to have thick skin and a sense of humor broad enough to not be offended by all the joshing and teasing that will come from other officers. This will never change, nor should it. But when officers are feeling unusually stressed or vulnerable over a professional or personal event causing them pain, this is a time to be more careful about what is said and a time to think about offering support. This can make all the difference in the world.

So why do some officers make insensitive comments during these sensitive times? Well, some are just jerks and that will never change, but happily they are few in number. The majority of hurtful comments are made out of ignorance, mostly because the speaker doesn't know what to say. This is the same reason some officers ignore or avoid their peers who are going through a bad time. Fortunately, a little education can go a long way toward helping officers know how to be there for each other.

If you are involved in a shooting or other traumatic event, seek out peer support from officers you trust. Call upon your agency's peer support teams or your friends and peers who have experienced a traumatic event.

Suggestions for Supporting Fellow Officers Who Have Been Traumatized

- Initiate contact in the form of a phone call or a note to let the officer know you are concerned and available for support or help. In the case of a shooting, remember that those officers at the scene who didn't shoot are often just as likely to be affected as those who did. And always remember that there are many other events besides shootings that can traumatize an officer.

- If an officer lives by himself, offer to stay with him the first few days after his traumatic event. If you can't, help him find another friend who can.
- Let the officer decide how much contact he wants to have with you. He may be overwhelmed with phone calls, and it could take a while for him to return your call. Understand that he may want some "down time" with minimal interruptions.
- Don't ask for an account of the shooting, but let him know you are willing to listen to whatever he wants to talk about. Officers often get tired of repeating the story, and they find curiosity seekers distasteful. There is also the legal problem of lack of privileged confidentiality in peer discussions.
- Ask questions that show support and acceptance, such as "How are you doing?" and "Is there anything I can do help you or your family?"
- Accept the officer's reaction to his event as normal for him, and avoid suggesting how he should be feeling. Remember that officers have a wide range of reactions to different traumatic incidents.
- Remember to apply nonjudgmental listening.
- Do feel free to offer a brief sharing of a similar experience that you might have had to help him feel like he is not alone and to show that you understand what he has been through. This is not the time, however, to work on your own trauma issues. If your friend's event triggers emotions of your own, find someone else to talk to who can offer you support.
- Don't encourage the use of alcohol. Drink coffee when you go out. In the aftermath of trauma, it's best to avoid all use of alcohol for a few weeks so officers can process what has happened with a clear head and with true feelings.
- Don't congratulate the officer on his shooting, call him "killer" or "terminator" (even as a joke), or make light-hearted or judgmental comments about his shooting or lack of shooting. Officers often have mixed feelings about

these traumatic events and may find such comments offensive.

- Offer positive statements about the officer, such as, "I'm glad you're OK."
- Although you are likely to find yourself second-guessing a shooting, keep your comments to yourself. They have a way of getting back to the involved officer and may do additional harm as he struggles to recover. Besides, second-guessing is usually wrong.
- Do encourage the officer to take care of himself. Be supportive of his need to take off as much time as he needs, and encourage him to participate in debriefing procedures and professional counseling.
- Do gently confront the officer with his negative behavioral or emotional changes, especially if they persist longer than one month. Encourage him to seek professional help.
- Don't refer to an officer who is having psychological problems as "mental" or other derogatory terms. Stigmatizing each other encourages officers to deny their psychological injuries and not get the help they need.
- Do educate yourself about trauma reactions by reading written material or consulting with someone who knows the topic.
- The officer wants to return to normality when possible. Don't pretend like the event didn't happen, avoid him, treat him as fragile, or otherwise drastically change your behavior toward him. Simply continue to treat him like you always have.
- Do remember that your mother was right when she said, "If you don't have anything nice to say, don't say anything at all."

Volunteer Support Systems

Another excellent way to encourage peer support in your agency is to form volunteer peer-support teams. These can be trained in a variety of areas and go by such titles as, Traumatic-Incident Support Team, Disabled-Officers Support Team, Peer-

Adviser Support Team, Alcohol-Recovery Support Team, and Family-Trauma Support Team. Family- and officer-trauma support teams can be useful for offering logistical and emotional support (many have members that volunteer to be paged when an incident occurs and throughout the aftermath).

The Psychological Services Section of the International Association of Police has formulated guidelines that can be useful for officers and agencies in the formation and running of peer-support teams.

POLICE PSYCHOLOGICAL SERVICES SECTION
International Association of Chiefs of Police

Peer Support Guidelines

Adopted by the IACP Psychological Services Section at the 1993 Annual Section Meeting.

PHILOSOPHY

1. The goal of peer support is to provide all public safety employees within an agency the opportunity to receive emotional and tangible peer support through times of personal or professional crises and to help anticipate and address potential difficulties. A peer support program must have a procedure for mental health consultation and training. A peer support program is developed and implemented under the organizational structure of the parent agency.

2. To ensure maximum utilization of the program and to support assurances of confidentiality, there should be participation on the Steering Committee of relevant employee organizations, mental health professionals and police administrators, during planning and subsequent stages. Membership on the Steering Committee should have a wide representation of involved sworn and nonsworn parties.

3. Sworn peer support officers are officers first and peer supporters second. Any conflicts of roles should be resolved in that context.

4. A Peer Support Person (PSP), sworn or nonsworn, is a specifically trained colleague, not a counselor or therapist. A peer support program can augment outreach programs, e.g., employee assistance programs and in-house treatment programs, but not replace them. PSPs should refer cases that require professional intervention to a mental health professional. A procedure should be in place for mental health consultations and training.

SELECTION

1. PSPs should be chosen from volunteers who are currently in good standing with their departments and who have received recommendations from their superiors and/or peers.

2. Considerations for selection of PSP candidates include, but are not limited to, previous education and training; resolved traumatic experiences; and desirable interpersonal qualities, such as maturity, judgment, and personal and professional credibility.

TRAINING

1. Relevant introductory and continuing training for a PSP could include the following:

A.	Confidentiality Issues	J.	AIDS Information
B.	Communication Facilitation and Listening Skills	K.	Suicide Assessment
		L.	Depression and Burn-Out
C.	Ethical Issues	M.	Grief Management
D.	Problem Assessment	N.	Domestic Violence
E.	Problem Solving Skills	O.	Crisis Management
F.	Alcohol and Substance Abuse	P.	Nonverbal Communication
G.	Cross-Cultural Issues	Q.	When to Seek Mental Health Consultation and Referral Information
H.	Medical Conditions Often Confused with Psychiatric Disorders	R.	Traumatic Intervention
I	Stress Management	S.	Limits and Liability.

ADMINISTRATION

1. A formal policy statement should be included in the departmental policy manual that gives written assurances that, within limits of confidentiality, a PSP will not be asked to give information about members they support. The only information that management may require about peer support cases is the anonymous statistical information regarding the utilization of a PSP.

2. A peer support program shall be governed by a written procedures manual that is available to all personnel.

3. Individuals receiving peer support may voluntarily choose or reject a PSP by any criteria they believe are important.

4. Management could provide noncompensatory support for the PSP program.

5. Departments are encouraged to train as many employees as possible in peer support skills.

6. A peer support program coordinator should be identified who has a block of time devoted to program logistics and development. This individual would coordinate referrals to mental health professionals, collect utilization data, and coordinate training and meetings.

7. The peer support program is not an alternative to discipline. A PSP does not intervene in the disciplinary process, even at a member's request.

8. The steering committee shall identify appropriate ongoing training for PSPs.

CONSULTATION SERVICES FROM MENTAL HEALTH PROFESSIONALS

1. PSPs must have a mental health professional with whom to consult.

2. PSPs should be aware of their personal limitations and should seek consultation when determining when to disqualify themselves from working with individuals who have problems for which they have not been trained or for problems about which they may have strong personal beliefs.

3. PSPs should be required to advance their skills through continuing training as scheduled by the program coordinator.

CONFIDENTIALITY

1. PSPs must inform department members of the limits of their confidentiality and consider potential role conflicts (e.g., supervisor providing peer support). These should be consistent with law and departmental policy and may include the following:

   A.   threats to self
   B.   threats to specific people
   C.   felonies as specified by the department
   D.   serious misdemeanors as specified by the department
   E.   child, spouse, and elder abuse

2. PSPs should be trained to be sensitive to role conflicts that could affect future decisions and recommendations on assignment, e.g., to investigations, transfers, and promotions. PSPs cannot abdicate their job responsibility as officers by participating in the program.

3. PSPs do not volunteer information to supervisors and should advise supervisors of the confidentiality guidelines established by the department.

4. PSPs must advise members that information told to them is not protected by legal privilege and that confidentiality is administratively provided and may not be recognized in court proceedings.

5. PSPs should avoid conflicting peer support relationships. For example, PSPs should not develop peer support relationships with supervisors, subordinates, or relatives. PSPs should avoid religious, sexual, or financial entanglements with receivers of peer support and avoid espousing particular values, moral standards, and philosophies.

6. A PSP must not keep written formal or private records of supportive contacts.

GOOD LEADERSHIP AND SUPERVISION

One painful aspect of talking to police officers who have struggled to cope with traumatic incidents is listening to one story after another about how they were neglected or mistreated by their command staff. Although complaints about bad supervision and poor leadership are common, the fact that these officers were let down by their leaders at a time when they were most vulnerable is particularly poignant.

I had been on the force for only three years when I got shot in the chest with a rifle. I thought I was dying. Had it not been for my body armor, I would not be here today. That was about 20 years ago in the days when there was no counseling, so I just sucked it up and spent the next 20 years working the streets as hard as I could. However, the incident kept haunting me and over the years other nasty events kept getting stuffed away instead of being dealt with. I never told anyone about my bad feelings, not even my wife. It wasn't considered "manly."

It all came to head a few years ago when a friend of mine got involved in a shooting. I heard it go down over the radio and I rushed to the scene fearing my friend had been shot. I got there shortly after and helped secure the scene. After determining that my friend was okay, I went over to look at the shot suspect. As I was looking down at him, I saw myself, in uniform, lying on the floor bleeding and dying. I felt horrible fear and sadness. As we were walking away from the fatally wounded suspect, one of the sergeants ordered me to get back out on patrol.

I was never offered any kind of debriefing or counseling. I felt devastated and betrayed. I knew something was wrong with me but I didn't know what it was or what to do about it. I did know I needed to get off the street for a while. My friend who had been involved in the shooting was also having a hard time. We went to the sergeant and requested a transfer to a quieter assignment so we could get some relief from the heavy street action.

The sergeant refused our request. His refusal and his unwillingness to acknowledge that we needed help was basically the end of my career as a police officer. Several weeks later we both went off on sick leave because we couldn't function on the street any more. I felt humiliated and embarrassed. I cleaned out my locker at night in the middle of a shift so no one would see me. I expected to get some calls from the command staff who might at least be curious about what was going on with me. I got nothing except a call from the sergeant chewing me out for abusing sick time. Up until that time I had a virtually perfect attendance record.

The only member of the command staff who called me out of concern was the new precinct commander who assumed command three weeks after I'd left. When he heard what was going on with me, he said I didn't need to be burning my sick time and I should apply for a work-related stress disability. I had always scorned officers who went out on stress leaves; I never thought I would be one of them. But I knew I probably could never go back on the street again so I swallowed my pride and applied for disability.

The director of the disability board, a former cop, called me into his office and told me I didn't have any emotional problems and implied I was faking. I was stunned. The sergeant had apparently told him this and he chose to believe it. Fortunately, a mental health professional disagreed with them and they were forced to accept my claim. But the contempt of the sergeant and the director of the disability board was emotionally devastating. I went deeper and deeper into my shell, full of shame and guilt over my condition. No one called to ask me how I was. Whenever I saw a police car I'd go in the other direction, dreading I'd be seen. I was afraid I'd get fired and I even sold my house for fear I wouldn't be able to keep up the payments when they fired me.

I kept going downhill. Finally, some officers persuaded me to go see a police psychologist. But I was reluctant, fearing further rejection. But it was the turning point for me. The psychologist educated me about my condition and helped me start my slow climb out of the deep, black pit I had fallen into.

If I had received some compassion and encouragement to get help from the command staff I think I could have come to grips with my problems and finished my career out on the street like I had always dreamed. Instead, I feel like they kicked me when I was down.

I hope they become educated to treat the next guy better than they treated me.

There are too many stories like this one. Are officers just a bunch of whiners? Are their leaders particularly bad? No. Unfortunately, poor leadership is not unusual in organizations.

In the June 1994 issue of *The American Psychologist*, Hogan, Curphy, and Hogan wrote a major review article on organizational leadership entitled, "What We Know About Leadership." To write the piece, they reviewed about 120 articles and books on management and leadership. Here is a quotation from it.

"R. Hogan, Raskin, and Fazzini (1990) noted that organizational climate studies from the mid-1950s to the present, routinely show that 60% to 75% of the employees in any organization—no matter when or where the survey was completed and no matter what occupational group was involved—report that the worst or most stressful aspect of their job is their immediate supervisor. Good leaders may put pressure on their people, but abusive and incompetent management creates billions of dollars of lost productivity each year . . . To stimulate research on the topic of inept management, R. Hogan et al. (1990) proposed that the base rate for managerial incompetence in America is between 60% and 75%."

Not all the officers we talked with were mistreated by their command staff. Some were fortunate to have caring and competent leaders, and those lucky officers will always remember and be grateful to them for their fairness and compassion during a very difficult time.

The causes and possible cures of incompetent leadership are obviously way beyond the scope of this book. We mention it here because the way an officer is treated by his command staff after a traumatic incident is a major factor in his ability to recover. Most officers can distinctly remember what every person in their chain of command did or did not do after the shooting. They remember who didn't call them and who went out of their way to make sure they and their family were being taken care of.

If you are a command-level person, we hope that you will read and follow the *Administrative Guidelines for Dealing with Officers Involved in On-Duty Shooting Situations* written by the

Psychological Services Section of the International Association of Chiefs of Police, reproduced in Chapter 9. These guidelines will help you facilitate the recovery of officers entrusted to your command. We also encourage you to learn all that you can about leaderships skills, which an officer develops through training and experience. Regularly check your agency's training unit and your teletype service for leadership training programs. The Internet is another great source of information. Go to the law enforcement sites listed in Chapter 5 and check out the books, videotapes, and articles written on leadership skills, and look for news groups where police officers hold discussions and seminars on leadership techniques, traits, and principles. The simple fact is that the more you avail yourself of knowledge about leadership, the better you will do your job and the more the officers under your command will benefit.

If you are an officer, we encourage you to not feel like a professional victim of poor leadership. You are in the same boat with the majority of American workers everywhere, and whether it's fair or not, it's up to you to find constructive ways of coping with this problem.

One thing you can do right away is to not take it personally. This can be hard, but to do otherwise will interfere with your ability to find an objective solution. If you feel emotionally affected to the extent that it's hard for you to function or think of a constructive solution, then ask for help. Consider asking for support and feedback from level-headed friends or seek professional counseling. These are two arenas where you can safely vent your feelings and start to explore options. Know that chronic complaining and demonstrating negative behavior at work will only make things worse. While the specific solutions will obviously depend on the situation, the important thing is to stop thinking *victim* and start thinking *solution*.

What can you do as an officer to encourage good leadership? There is one simple behavior that everyone can do that is too often overlooked: simply tell the good supervisors

"Thanks." Good supervisors who care about their troops, who take the extra time and effort to mentor, challenge, and treat them with honesty and fairness, are worth their weight in gold to the officers and the organizations they work for.

Unfortunately, they are not always rewarded or promoted for their efforts in this regard. As Hogan, Curphy, and Hogan point out in their article, bosses' ratings of a manager's effectiveness are largely influenced by judgments of the manager's technical competence, whereas subordinates' ratings of a manager's effectiveness are largely influenced by judgments of the manager's integrity and trustworthiness. Since good managers can't count on being rewarded by the organization for looking out for you, let them at least count on being thanked by you.

This may not sound like much, but you can rest assured that your thanks will mean a great deal to those supervisors who really do care. We would encourage you to even thank a lousy supervisor when they actually do something positive for you. Whether it's from supervisor to officer or the other way around, a little positive reinforcement can go a long way,

MENTAL HEALTH PROFESSIONALS

There are a number of reasons why some police officers don't like shrinks or other touchy-feeley mental health professionals. They see them as bleeding heart liberals who, because they have little understanding of the world police officers work in, have little to offer. Officers' experiences might also be negative because of the testing and interviewing done by MHPs during their pre-employment screening process. And there are officers who have negative opinions because of their experience or a friend's experience of being sent for a fitness-for-duty evaluation. Though these are valuable services that MHPs provide to agencies, they are not warm and fuzzy experiences likely to leave officers looking forward to the next one.

So what do they have to offer? Well, the answer depends

on the individual MHP's training and experience. MHPs come from a variety of disciplines: psychologists, psychiatrists, social workers, chaplains, nurse practitioners, and others. While each discipline offers something unique, the common theme among all of them is their professional training and experience in helping people with a range of mental and emotional problems. Like in every other profession, some are effective and some are not.

If you can find an MHP who has taken the time and effort to seek out the types of experiences and training that allows him to understand the unique world of law enforcement, he can be a valuable resource to you and your family. A MHP who understands police officers can also provide counseling in other areas, such as coping with abusive supervisors, troubled relationships, excessive fear level while on duty, depression, conflicts with co-workers, and problems with their children.

A MHP who understands police officers will not just sit and look inscrutable for six months while you spill your guts. He knows you are looking for concrete options to make your life better. While he can't tell you how to run your life, he will give you feedback and help you explore options and solutions that might work for you. Whether you take the ball and run with it is, of course, up to you.

MHPs can also play an important role in helping to train officers and agencies in a variety of topics, such as mental preparation to survive deadly force encounters, the emotional and legal implications of perceptual distortions, traumatic stress reactions in officers and family members and how to take care of them, peer-support training and supervision, stress management, supervision skills, and mental health issues.

Sadly, our society still stigmatizes mental health problems and harbors irrational fears about them. We take it for granted that our bodies are not perfect and that they will periodically malfunction due to traumatic injury, chronic stress, poor health habits, infectious diseases, and faulty genetic programming. While people might be annoyed and frustrated about having a broken leg, heart disease, diabetes, meningitis, cancer, or the flu, they don't usually feel ashamed of it, and most will be responsible in seeking treatment from health care professionals. So why should they assume that their mental and emotional functioning be perfect when their bodies are not?

They shouldn't, nor should they feel shame about mental illness and refuse treatment. As with physical illnesses, we still have much to learn about mental illness. The good news is that we are making progress all the time in understanding and effectively treating mental health problems.

Many officers in this book have had counseling. For some it may have been just one session where they were reassured by a simple comment from the MHP like, "Your feelings are normal and you're doing fine. Feel free to call me if anything else comes up." Others have been in extended counseling for a variety of things that have troubled them. Nearly all of these officers spoke freely with others about their counseling, and their message to you is this: *You don't need to buy into feeling guilty or ashamed about having feelings and problems. Counseling worked for us and it might work for you.*

Family
and
Trauma

12

Several years ago, my partner and I shot it out with a holdup man. My partner got shot in the face and damn near died. This was years before our agency got sensitive to officers involved in traumatic incidents and the families of the officers. I remember when I got home that night my wife acted pretty strange, like she didn't know what to do. She treated me like I was sick: waiting on me hand and foot.

Two days later when I had to go back to work and pull the evening shift, I could see that my wife was anxious throughout the day. When I put on my coat and gave her a good-bye kiss, she wouldn't let go of me. I pried her loose and headed for the door, but she latched onto my arm and held on tight. I kept telling her that I would be all right and that the shooting was a rare occurrence, but she just wouldn't let go. She clung to me as I worked my way out to the driveway and I had to pry her loose so I could get into the car.

I still remember how she looked as I drove away: scared and alone.

When an officer is involved in a traumatic event, all who care about him will also be affected. The following two stories are representative of what can happen to families after a deadly force encounter.

THE BLACK HOLE

"Ted's shooting was a black hole that sucked the whole family into seven years of hell."

Jean Higa is married to Ted Higa, whose story is told in Part Two, "THE BACK YARD." Jean is no shrinking violet. She has a rapier sharp wit, a ready laugh, and a lively presence that fills the room around her. Formerly a police dispatcher, she was no stranger to the world of law enforcement when Ted got into his shooting. Still, her experiences had not prepared her for the impact that it would have on Ted and the entire family.

Jean's first hint that something was wrong was when Ted didn't come home at the end of his shift. Her expressive face gave eloquent emphasis to her recounting of that painful night. *"He didn't even call me and that's not like him at all. I knew something was terribly wrong. Since I used to be a dispatcher, I called the radio center to try to find out what might have happened. They told me there had been a shooting but refused to give me any more information, which made me even more upset. Finally, hours later, I got a call from Ted from the detective's division. He told me there had been a shooting of an elderly woman. When I asked him when he was coming home, he said he couldn't. I asked why not and he replied in a sad whisper, 'I shot her.'*

"My heart sank; he sounded awful. I asked him if he was under arrest and he said they had read him his Miranda rights. I told him I was coming right down there but he told me to stay home, that I wouldn't be allowed to see him anyway."

People who know Jean could tell you two things about her: first, don't waste your time telling her she can't do something unless you have a damn good reason. Secondly, she is a caring person who puts her money where her mouth is. So, of course, she went down to detectives.

"When I got there I was only allowed to see Ted from a distance. He was surrounded by people but he looked so sad and alone. I felt awful and I wanted to do something to help him but I wasn't sure what that was. Later on, we both drove ourselves home."

Things were never the same for Ted and Jean after that night. From then on, they had two conflicting needs: Ted wanted to be left alone, and Jean wanted to help him. She remembers how painful that was. *"Ted wanted to be alone most of the time but I was worried sick about him. I'd heard stories of how some officers went crazy after being in a shooting and I followed him around looking for signs that he might be cracking. I was ready to help in any way I could. But it only annoyed him and I felt confused and rejected. My hurt feelings were compounded by the fact that although Ted wouldn't talk to me about it, when officers called, he would spill his guts to them. I felt like my role as the main person who was supposed to love and take care of him was being totally ignored.*

"It broke my heart as I watched him suffer, but there was nothing I could do. I felt helpless, incompetent as a wife, and guilty that somehow I wasn't figuring out the right thing to do to fix him. I felt like there was something missing in me and I lost my whole belief system."

Besides feeling confused about her role in Ted's recovery, Jean, like too many family members, was ignored by the agency and other officers: *"After the shooting, Ted got lots of phone calls from his fellow officers. I was glad they were reaching out to him but if I answered the phone, all they did was ask to speak to Ted. No one ever asked how me or the kids were doing. No one reached out to us. Back in those days there were no debriefings or support of any kind. I felt alone and increasingly isolated. It was like the family didn't exist. No one noticed or acknowledged that this traumatic event might have an impact on Ted's family."*

Ted and Jean's conflicting needs tore at them for the next seven years. Ted withdrew and silently struggled to cope with the emotional damage of the shooting as Jean felt abandoned and rejected. *"I didn't know how much the shooting bothered him because he couldn't talk about it. His body was home, but his heart, soul, and spirit were gone for seven years. We fought all the time. Ted would pick fights just to get away from me so he could retreat into that wall of silence he had built up around himself after the shooting. And I was terrified when he went back out on the street. I* had nightmares and my anxiety level skyrocketed, but I couldn't talk to him about it. I could see he was already struggling and didn't want to add my anxiety on top of his own.

"Things were also very tense at home. The kids and I couldn't relax because Ted had become irritable, extremely controlling, and he had little frustration tolerance. Instead of talking with us, he'd interrogate us. He could no longer separate the street from home. We felt like we were walking around on eggshells much of the time. This was not at all like Ted's normal personality and I was baffled why the nice man I had fallen in love with had turned into basically an asshole."

The shooting almost destroyed their marriage. At one point they separated for nearly a year, but love and respect somehow held them together. Seven years after the shooting, Jean and Ted attended a training seminar on how traumatic incidents affect police officers and family members. Jean said, "As the psychologist was talking about post-traumatic stress disorder, a huge light bulb came on in my head. For the first time I started to understand what had happened to Ted and the rest of us."

The healing of their marriage and their own individual psyches had begun. Jean became an early member of a new support team formed for family members. She wanted to help ensure that other families in her agency would not feel as alone, lost, and isolated as she had. The family-support team was a place she could talk freely about her feelings to other police families, people who understood how she felt. Besides providing peer-family support, Jean also volunteers to be a co-instructor in classes where the dynamic presentation of her family's journey into and out of the black hole commands rapt attention.

Jean said that just before she was interviewed for this book she looked at some photos taken at the scene of Ted's shooting. Her eyes grew misty as she recounted how it made her feel to see them. "You can actually see bullet holes in the leaves that were right above Ted's head. As time goes on, I am still getting in touch with how close I came to losing him to the suspect's bullets, and how close we came to losing each other in the emotional devastation that followed. I am so grateful that he survived and we survived."

Jean said that during the past year Ted has thanked her for sticking by him through that black hole. They are now able to talk openly with each other about the shooting and how it made them feel about themselves and each other. Although Jean had felt like a failure as a wife because she couldn't "fix" Ted, he said that her willingness to just stay with him during that confusing time has caused him to love and respect her more than ever. Jean and Ted plan to renew their wedding vows in the future. It will be a celebration of the love and commitment that held them together.

THE WOMAN WHO REFUSED TO BE IGNORED

Although Detective Marie Nordin is in law enforcement, she still experienced some of the same problems after the incident, whose story is told in Part Two "THREE SHOOTINGS," that other officers' non-police spouses have experienced.

Marie is an intense woman with a ready sense of humor, a hearty laugh, and a gift for telling a good story. She is also a force to contend with when she gets her dander up. Woe be unto those who would push her aside when the fate of those she cares about is at stake.

Her husband called and told her about the first shooting shortly after it occurred and she marched right down to the detective's division where he was being interviewed. Her eyes twinkled as she remembers, *"They couldn't throw me out because I'm a cop too. When I saw Bill, I felt fiercely protective of him and wound up overstepping my boundaries. Fortunately, a detective on the case was kind to me and helped me back off and withdraw from the situation. But at least I was there. It was important to me to actually see Bill with my own eyes to be reassured that he was OK."*

Over the next several years, Marie had two more opportunities to learn about how she and Bill process these traumatic events. *"Even though I'm a cop, Bill hasn't really talked to me in much detail about his shootings. He prefers to talk to other cops who have also been involved in deadly force encounters. He's a pretty verbal person and I had to get used to the phone ringing off the hook*

*after the shootings and listen to him talk and talk over the next 24
hours until the adrenaline cleared out of his system. After the adrenaline wears off, he also tends to spend time alone in the garage, which
is his cave that he retreats to when he feels stressed.*

*"I had to learn to not take it personally and to realize that it was
just his way of processing what had happened to him. I learned that
it was necessary for me to talk about my own feelings and reactions
to people other than just him."*

Marie's opportunity to practice her considerable assertive-
ness skills came during Bill's second shooting. She was on
duty when he was called out on the SWAT team to rescue a
hostage at a bank. She heard that a SWAT officer had been
shot and was being taken to the hospital; she was told it was
Bill. Marie was at a fire station when she heard the news and
she remembers being embarrassed about being in uniform
and crying on the phone as she tried to find out where he was
and if he was OK.

Another female officer friend who was on duty picked up
Marie and sped, lights and siren, to the hospital where Bill
supposedly had been taken. As Marie desperately looked for
her husband, she saw an emergency medical technician she
knew and asked where Bill was. He made the mistake of
ignoring her. *"I didn't know if Bill was dead or alive and this guy
won't even talk to me. I grabbed him by the shirt and shoved him
against a wall and demanded that he tell me where my husband was.
He finally told me that it was actually another SWAT officer who
had been wounded. The police grapevine can work for you or against
you. This time it was wrong and I was so happy.*

*"Then I saw the other shot officer's wife there, a woman I have
known for years. I had to instantly switch from my fear for Bill, to
relief that he was probably OK, then to compassion for the other officer's wife as I tried to comfort her. It was a wild, emotional roller
coaster ride.*

*"After this shooting we realized it was important for us to have
a plan in case this ever happened again. I told him that I preferred
that he call or page me immediately from the scene of the shooting
and stay until I arrived. That way I would know exactly where he*

was and could see and touch him and know that he was OK."

Less than 30 days later, Bill was involved in a third shooting while serving a search warrant. Marie was also working that day and went to the scene to look for him. *"When I saw him it was like a surrealistic scene out of a movie as he eerily emerged out of the smoke and haze left over from the flash-bangs and gunfire. I ran to him and we hugged each other, though neither one of us could feel it through our body armor. I found out later that others had tried to take him away, but he stubbornly refused because he had promised me he would not leave the scene of a shooting until I arrived. The fact that he waited has always meant a lot to me."*

Marie said that each incident brought up different emotions. After the third shooting, the agency was sued in civil court and she found the trial emotionally stressful. She said it was like going through the shooting all over, except worse. Each event required new adjustments and adaptations. At one point Marie asked Bill to not be the lead man on the SWAT entry team for a while and he respected her wishes. They also came up with an agreement that Bill would always call her after every SWAT call-out, even if no shots were fired, just to let her know that it was over and everyone was OK.

Marie belongs to her agency's family-trauma support team and has been active in supporting other family members through traumatic events and helping train them in coping skills. She said that at times it has been difficult for the family-support team to gain official recognition and acceptance. Again, she had to set others straight when they tried to ignore the importance of the team's mission. *"Early in our formation,"* Marie said, *"a member of management actually had the audacity to ask us to bake cookies to bring as if we were some kind of women's auxiliary. Can you imagine asking the officer-trauma support team to bake cookies? Our function is to help people get through emotional trauma. We told him in no uncertain terms that he should call a caterer if they wanted food."*

Though Marie is a police officer, she can still identify with what family members go through who don't have that advantage. She knows how important it is for them to support each other and get whatever professional help they need. As a formidable member of the family-trauma support team, she is doing her part to make sure they are not ignored, and she does it well.

FAMILY MEMBER'S RESPONSES MAY VARY

As with officers, each family and each family member will respond differently after a shooting. The response will depend on each individual, the family dynamics, the education and preparation the family has before the incident, and the support they get afterward. Some will bounce back quickly and be relatively unaffected, while others may be devastated.

Since family members can develop post-traumatic stress disorder, they should be educated about trauma reactions by the agency, have access to debriefings, receive counseling, and be involved in the agency's family-trauma peer support teams.

The love and empathy that family members feel for each other can be a strength and a liability after a deadly force encounter. While there is no question that officers and their significant others can benefit by talking about the event and their feelings about it, it's important to understand there may be times when they will be more willing to talk to others outside the family. This is normal and doesn't necessarily suggest rejection or lack of trust.

Officers may be reluctant to discuss the gory details of an event and their reaction to it for fear of increasing their family's anxiety level even more. Members of the family may be reluctant to discuss their anxieties with the officer for the same reason. Therefore, both the officers and family members may hold back some of their feelings to protect each other. This can be a double-edged sword because it might cause the others to feel left out or ignored.

Officers often feel most comfortable talking to other officers who have also been involved in a deadly force encounter. Family members may be most comfortable talking to other police family members who have been through a similar event. This is why peer-support teams for officers and family members are a valuable resource to many people who have been through a traumatic event.

As with everything else, it's important for family members to respect individual differences in how each person copes with traumatic events. Officer Suzanne Kirk's husband has been involved in five SWAT shootings. She is a lively, enthusiastic woman who freely expresses her emotions, and her husband is known for his reserved and laconic demeanor. She talked about their differences.

"Mike is a very calm, grounded person who is not emotional and talkative like I am. Even so, I worried that he seemed so unaffected by his shootings. The only time I saw him get upset was when someone in the media called him "Terminator." He was upset because he was afraid of how our daughter would be affected if she ever heard that. Fortunately, she was only three-years-old then and we could keep that publicity away from her.

"At one point I consulted a psychologist to ask if Mike's lack of reaction to his shootings was normal. I worried he might be stuffing it all and having it eat away at him. The psychologist explained that since Mike has always been a calm, nontalkative person, it was quite possible he was taking it all in stride and encouraged me to not worry about it unless I noticed negative changes in his behavior.

"Mike was acting just like he always had, so I stopped worrying. At one point I asked him if he knew why the shootings hadn't bothered him. After thinking about it for a day he said that since all his shootings had been SWAT shootings, he'd always had planning time to mentally prepare for something bad happening. This took away the shock factor for him. He thought it might be different if any of them had happened suddenly and unexpectedly when he was on regular patrol. He promised me he would tell me if they ever started to bother him.

"Unlike Mike, it's real important for me to talk to others when dealing with my feelings. The support of my women friends, some of whose husbands have also been in shootings, has been invaluable. They're glad to listen to me rattle on about it in a way that would be hard for Mike to do.

• • • • •

"I sought counseling for an incident I was involved in and it made a big difference."

Officer Emma Mills is one of those solid, no-nonsense women whom you could easily imagine as a leader in a wagon train heading west. She tells her story with confidence and gentle, self-deprecating humor.

"I was one of several officers involved in capturing an armed robber who had a long criminal record. I found him hiding in a restaurant and wound up in a foot pursuit after he fled the building. He ran over to my patrol car and tried to steal it but fortunately I had the keys on me. It turns out he had stolen another agency's patrol car the week before.

"I was chasing him on a busy, crowded avenue in the middle of the day. At one point, he and I chased each other around a car, taking pot shots at each other. Other officers showed up, one of whom fired rounds at the suspect. He was finally taken into custody without anyone getting hurt.

"The whole thing was pretty wild and I was wired for three days before my body finally ran out of steam and I suddenly felt exhausted. My agency took good care of us with debriefings, counseling, and time off. Once the grand jury was over, I was fine and it hasn't bothered me much since. But it was a different story for my mother. She was never fond of me becoming a cop, and one time asked, 'Why can't you get a real job like your sister?' I told her, 'Mom, this is about as real as it gets!'

"After the shooting, she became more fearful for my safety, sometimes to the point of tears. My sister, whose 'real job' is a secretary, said that to this day whenever her phone rings she has some anxiety that it might be someone telling her that I've been shot and killed.

"In spite of their fears, they know I love being a cop and they support me as best they can. After the shooting the family-trauma team contacted my mother and she found it very helpful."

CHILDREN'S REACTIONS

Children can also be affected to differing degrees. In Part

Two, "How Many Lives Do I Have?", Tony Petterson talked about his close relationship with his children, how his four shootings might affect them, and his relief that all the talking and preparation he has done with them is working well to inoculate them from the stress of these events.

Suzanne's children have also weathered Mike's shootings, but she was surprised when her ten-year-old daughter showed the first sign of being affected. Suzanne said, *"Our children have done well through all of Mike's shootings. But it was the shooting of another officer that wound up creating anxiety for our daughter. One of the other SWAT members was shot and wounded during a shoot-out. For six months after that, our daughter insisted on sleeping on the couch every night because it was closer to our bedroom and she could be closer to Mike. The officer who was shot said that some of the children of the other SWAT members were also showing anxiety and he felt badly about it even though he knew it wasn't his fault."*

Police families sometimes wonder how much to tell their children. This depends on their age, maturity, and temperament, but a good rule of thumb is to tell them the facts in a calm, neutral, reassuring manner, then ask if they have questions. Children will often let you know how much they need to know by their questions. Keep the lines of communication open and look for any changes in their behavior. Counseling is always an option if significant problems develop down the road.

PREPARING FAMILY MEMBERS
FOR A TRAUMATIC EVENT

How can family members cope with the stress of these traumatic events? While each family will have it's own unique style, here are suggestions that will work for many.

- Prepare ahead of time. Make a plan what each person will do, such as:

1. How will family and friends be notified?

2. Where will the officer be and will family members go there or wait at home?
3. Who will look after the children?
4. How will other friends and family members be notified?

- To minimize uncomfortable surprises, familiarize yourself with all that may happen after a shooting, such as:

1. Media responses
2. Criminal investigations
3. Grand juries
4. Civil litigation

- If it's desired, see that everyone in the family has access to a debriefing and counseling with mental health professionals.
- Seek out your agency's family-peer support team.
- Allow for individual differences in how family members cope with the event. For example, one person may cherish personal privacy and feel threatened if another member needs to talk about the event and its aftermath with others outside the family. Try to allow for everyone's needs to be reasonably met with a respectful compromise.
- Open communication is always helpful to families, both within and outside the family.
- An excellent resource for police families is Dr. Ellen Kirschman's book, *I Love A Cop: What Police Families Need To Know.* Her book is packed with information about coping with the whole range of stressors and issues that police families face.

FAMILY SUPPORT TEAMS

Family-trauma support teams are a valuable resource, and the IACP "Peer Support Guidelines" in Chapter 11 are applicable for family teams, too. Although it may be harder to gain acceptance within the agency than it is for officer teams, the following tips have worked for some family-support teams.

- Team members who are also officers can help the team negotiate agency policies and politics.
- Gain the support of an inside "sponsor," who has influence.
- Advocate for and volunteer to help with in-service training concerning family trauma issues.
- Be clear about your purpose and express that to others.
- Since family members are more likely to be isolated from each other than officers are, you may have to make that extra effort to reach out to help them overcome this isolation.
- All "significant others" should be invited to participate in the team's support activities. This would include men and women, spouses, parents, siblings, gay partners, close friends, cousins, and so on.
- Those officers who are protective of family members and try to keep their work separate from their home life may feel intruded upon if others try to contact their family members. Tact, respect, and sensitivity are needed to avoid having those officers feel like you are "interfering" with their families.

LINE OF DUTY DEATHS

Most agencies do an excellent job of providing a moving and stately tribute to an officer who has made the supreme sacrifice for his community. These rituals are an important part of healing for everyone, but they are only the beginning of the grieving process that will usually take at least one or two years for those who cared for the officer. Even when the grieving is completed, the world will never be the same without the officer in it. Learning to adjust to this reality is a long-term process.

It is important that peers, friends, and family be given the support and help they need to walk through this painful journey. Besides the memorial service, agencies should see that all those affected have access to whatever grief counseling they may want or need.

The mutual support of friends, peers, and family is important. There is a nonprofit organization called Concerns Of Police Survivors, Inc. (COPS) that offers and facilitates this mutual support. Many of those who have loved and lost a police officer have found solace and comfort through this organization that is devoted to "reaching out to the surviving families of America's fallen law enforcement heroes." To find out more about the services offered through COPS and to locate a local chapter in your area, call or write to:

CONCERNS OF POLICE SURVIVORS, INC.
South Highway 5
P.O. Box 3199
Camdenton, MO 65020
(573) 346-1414

Investigating Officer-Involved Shootings

13

He came out the door aiming his rifle at the closest officer. A half dozen of us opened fire on him and when it was all over, he had been hit 25 times and looked like a pile of ground burger. After the autopsy and the crime lab had done their investigation, the detectives called me up and said that it was my bullet that had killed the man.

I was already feeling pretty shook about the shooting. Then, when the detectives told me that out of all the rounds that hit, mine was the fatal shot, I was devastated. I'm a Christian and I believe that taking a human life is wrong, plain and simple.

Why did they have to tell me? It took a long time for me to come to terms with the shooting.

A MESSAGE TO OFFICERS

The investigation of officer-involved shootings can be stressful for the officers and the investigators. Know that a good investigator is not your enemy. Since there is an outstanding chance that your shooting will be found justified, a good investigator who does a meticulous and accurate investigation is working in your best interest.

It's becoming increasingly common to encourage officers to retain their own attorney before talking to anyone about their shooting. You should educate yourself about how legal representation is handled in your jurisdiction and develop a plan *now*, before you get involved in a deadly force encounter.

It's also becoming common to not require officers to write their own reports or to give a statement immediately after the incident. This is because officers who have been traumatized by the event may not be in any shape to give a coherent story until they have had a chance to rest and calm down. Again, you should educate yourself about how this is handled in your jurisdiction and be prepared to advocate for yourself about when you are ready to make a statement. You may feel relatively clearheaded right after the incident and want to give your statement right away and get it over with, or you may want to wait. To the extent possible, make this your decision.

A MESSAGE TO INVESTIGATORS

One of the most important things to remember about investigating shootings or any incident is that human memory is fallible. Few people have a photographic memory that is a totally accurate representation of reality. Human memory is subject to distortions and omissions even under nonstressful circumstances, and the stress of a traumatic incident only makes it worse. Memory distortions can be minor, or they can be extreme. Participants and witnesses may be unable to recall events, or their minds may invent complex sequences as to their behavior and what they perceive others have done.

Improperly trained investigators have taken it upon themselves to decide that "no one could forget something like that" or "that obviously never happened, he must be lying." Too many honest officers and witnesses have been falsely branded as liars because their reports were not consistent with evidence. Police officers have been disciplined and even terminated for being untruthful, when in fact they were telling the truth as they knew it.

No one can tell you what *really* happened. They can only tell you what they *perceived*. The bottom line is, a truthful participant or a witness may be able to give you a totally accurate account of what happened, or he may not. This will vary from person to person and situation to situation.

It is also normal for memories to change over time. As people talk with others or mull over the event in their minds, their memories will often become altered and they may start to remember details they hadn't recalled before. These alterations may or may not be closer to reality than their previous versions. So if an officer's memory is not rigidly consistent, don't automatically assume he is being untruthful.

You have a difficult job when you get conflicting eyewitness accounts, and you must be careful not to jump to conclusions. Learning what actually happened may be difficult or even impossible. Trying to determine if someone is deliberately lying is a difficult, complex judgment call involving many factors. If you make a hasty conclusion about an officer's truthfulness, an innocent person may get hurt.

As an investigator, it's important for you to understand the perceptual and cognitive distortions that are the result of the high arousal state that occurs during any emotional event. Carefully read Chapter 5 and consider this information when conducting your interviews and investigations.

When you are investigating an officer-involved shooting, "cognitive interview" techniques can be helpful in maximizing the ability of the officers and the witnesses to recall their perceptions of the event. Seek out training in these techniques if you haven't already had it. Fisher and Geiselman have written a book on the cognitive interview titled, *Memory-Enhancing Techniques for Investigative Interviewing*.

SUGGESTIONS FOR INVESTIGATING OFFICER-INVOLVED SHOOTINGS

Keep in mind that these are only suggestions on how to deal effectively with the psychological consequences of trauma on officers. Every situation is different, and your decisions must be responsive to the circumstances and the requirements of your agency. Investigative techniques and psychological issues are inevitably intertwined and cannot be separated. While some of the following may not be your direct responsibility, it would be helpful if you could facilitate them if they are not happening.

- When you first contact an officer, tell him what the procedures are and what will happen from that point on. Keep him informed throughout the process about what is happening. It's anxiety provoking to the officers to not know what is going on. Don't make any assumptions about their knowledge of post-shooting procedures.
- Ask the officer if arrangements have been made to contact his family or friends. Help him do it if he wants.
- If your agency has officer- and family-peer support teams, find out if they have been contacted. If not, do so.
- The officer should have an uninvolved peer-support person or friend of his choice available immediately after the shooting, though he should not discuss details of the shooting with this person. If this is another officer, he should not be given any orders or duties beyond the role of support person.
- It's often helpful for the officer's memory to view the scene and do a "walk through." He may want to do it right after the shooting or later, but he should not discuss the details of the event with you or anyone else until he has had an opportunity to talk with his attorney. Having an on-call list of attorneys who can respond instantly after a shooting can be a useful tool. The attorney can accompany the officer on the walk-through and then provide information to you that will help delineate the scene for evidence collection. This way the officer will not be put in the position of giving statements without legal representation, and you will get on-scene information that will help you with your investigation.
- Don't confiscate the officer's weapon unless it's absolutely necessary or required by agency policy. If this must be done, make sure he gets an exact replacement when possi-

ble and let him know when this will occur. Make it your responsibility to see that his personal weapon is returned. If an officer must give up his weapon at the scene and a replacement is not available, see that an armed officer, who the involved officer feels comfortable with, is assigned to be his personal bodyguard until he gets home.

- Remember that officers who were present at the shooting, though they didn't shoot, may be just as traumatized as the shooter. Supervisors and command staff who might have been on the scene during the shooting are not immune either. Expect a wide range of emotional reactions from on-scene personnel. All should be observed for signs of emotional distress and given support as needed by mental health providers and peer-support personnel.

- The officer should not have to drive himself anywhere after the incident. A driver should be provided to take him to detectives, home, wherever. Family members may also need transportation.

- The post-shooting interview should occur at the discretion of the officer after he has had an opportunity to talk to his attorney. Some officers want to get it over with right away, others prefer to wait for varying lengths of time. It will depend on a variety of factors, especially the psychological status of the officer.

- Some officers may find it helpful to exercise before being interviewed or going home so they can unwind and dissipate the excess energy caused by the adrenaline surge. Arrange this for them if necessary.

- If the officer chooses to be interviewed right after the shooting, offer him the opportunity to shower and change clothes first.

- The interviews should take place in a comfortable room, such as a conference room. Avoid conducting officer interviews in rooms used for interviewing suspects. Don't isolate him. The officer should have access to friends, family, and support personnel. To the extent that it's appropriate, allow him leeway about where he wants to be after the shooting.

- If the interview is conducted right after the shooting, it may be hard for the officer to sit still due to the excess energy from his recent adrenaline surge. Don't stuff him into a room for long periods. He needs to be allowed to stand or pace.
- Arrange to have appropriate beverages and food available. Choose easy to digest food (low fat, not spicy, not too much sugar). Have a choice of nonstimulant type beverages so the officer who is already wound up can choose something other than coffee.
- There is likely to be a convergence of many people at the scene and at the location of the investigative interview. Since this may be overwhelming to an officer, be sensitive to his reactions and allow him appropriate leeway about who has access to him. It would be helpful to have a "quiet room" where he (and his family members) can retreat to get temporary relief from the commotion.
- Sometimes people with different roles during the post-shooting investigation can disagree with each other. Know that it can be destructive when this happens in the presence of an involved officer and his family. When disagreements arise, everyone should try to resolve them as quickly as possible, then problem solve so the same conflict will not occur again.
- As discussed earlier, an officer can only report what he perceived, not what actually happened. If an officer's perceptions differ from the physical evidence, from other officers, or other witness accounts, it doesn't necessarily mean he is lying. Differing or fragmented memories of the event are the result of cognitive, sensory, and perceptual distortions that are the inevitable result of physical changes in the body due to high arousal states during the event.
- Sometimes an officer may feel pressured to provide specific details to detectives' questions, though he can't remember them. It's better for him to admit that he didn't notice or cannot clearly remember what happened. You can facilitate honesty by being aware that perceptual and

cognitive distortions are a normal part of traumatic events. Don't pressure the officer or imply that he is being incompetent, evasive, or dishonest when he reports memory gaps or confusion.

- The sensory, perceptual, and cognitive distortions caused by high arousal states will result in each officer having tunnel vision. This, coupled with intense emotions caused by the event, can lead an officer to second-guess himself and others. This second-guessing is an inevitable consequence of any trauma (not just shootings) and should not be interpreted as evidence that they, or anyone else, has necessarily acted inappropriately.

- Since the individual reactions of each officer will vary widely in the hours after a shooting, the pacing of the interview should be responsive to the needs of each officer.

- It's common that an officer might remember additional details of the shooting in the days or weeks following the event. If he is interviewed right after the shooting, it would be wise to allow him to amend his statements as he later begins to recall further details. If his recall improves or changes over time, know that this doesn't necessarily mean his first statement was untruthful.

- Interviewing a fellow officer regarding a traumatic event is one of the most demanding and difficult jobs you may face. The officer deserves and needs the most professional, thorough, and accurate investigation you can do, and he needs the respect and compassion you would show any person who has experienced a traumatic event.

- Know that these traumatic events may have an emotional impact on you. Take care of yourself and your family by seeking out peer-support, supervision, and psychological debriefing from a mental health professional as the need arises.

Conclusion: Components of a Police Trauma Survival Program

This last section has been designed to give you an easy reference to the components of trauma survival that can help officers, agencies, and family members prepare to survive a traumatic event.

As an officer, you need to be concerned about three areas of survival in a deadly force situation: physical, legal, and psychological. As mentioned frequently throughout this text, many officers say that what happened to them and their family in the weeks, months, and even years following their incident was much worse than the incident itself. We cannot emphasize enough the importance of preparing for your legal and psychological survival.

And always keep in mind that while discussions of trauma usually focus on deadly force encounters, there are many kinds of nondeadly force events that can be traumatic. These too should be taken seriously in terms of the psychological impact on you and your family.

BEFORE THE TRAUMA

These suggestions can help you, your family, and your agency to better prepare for traumatic events before they happen.

Officer's Physical Training
- Research the most up to date police tactics.
- Develop physical skill in those techniques.
- Maintaining optimum physical fitness.

Officer's Psychological Survival Skills
- Master mental rehearsal and visualization techniques.
- Fully understand the dynamics of fear and high arousal states.
- Fully understand the aftermath of trauma and how to cope with it (including its affect on family members).

Officer's Legal And Administrative Survival Skills
- Always know when and how to give statements.
- Always know what procedures the agency will follow.
- Always know what procedure the community will follow (public inquest, grand juries, etc.).
- Always know your officers' legal rights and responsibilities.
- Always know the legal risks to the officer and how to cope with them.

Mental Health Fitness Training
- Officers can participate in "wellness" training aimed at early detection and treatment of the types of problems that can put officers at risk, such as untreated alcoholism, depression, post-traumatic stress disorder, anxiety disorders, sleep disorders, and so on.

Peer-Support Training
- This will provide officers with the information and skills needed to support each other.
- This facilitates the formation and clinical supervision of peer-support teams, such as the:

1. Traumatic Incident Support Team
2. Alcohol Recovery Support Team
3. Family Support Team

4. Disabled Officers Support Team
5. Peer Counseling Team

EDUCATING FAMILY MEMBERS

- Family members of police officers should be educated in what to expect and how to cope with the demands that police work will make on the officers and their families.
- Officers and family members should be encouraged to discuss and plan what they want to do if the officer is involved in a shooting.

TRAINING SUPERVISORS, COACHES, AND COMMAND STAFF

Knowledge Of Physical Tactics
- Supervisors and command staff should stay current on all the physical tactics training received by line officers.

Mental Health Awareness Training
- Supervisors and command staff should understand and promote mental health fitness among their officers. They should be trained in how to recognize distressed officers and how to help them in a positive and constructive manner.

Supervision Skills Training
- Supervisors should participate in ongoing training in people-oriented supervisory and leadership skills.

ESTABLISHMENT OF PROCEDURES AND PROTOCOLS

- Agencies need to develop or update established procedures and protocols (legal, administrative, psychological) on how to deal with officers and family members after a deadly force encounter.before a traumatic incident The chaotic aftermath of a shooting or other trauma is not a good time to "wing it."

- Post-deadly force protocols need to be coordinated smoothly among all the factions involved, such as unions, attorneys, command staff, DA's office, peer- and family-support teams, and mental health professionals.

ESTABLISHMENT OF AN EMPLOYEE ASSISTANCE PROGRAM

- There needs to be an EAP that officers can trust and will use as a confidential source of referral information for help with personal and work problems.

TRAINING INVESTIGATORS

- Investigators should be trained in the effects of trauma on perception, memory, thinking, and emotions to ensure the investigation is accurate and to avoid further traumatization of officers and family members.
- They should also be trained in all administrative and legal issues involved, ensuring that the officers receive full legal protection during post-shooting investigations, hearings, civil litigation, and so on.
- Investigators should be selected for their motivation and willingness to investigate officer involved shootings.
- They should be trained to cope with the added stress of investigating fellow officers.

TRAINING POLICE UNION OFFICIALS AND REPRESENTATIVES

- Union officials and representatives should be trained in all the legal and emotional risks that their officers may encounter after using deadly force.
- Union officials need to ensure that officers and family members are receiving the training, support, and treatment they need to survive and fully recover.

TRAINING THE COMMUNITY

Citizens' Academy

- Citizen support (or the lack of) can have a significant emotional impact on officers and family members after a shooting.
- Citizens can be put through a miniversion of the basic police academy training to give them a more realistic idea of what police officers must contend with on their job.
- Classes that may be particularly useful for helping them understand deadly force encounters include firearms training, training on simulators such as the FATS machine, and classes on the psychological impact of shootings.
- Once citizens understand these issues better, they will be less likely to criticize officers for doing their job.

Educating Community Groups

- There are many community groups, such as civic organizations, neighborhood associations, and school groups, that would benefit from an education that gave them a better understanding of police work and therefore make it more likely that they will support police officers.

AFTER THE INCIDENT

When all the above preparation is met before a traumatic incident, the following steps should fall into place afterwards.

Support from All Supervisors and Command Staff

- Members of the chain of command should call the involved officers and their family members at least once within a day or two after the event with sincere offers of support and assistance.

Mobilization of Peer-Support Teams

- Officer and family support teams should be on call and ready to offer assistance 24 hours a day.

Smooth Functioning of Procedures and Protocols

- Officers and family members should be kept informed about what to expect.
- Any conflict about how the incident is handled should be kept minimal around them.

Mandatory Paid Administrative Leave

- A common mistake is for officers to return to work too soon.
- They should get a minimum of three days off, though more will usually be needed.
- It's strongly recommended that officers not go back to street duty until all investigations and any other reviews or legal procedures are completed.
- Command staff and peers should support officers taking time off so they can fully recover emotionally.

Debriefings

- Individual psychological debriefing (mandatory and confidential)
- Group psychological debriefing
- Group tactical debriefing
- Incident clarification

Review of Procedures and Protocols

- Review all procedures after each shooting to evaluate their effectiveness and make changes as needed.
- It would be helpful to have a review board of all the interested parties: peer- and family-support teams, mental health professionals, command staff, a union official, DA's office, attorneys, and any others to examine each incident to ensure officers and family members were taken care of.

Ongoing Counseling as Needed

- Officers and family members are provided access to confidential follow-up counseling as needed.

Long-Term Follow-Up

- Involved officers, family members, peers, supervisors, command staff, and the Employee Assistance Program person should be aware of the potential for the flare-up of past psychological injuries, especially during "trigger" events, such as civil trials, anniversary dates of traumatic events, news coverage, and similar recent events.
- Further counseling and debriefings are arranged for those whose psychological injuries become aggravated.

• • • • •

May your journey be a safe and healthy one.

References and Suggested Readings

Aitchison, W. (1996). *The Rights of Law Enforcement Officers* (Third Edition). Labor Relations Information Systems, 3021 NE Broadway, Portland OR 97232-1810.

American Psychiatric Association (1994). *Diagnostic and Statistical Manual of Mental Disorders*, Fourth Edition. Washington, D.C.

Anderson, W., Swenson, D., & Clay, D. (1995). *Stress Management for Law Enforcement Officers*. Englewood Cliffs, N.J.: Prentice Hall.

Ayoob, M. (1995). *The Ayoob Files: The Book*. Concord, NH: Police Bookshelf.

Blau, T. (1994). *Psychological Services for Law Enforcement*. New York: John Wiley & Sons, Inc.

Bureau of Justice Assistance. *Fear: It Kills!* Washington, D.C.

Christensen, Loren W., (1996) *Speed Training: How To Develop Your Maximum Speed For Martial Arts*, Boulder, Colorado: Paladin Press

Christensen, Loren W. (1987). *The Way Alone: Your Path To Excellence In The Martial Arts*, Boulder, Colorado: Paladin Press.

Davidson, J.R.T. & Foa, E.B. (1993). *Posttraumatic Stress Disorder: DSM-IV and Beyond*. Washington, D.C.: American Psychiatric Press.

Epstein, S. (1994). *Integration of the Cognivitve and Psychodynamic Unconscious*. American Psychologist, 49. 709-721.

Epstein, S. (1983). *Natural Healing Processes of the Mind*. Meichenbaum, D. & Jaremko, M.E., (Eds.) Stress Reduction and Prevention. New York: Plenum Press.

Fisher, R.P. & Geiselman, M.S. (1992). *Memory-Enhancing Techniques for Investigative Interviewing*. Springfield, IL: Charles C. Thomas.

Geller, W.A. & Scott, M.S.,(1992). *Deadly Force: What We Know*. Washington, D.C.: Police Executive Research Forum.

Herman, J.L. (1992). *Trauma and Recovery*. New York: Basic Books.

Hogan, R., Curphy, J.D., & Hogan, J. (1994). *What We Know About Leadership*. American Psychologist, 49, 493-505.

Kirschman, E. (1997). *I Love A Cop: What Police Families Need To Know*. New York: Guilford Press.

Kurke, M.I. & Scrivner, E.M. (Eds.) (1995). *Police Psychology Into the 21st Century*. Hillsdale, N.J.: Lawrence Erlbaum Associates.

Meichenbaum, D. (1985). *Stress Inoculation Training*. Boston: Allyn & Bacon.

Meichenbaum, D. (1994). *Treating Patients with Posttraumatic Stress Disorder*. Lecture and Workshop Syllabus sponsored by Institute for Advancement of Human Behavior.

Reese, J.T., Horn, J.M., & Dunning, C. (Eds.) (1991). *Critical Incidents in Policing*. Washington, D.C.: Federal Bureau of Investigation.

Reese, J.T., & Goldstein, H. (Eds.) (1986). *Psychological Services for Law Enforcement*. Washington, D.C.: Federal Bureau of Investigation

Siebert, A. (1994). *The Survivor Personality*. Portland, OR: Practical Psychology Press.

van der Kolk, B. (1987) *Psychological Trauma*. Washington, D.C.: American Psychiatric Press

van der Holk, B., McFarlane, A.C., & Weisaeth, L. (Eds.) (1996). *Traumatic Stress*. New York: Guilford Press.

Violanti, J. (1996). *Police Suicide: Epidemic In Blue*. Springfield, IL: Charles C. Thomas.

Wolf, M.E., & Mosnaim, A.D. (1990). *Posttraumatic Stress Disorder*. Washington, D.C.: American Psychiatric Press.

About the Authors

Alexis Artwohl, Ph.D., is a clinical psychologist in private practice in Portland, Oregon. She was initiated into the world of trauma through her work with combat veterans during her internship in a veteran's hospital, then later with survivors of other traumas, such as child abuse, crime, domestic violence, accidents, and disasters. As a police psychologist, she has provided psychotherapy and debriefings to countless officers and family members after traumatic events.

Dr. Artwohl consistently receives excellent ratings for the law enforcement training she provides to agencies around the country in such subjects as how to survive deadly force encounters, how to investigate officer-involved shootings, awareness of mental health issues for police supervisors, how to conduct debriefings, how to manage stress, the importance of peer support, understanding the components of a trauma survival program, and training citizens on the impact of traumatic events on officers and their families.

Loren W. Christensen has been in law enforcement since 1967. He has been a police officer with the Portland Police Bureau since 1972, where he has worked a variety of assignments. It was his personal experience with post-traumatic stress 10 years after his return from Vietnam, and his experience seeing so many of his fellow officers traumatized after they had been involved in shootings, that sparked his interest in this writing project.

A prolific writer, Christensen has authored dozens of magazine articles, nine books on the martial arts, two books on street gangs, one book on missing children, and one on personal safety. He is also the editor of an award-winning, monthly police newspaper called *The Rap Sheet*.

The authors have nearly 40 years of combined experience working with law enforcement officers.